PQ   Clarke, Henry
6037   Butler, 1863-1904.
C5
1970   Spanish literature

DATE			
MAY 3 '82			

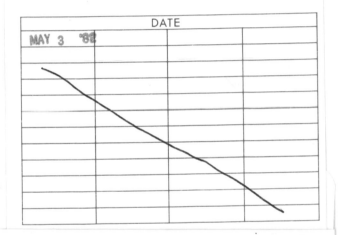

SPANISH LITERATURE

SPANISH LITERATURE

AN ELEMENTARY HANDBOOK

BY

H. BUTLER CLARKE, M.A.

KENNIKAT PRESS
Port Washington, N. Y./London

First published in 1893
Reissued in 1970 by Kennikat Press
Library of Congress Catalog Card No: 77-103220
SBN 8046-0857-1

Manufactured by Taylor Publishing Company   Dallas, Texas

First published in 1893
Reissued in 1970 by Kennikat Press
Library of Congress Catalog Card No: 77-103220
SBN 8046-0857-1

Manufactured by Taylor Publishing Company   Dallas, Texas

SPANISH LITERATURE

SPANISH LITERATURE

SPANISH LITERATURE

PREFACE

Dᴜʀɪɴɢ the time that I have held the Taylorian Teachership of Spanish at Oxford, I have frequently received letters asking what there is to read in Spanish besides Cervantes and Calderón, and what editions should be used. The present volume is intended to answer these questions, and to show the position occupied by the great writers in the general scheme of the literature of their country. The various divisions of this great subject have been exhaustively treated up to their several dates by Nicolás Antonio, Ticknor, Amador de los Ríos, Schack and Wolf, to whose books I beg to acknowledge my many obligations, hoping at the same time that the present general sketch may be useful to the general reader, and to the beginner, and may serve as an introduction to more extensive works.

I am aware that a few short extracts, however well chosen, can give no adequate idea of the manner of a great writer or of the merits of a great book, and that translations, even by the most skilful hands, are wont to reproduce the defects rather than the beauties of their original. The extracts here printed are intended to relieve the monotony of a long list of short notices of authors, and to illustrate the development of the language and the progress of literary method ; they are, as far as possible, characteristically Spanish in subject and, it is hoped, of sufficient interest to induce readers to refer to the books from which they are taken. The translations are literal rather than literary, and are meant to assist beginners in reading the extracts without the help of a dictionary. My aim has been to stimulate inquiry rather than to satisfy it. I have given brief outlines of well-known stories, such as that of the Cid, in order that on opening the *Romancero del Cid*, or meeting with an allusion to it, the reader may at once recognise his whereabouts.

If the literature of a country forms an organic whole, all divisions into periods must necessarily be somewhat arbitrary. I have avoided them as much as possible. The short chapter on the novel ranges from the fifteenth to the seventeenth century, from the period preceding the Golden Age of Spanish literature to its decadence. As a mere aid to memory a division into five periods may be adopted. The first period extends from the earliest documents in the language to the beginning of the fifteenth century ; the second brings us down to Garcilaso de la Vega ; the Golden Age reaches from the middle of the sixteenth century to the death of Calderón ; it is followed by a period of stagnation which prevailed until late in the last century ; the fifth period includes the last hundred years. The eighteenth century has been passed over in a few pages because of the lack of originality in its colourless writings. Of contemporary authors few only have been mentioned, for the Spanish literature of the present day cannot vie with that of a more glorious age.

English booksellers are generally almost entirely ignorant of Spanish books. Existing bibliographies are chiefly occupied with the rare editions dear to collectors. It was my original intention to give a select bibliography of all authors mentioned. Finding, however, that it took up too much space, and was likely to confuse the beginner without satisfying the student, I have merely appended a list of the cheap and easily obtainable editions of the books best suited for a preliminary course of Spanish reading. For help in its compilation I beg to thank Señor Murillo of Madrid, the most learned and courteous of Spanish booksellers.

A list of some of the principal writers on Spanish literature is added for those who wish to continue the study of the subject.

My best thanks are due to Miss Florence Freeman whose help in revising proofs has been invaluable, to Mr. York-Powell for advice and encouragement, and to other friends.

We have good reason to be proud of the illustrious English-speaking men of letters who have devoted themselves to Spanish subjects. Most of them, however, are primarily though not exclusively students of Cervantes or Calderón; it is to be hoped that, without neglecting the greatest writers, some one will come forward to bring up our knowledge of the more illustrious of their rivals to the same level of perfection. A large amount of treasures lie ready for him who will seek in the rich storehouses of our great libraries. I have recently discovered in the library of Wadham College, Oxford, a manuscript of parts of the works of Luís de León, some twenty years older than the first edition and containing some interesting variants.

Writing in sight of the Spanish hills, with my memory full of Spanish kindness, and the echo of the most stately of languages still in my ears, I hope that the time is approaching for a better understanding between my own country and what was once the greatest, and is still the most chivalrous, nation upon earth. If, by aiding the study of the ancient literature, the present volume in any degree furthers this great end, its author's purpose will have been amply fulfilled.

H. B. C.

St. Jean de Luz,
    1st January 1893.

CONTENTS

CHAPTER I

Remarks on the History of Spain down to the Time of the earliest Writers in the Vernacular. Local Distinctions of Language and Character

AMONG the histories of the great nations of the world, it would be difficult to find any one more characteristic and interesting than that of Spain. Its interest, however, is romantic rather than political or social; it is the history of great individuals and of great deeds rather than of corporate bodies and of great ideas. In spite of the by no means unimportant part taken by Spain in the struggle for liberty against oppressors from within, her constitutional development has been irregular, and her present position is far from satisfactory. But the history of the Spanish municipalities, of the liberties of Aragón and of other provinces, of the war of the *Comunidades* (guilds) in the sixteenth century, and of the bitter contest that marked the beginning of the present century, affords sufficient proof of her free spirit and of her sturdy independence.

Except during the centuries of the Roman occupation, and the short and fictitiously brilliant period during which she herself was the most powerful country in the world, Spain has, as it were, stood apart from what have been at different times

the centres of civilisation. Her development and her success,
her struggles and her failures, have been the work of her own
sons ; she has stood or fallen alone. To this may be attributed
the romantic charm which she has exercised, and continues to
exercise, over the minds of most of those to whom her history
and literature, her art and national characteristics, are familiar.

From the first the Western Land was a land of mystery, the
land from which came the gold, and of whose riches fabulous
accounts were given by the Phœnician and Greek traders whose
factories fringed her coasts. The interior remained unknown
to them, and beyond lay the great encircling ocean and the
Islands of the Blessed.

The Roman conquest here, as elsewhere, introduced order
amongst a host of contending elements, but it cost centuries to
carry it out. The north, the traditional mountain home of
Spanish liberty, was indeed never thoroughly subdued. In
other parts of the country repeated rebellions gave rise to
bloody and obstinately contested wars, which taught the conquerors to respect the proud and warlike spirit of their subjects.
When resistance became hopeless, the Iberian and Celtic inhabitants rapidly and thoroughly assimilated the language, laws,
and manners of the Romans. It is certain, however, that the
native languages were still spoken side by side with Latin.
Money with Celt-Iberian inscriptions was coined in the time of
Augustus, and Cicero mentions a Spanish tongue unintelligible
to the Romans ; but the thoroughness with which the central-
ising process was carried out is best proved by the list of
distinguished writers, natives of Spain, who contributed to the
Latin literature of the Silver Age. Quintilian, Martial, Lucan,
and Seneca, were Spaniards ; Latin names are borne by many of
the principal towns of the peninsula, and the gigantic public works
by which the Mistress of the World adorned and strengthened her
empire may still be seen in almost every part of the country.

Once pacified Spain rose rapidly to the position of one of

the most prosperous provinces of the Empire. The almost incredible amount of wealth that flowed yearly from her mines and fields to the Imperial treasury seems to have been incapable of exhausting her marvellous resources. Agriculture, mining, manufactures, and commerce flourished ; Christianity was introduced and spread rapidly. The last three centuries of Roman rule are almost qualified to rank among the happy class that have no history.

With the dismemberment of the Empire Spain shared the fate of the other Roman provinces. Successive armies of conquering Teutonic tribes overran the land. Some of these passed through on their way to Africa, as the Vandals who have left their name in (V)andalucía. Others remained to carve out for themselves an empire amongst a people which, under the powerful protection of its former masters, had lost the habit of carrying arms and, with it, the power of defending its own independence. The numerical importance of the so-called Gothic conquerors of Spain seems to have been as greatly over-rated as their level of civilisation has been under-rated. The bodies of aliens that settled in the country were rather armies than tribes. For some generations they maintained their position as a conquering and privileged race by means of laws forbidding intermarriage with their subjects. Of Gothic blood there remains little trace in the present population of the Peninsula. The Teutonic conquerors of Spain had, for the most part, been for some time established in Gaul before they crossed the Pyrenees, and they had adopted the more civilised customs as well as the laws and language of the people amongst whom they had settled. In Spain they have not left a single Teutonic inscription or monument, and it is doubtful if to them can be traced the origin of any of the few Gothic words existing in the languages now spoken in the Peninsula. The *fuero juzgo*, the so-called Gothic code of law, is almost entirely Roman in character.

The government of the Gothic kings was feeble and suspicious. They acted on the system of weakening the subject race, in order that they themselves might be proportionately stronger. All their efforts were powerless to prevent their absorption into the larger body of Celt-Iberian people. When, in the eighth century, the Saracens arrived, they conquered the whole country in a single battle, and at once parcelled it out into a number of states owning a more or less nominal allegiance to the Califs of Bagdad. Coming from the warm southern countries, the Moors found the climate of the north of Spain unsuited to them, and the mountainous region, inhabited by rough and warlike shepherds, not worth the trouble of conquest. Here, in the mountain fastnesses of Cantabria, they left the germ of a hardy race that was fated in after times to exact from their descendants a bitter retribution for the invasion of its native land, and the subjection of its brethren. Almost immediately after the Saracen conquest, the war of liberation was begun by Pelayo's valiant band of refugees, sheltered in the cave of Covadonga, around which centre so many of the national traditions. After lasting for seven centuries, the struggle ended only when the miserable remnant of the Moors turned their backs on Granada, carrying with them to Africa the keys of their houses as relics of their beloved homes in Spain.

The rule of the Moors was by no means harsh. They found in the south a population accustomed to subjection, and allowed to it a considerable share in the administration of its own affairs. Patriotic historians have endeavoured to show that the Christians of the old stock persistently held aloof from their conquerors, and looked upon them as enemies throughout. This is far from being the truth. An ecclesiastical writer of the ninth century[1] complains that his co-religionists in

[1] Álvaro of Córdova. *Indiculum Luminosum.* Even Alvar Fañez, the companion of the Cid, signed his name in Arabic characters. The large body

Andalucía had so thoroughly adopted the Arabic tongue that they were unable to follow the services of the Church in their native Romance, but were capable of writing verse in the language of their so-called oppressors. These Christians of the south rose against the Moslems amongst whom they lived, only when summoned by the trumpet-call from the north. When freed by their more hardy compatriots, they were regarded by them with some suspicion, and did not always escape the opprobrious but well-deserved name of *Cristianos nuevos* (new Christians). Until the thirteenth century, and even later, it is by no means rare to find Christians fighting side by side with Moors against their fellow-Christians. The spirit of religious and national intolerance originated outside Spain with the Crusaders; it was cultivated by the Church, and was carried south by the early *conquistadores*. The sentiment expressed in the lines of the ballad

> [1] *Caballeros granadinos*
> *Aunque moros hijosdalgo*

probably belongs to a date when, after the completion of the re-conquest, the attribution of noble qualities to the vanquished became a means of glorifying the victor.

Of the civilisation and learning of the Moors very little filtered through to the rough Christian soldiers whom they successfully resisted when Islam was the common cause, but to whom they afforded an easy prey when, as so often happened, dissension prevailed amongst the Moslem states, or when single states were torn by internal division. More than half the land was already won back from the alien when, in the fourth century of this great war, Spanish literature begins.

The re-conquest, the story of which forms the history of

of Spanish documents written in Arabic characters are known as *Textos Aljamiados;* see the excellent little book bearing this name, by Pablo Gil. Zaragoza, 1888.

[1] " Knights of Granada—though Moors, yet gentlemen."

Spain during so many centuries, has left its lasting mark on the country. Those who won back the several provinces planted respectively their native dialects in them. The Castilian language, known to foreigners as Spanish, is spoken, with slight local variations, throughout three-fourths of the country included in the present boundaries of Spain. This tract is roughly equivalent to the district won back by the descendants of the refugees from the mountains of Asturias. Their language is the language in which is written almost the whole of the works that will come under consideration in the present volume; and well does it deserve the title that has been bestowed upon it of "noblest daughter of the Latin." For from Latin it derives seven-tenths of its vocabulary, and the whole of its syntax. Sonorous and cadenced more than other tongues, it is peculiarly fitted for lofty verse and oratorical prose, yet in spite of its grave and dignified character it can scarcely be equalled for tenderness and pathos. Galicia keeps a dialect of its own, closely resembling the Portuguese, but possessing little or no literature.[1] In Catalonia a dialect of Provençal is still spoken, but day by day it is adopting Castilian forms, in spite of the efforts of a small number of writers to revive a literature in the vernacular. In literature, as well as in ethnology and language, the Catalans belong rather to Provence than to Spain. (See chapter on Catalan Literature.)

Much misapprehension has been caused by regarding the inhabitants of the Peninsula as one people. Only in a political sense can they be properly so regarded. All general propositions about Spanish national character and customs must necessarily be false or only partially true. It would be as vain to seek a description which should apply equally to the national characteristics of Scotch and Irish, as to attempt to include in

---

[1] See p. 75. The best collection of modern Galician verse is contained in the *Cancionero Popular Gallego por José Perez Ballesteros con prólogo de Teófilo Braga.* Madrid, 1886.

a single portrait the distinctive features of Asturian and Andalucian. To those who believe in the influence of physical environment upon national character this will be evident from a glance at the map, or better still, by a visit to the country. The climate and productions of Galicia, and parts of Asturias, are not unlike those of the south-west of Ireland. In Murcia is found an almost rainless region, producing the date, sugar-cane, and rice, a region in which camels may be used as beasts of burden under an African sky. The lofty table-land, inter-sected by high mountain ranges, which forms almost the whole of the interior of the Peninsula, is bare, and in great part tree-less ; its bleak brown uplands are parched by bitter winds in winter, and by a burning sun in summer, yet they produce corn, wine, and oil in abundance, and are capable, with the help of irrigation, of yielding the most delicious fruits and the most brilliant flowers.

The inhabitants of this country vary as much as the land in which they live. Brave, sober, honest, and persever-ing, but somewhat heavy and slow-witted as compared with his Andalucian cousin, the Asturian possesses in a marked degree the qualities common to mountaineers. His pride lies in his descent from the old stock, alike unconquered by Roman, Goth, or Moor. Writers of all times have made him a subject for good-natured ridicule on account of his claim to a long pedi-gree, his habit of presuming on his nobility, and his extreme poverty. Asturias now provides the men of letters, and, in conjunction with Aragón, the lawyers of Spain ; almost all the noble houses trace their origin to the *montaña*.

The Galician is somewhat similar to the Asturian ; in spite of his large share of Celtic blood he is sluggish, and on the Spanish stage he figures as the Auvergnat on the French stage. He is a hewer of wood and a drawer of water, yet with a strong vein of poetry underlying his rough exterior, and honest and reliable withal.

The Spaniard, with whose caricature the French and English stage have made us familiar, the Spaniard of pictures and painted fans, the man with the broad hat, red sash, and guitar, is the Andalucian, the most picturesque and brightest figure of the nation. Inhabiting a country in which the bounty of nature has reduced the necessity for labour to a very slight burden, the Andalucian has not been slow to take advantage of her kindness, and to make the best of life. Passionate, gay, communicative, and idle, the bulk of the population of this lovely region lead, so far as it is possible for a large body of ordinary human beings, a butterfly existence. In their blood, as on their manners and mode of life, the Eastern conquerors have left deep traces, without imparting to them anything of the gravity of Orientals. Their virtues and vices alike spring direct from the heart, and owe nothing either to moral training or to deliberate depravity.

The qualities, good and bad, of the Catalán are of a commercial and industrial kind; he is the manufacturer of Spain, and betrays his separate origin by possessing, only in a modified degree, the two qualities which make all genuine Spaniards akin ; these are deep religious feeling in an exclusively Catholic sense, and a lofty idea of personal dignity.

These two characteristics are particularly prominent in the Castilians, and under this name may be included for our present purpose the inhabitants of the country from León to La Mancha, and from Extremadura to Aragón. These form the backbone of the nation, the men who won back the country from the Moors, the men who discovered and colonised so large a part of America, and who once, as champions of the Catholic Faith, overawed or overran the greater part of civilised Europe. Noble and independent in bearing, they are grave without stolidity, and courteous in manner even to foreigners, in spite of their innate prejudices against strangers. They are sober, laborious, and thrifty, yet neither inhospitable nor sordid. The popular songs (see p. 267) which, at the present day, have replaced the ballads of a more heroic age, show how intense is their appreciation of the beautiful, and more particularly of poetry. Their good qualities, alike with their defects, have an old-world flavour that renders their possessors unfit to excel in an inartistic, commercial, democratic, and sceptical age. The charge of dishonesty and peculation that has been so often brought against them is well founded only in so far as it applies to public life. Years of misgovernment have made corruption universal throughout the official classes, and from the official world the commercial has taken its tone. But in this respect, as in others, signs of improvement and progress are now everywhere apparent, and haply the day is not far distant when Spain will again take, amongst the nations of Europe, the position which is hers by right, not only of glorious traditions, but of noble and sterling qualities.

The pattern and type of Castilian character is Rodrigo or Ruy Diaz de Bivar, the Cid, the hero in whom the popular fancy has summed up the virtues that go to form the national ideal. In the successive developments of his story and character may be traced the strong lasting elements of this ideal, as well as the weaker but no less chivalrous ones that vary with varying circumstances. It was by such men and for such men that a great part of the older Spanish literature was created, and it is with the Cid's story that it begins.

CHAPTER II

FORMATION OF THE SPANISH LANGUAGE AND BEGINNING OF SPANISH LITERATURE

FOR eight centuries after the abolition of Roman rule in Spain, Latin continued in use as the written language employed by native Spanish authors. A considerable number of important Latin works, mostly ecclesiastical, and written between the fifth and twelfth centuries, has come down to us. But these in no sense come under the heading of Spanish Literature. Between them and the earliest books in the vernacular there is no continuity, nor can any development be traced from the one to the other. The employment of the popular speech for literary purposes marks an entirely new departure, in which almost all the traditions of the past were cast aside. An examination, therefore, of the Spanish-Latin literature does not enter into the province of the present volume.

Equally little have we to do with the Arabic authors who flourished in Spain at a time anterior to that of the earliest Spanish writings. These brought with them from the East their own literary and artistic traditions, and continued to hand them down with oriental immutability.[1] The Arabic and Spanish literature ran parallel for a time, but in distinctly separate channels, and it is only in rare translations or adaptations that their currents mingle. Each has its own distinct ideals and methods.

[1] See Schack, *Poesía y Arte de los Árabes*, trans. Juan Valera. Madrid, 1872.

Whilst educated men, despising the speech of the vulgar, continued to write in literary Latin, Spanish was slowly developing from the popular language which had been planted in the country by the Roman legionaries, and is known as the *lingua romana rustica*. Except in such books as the *Etymologies* of St. Isidor of Seville, and in certain documents written in a mixture of the two languages, we have but little evidence as to how the change went on. But in the earliest Spanish writings we find that a wonderful change has taken place. The Spanish of the thirteenth century differs but little from the Spanish of to-day. The old Latin vocabulary is here almost complete, but supplemented by a large number of Arabic words relating mostly to agriculture and to the new arts and sciences brought from the East. The familiar Latin words, however, have undergone a transformation. The case-endings are gone, and their place has been taken by prepositions : the Latin tonic *o* and *e* have become split up into *ue* and *ie* respectively : *h* is rapidly taking the place of the Latin initial *f : ct* has changed into *ch : t* between vowels into *d ;* and instead of the Latin initial *pl, fl, cl,* we find the peculiar Spanish *ll*.[1] Some tenses of the verb have disappeared, and their places have been filled by others, whose importance is thereby greatly magnified. The Latin Future has suffered the same fate as in France and Italy ; it has been given up, and in its place we have a new form constructed with the Infinitive and the verb *habere*, which did not become thoroughly welded together until the seventeenth century. The whole structure of the sentence has been vastly simplified, and a new instrument has been wrought from the material of the old to express the new ideas of a new age.

---

[1] The date of the introduction of the characteristic harsh guttural sound now represented by the Spanish *j* (*g*), and replacing the Latin *j, g, x, lj, cl,* is uncertain. Such evidence as is obtainable points to the sixteenth century.

The earliest literary work in Spanish, which is probably at the same time the earliest existing document in the language, is the *Poema de Myo Cid*, a short epic or *chanson de geste* of about four thousand lines. Its beginning is lost, and it comes to an end somewhat abruptly. Some critics have maintained that it is an agglomeration of several distinct ballads. This view is not confirmed by consideration of language or style, but the arguments drawn from internal evidence and from the lack of unity in its subject are strong enough to warrant it. The name of its author and the place in which it was composed are unknown; the most probable conjecture as to its date is that it belongs to the latter half of the twelfth century, and, consequently, was written about a century and a half after the death of its hero. The language of the poem is rude and uncouth, a language struggling into existence. The versification is barbarous and irregular; the normal lines are of fourteen syllables, with a strong cæsura after the eighth; many, however, fall short of this limit, and many exceed it; the same rhyme, more or less correct, is employed until exhausted, when another takes its place. The subject of the poem is the exile of My Cid;[1] his campaign against the Moors of Alcocer; his victory over the Count of Barcelona; his conquest of Valencia; his reconciliation with the king who had treated him with so much ingratitude; the marriage of his daughters with the Counts of Carrión, and the vengeance exacted by the Cid for the ill-treatment received by them at the hands of their husbands. That these verses were at one time recited by wandering minstrels is proved by the last lines which contain the request—

[2] *Dat nos del vino si non tenedes dineros.*

---

[1] For an outline of the traditional history of the Cid, see the chapter on the Ballads. In the *Poema*, Rodrigo de Bivar is generally called " My Cid," or " he who was born in a happy hour " (*el que en buen hora fué nado*).

[2] " Give us wine if ye have no money."

Apart from its value as the earliest monument of the language which, in after times, was to spread over so large a part of the earth, the *Poema* is worthy of attention and admiration by reason of its heroic simplicity, its rapid movement, the life-like pictures it presents of the turbulent times in which it was composed, and the free and light-hearted spirit which it breathes throughout. Here is chivalry indeed, without the false and sickly sentimentality with which it was corrupted in a later age. The Cid's notions of honour, nay, even of honesty, are somewhat hazy and not over refined, but, such as they are, he puts them into practice; he is a good husband and a good father, brave, loyal, and disinterested. The hero of the poem is also a scrupulously devout son of the Church [1] and a patriot, though it is more than doubtful whether the Cid of history could establish a claim to these virtues as nowadays understood. One of the most characteristic and animated passages, and one that has been most often quoted, is the description of how the Cid rescues his banner when in danger of falling into the hands of the Moors through the rashness of his standard-bearer, Pero Vermuez (lines 715-732). It runs as follows :—

> [2] Enbraçan los escudos delant los coraçones,
> Abaxan las lanças abuestas de los pendones,
> Enclinaron las caras de suso de los arzones.
> Yuan los ferir de fuertes coraçones.
> Á grandes vozes lama el que en buen hora nasco ;
> " Ferid los, caualleros, por amor de caridad :
> Yo so Rruy Diaz el Cid Campeador de Biuar ! "
> Todos fieren en el az do está Pero Vermuez.

[1] Cf. the curious references to auguries and other superstitious observances in which the poem abounds.

[2] "They clasp their shields before their hearts ;—their lances are levelled with pennants decked :—their heads they bent low over the saddle ;—to smite them they went with valiant hearts.—Loudly calls he who was born in happy hour,—'Strike them my knights for love of charity—I am Ruy Diaz the Cid Campeador of Bivar !'—One and all shower blows on the band

Treszientas lanças son, todos tienen pendones.
Seños moros mataron, todos de seños colpes ;
Á la tornada que fazen otros tantos son.
Veriedes tantas lanças premer é alçar,
Tanta adagara foradar é passar,
Tanta loriga falssa desmanchar,
Tantos pendones blancos salir vermeios en sangre
Tantos buenos cauallos sin sos duenos andar ;
Los moros laman Mafomat, los cristianos Sant Yague,
Cayen en un poco de logar moros muertos mill é C C C ya.

Two other very ancient compositions treat of the exploits of the favourite national hero. The first of these, the *Latin Chronicle*, gives practically the same version of the story as that found in the *General Chronicle* (see p. 21), and may either have been the source from which the *General Chronicle* drew its information, or have been itself compiled from this great work of Alfonso the Wise. The *Rhymed Chronicle*, the second of the two, has been supposed by some to be older than the *Poema*. The *Latin Chronicle* is written in most barbarous language, and in verses of irregular length ; its contents are of little interest, nor does it properly come under the heading of Spanish literature. Not so the *Crónica Rimada*. Less spirited in tone than the *Poema*, it deserves attention at the hands of the student of popular traditions, showing as it does how rapidly a real personality may be surrounded by myths of the most extravagant kind, until at last it becomes almost impossible to distinguish between the purely fictitious part and the real facts which so powerfully impressed the popular imagination. In it we find the germ of almost all the

round Pero Vermuez.—Three hundred lances are they, each with its pennant decked.—A Moor apiece they killed, each with a single blow,—and when they wheeled about they slew as many more.—There might one see many lances rise and sink again,—many a shield pierced and thrust through,—many a corselet burst and broken—many a white pennant come forth red in blood,—many a good horse run free without a master.—The Moors call on Mahomet, the Christians on St. Yague—in but a little space a thousand and three hundred Moors are slain."

Cid ballads of the fifteenth and sixteenth centuries, such as the story of Count Lozano, of the Cid's marriage, and of his expedition to France and victory over the twelve peers ; even the Pope himself is forced to submit to the overbearing insolence of the Castilian freebooter.   The fact that the Pope in question was probably unacquainted even with his name, and that the Cid apparently never left his native land, would weigh but little with the author of such a composition.

As Spanish literature begins appropriately with a poem celebrating heroic deeds, so it continues with a body of religious verse, thus giving, as it were, a clue to the two sides of the national character.   The question of priority of date among these pious compositions, known under the general name of *poemas de clerecía* (clerkly poems), is a disputed one ; it is, however, unimportant.   On the whole, preference may be given to the *Mystery of the Magian Kings*, a miracle-play of a type common in the middle ages, and interesting only for its bearing on the early history of the Drama (see p. 59).   A manuscript of the thirteenth century, now in the library of the Escurial, contains three poems of which the authors, like their predecessors, are unknown to us by name.   These are the *Book of Apollonius King of Tyre*, the *Life of Saint Mary the Egyptian*, and the *Adoration of the Three Holy Kings*.   Drawn from sources such as the *Gesta Romanorum* and the *Lives of the Saints*, which were the common property of mediæval writers, these and the later religious poems are interesting chiefly as showing the development of language and versification.   In them first appears the *cuaderna vía*, a system of metre consisting of lines of fourteen syllables, divided into stanzas of four lines, all ending with the same rhyme (see extract, p. 33).   This verse is extremely artificial and stiff, but it seems to have pleased the popular taste, as it continued in use for two centuries.

The *Life of Saint Mary the Egyptian* sometimes rises slightly above the prosaic tone general throughout these compositions.   The repentant sinner who was afterwards to become a saint thus addresses the Virgin, contrasting the saintly life of her patroness with her own :—

> Creyo bien en mi creyencia
> Que Dios fué en tu nasçençia,
>
> .   .   .
>
> Virgo, reina, creyo por tí
> Que si al tu fijo rogares por mı,
> Si tu pides aqueste don,
> Bien ssé que hauré perdón. . . .
>
> .   .   .
>
> Un nombre havemos yo é tí
> Mas mucho eres tu luenye de mí ;
> ꞌTu María é yo María,
> Mas non tenemos amas huna vía.

Here, and in the *Mystery of the Magian Kings*, we have the earliest examples of the eight-syllable lines, which constitute the most popular Spanish metre ; the system of rhyme, however, is wholly unlike that which was used later, and gives an entirely different character to the verses (see p. 44).

Passing by the *Disputation between the Body and the Soul* which may easily be paralleled, both as to form and matter, in the earlier literature of most European countries, we come to the first Castilian poet whose name and date we know.

Gonzalo de Berceo flourished during the first half of the thirteenth century.   A clerk of the monastery of San Millan, near Calahorra, he devoted the whole of his voluminous writings to religious subjects, using the *cuaderna vía* to relate the lives of several saints, the *Miracles of Our Lady*, the

---

[1] " Firmly I hold to my belief—that God Himself in thy birth took part, —O Virgin Queen, I believe that for thy sake,—if to thy Son thou shouldst pray for me,—if thou shouldst ask Him this boon,—certain it is I should obtain pardon.—One name we share both thou and I,—but thou art far removed from me ;—I am Mary and thou art Mary—but widely different are our ways."

Sacrifice of the Mass, the *Virgin's Lament*, and other works of a like character. He is the first who makes use of the *mester de clerecía* (clerkly verse), a more artificial and correct style of writing as compared with the free and barbarous *mester de yoglaría* (minstrel's verse) of earlier times and popular use; Berceo speaks of his writings as *dictados* (poems), to distinguish them from the minstrel's *cantares* (lays), but his verse is not worthy of the name of poetry; it is generally simply rhymed prose, and, if here and there he for a moment rises to a slightly higher level, he quickly falls back into his usual tameness.

Three more poems must be mentioned before we come to the earliest Spanish prose and to the great works of Alfonso el Sabio. Though posterior in point of time to the founder of Castilian prose, they do not share in the vast improvements in style and literary method that originated with the "Wise" or rather "Learned" King, who lacked so entirely the practical wisdom known to his countrymen as *gramática parda* (gray grammar).

Juan Lorenzo Segura devoted his poetical talents to the glorification of a personage so far removed in time and place from himself and his native land as Alexander the Great. His hero, however, though he bears this famous name, and performs many of the impossible exploits popularly ascribed in the Middle Ages to the Macedonian conqueror, is not only a Spaniard, but a Spanish paladin of the period in which the author wrote. In so far as Segura departs from genuine history, and from the tradition of the writers of the French *fabliaux*, his work is interesting. Alexander is not unworthy of attention when he hears mass, and visits the depths of the ocean.

The *Libro de Jusuf* is an early specimen of *aljamia*, or Castilian, written in Arabic characters, and interspersed with Arabic words and expressions. This version of the story of Joseph, the son of Jacob, differs in important particulars from the Biblical narrative. Its interest is chiefly antiquarian and philological. Though ascribed by some critics to a much later date, the circumstance that it is written in *cuaderna vía* (see p. 15) forms of itself a strong presumption that it belongs to a comparatively early age.

The *Poem of Fernan-Gonzalez*, the famous count of Castile, is national both in subject and in form ; but in spite of this, and in spite of the fact that it contains the earliest version of some beautiful legends concerning the foundation of the kingdom of Castile, the tameness and monotony of its style greatly lessen its interest.

This series of diffuse and prosaic poems would be hardly worth the attention of the student of literature were it not for the quaint details in which some of them abound, and for the opportunity here and there afforded of feeling deep down below their formal surface the throb of the pulse of a great nation, which was still too deeply engaged in the struggle that was to furnish a theme for the poetry of a later date to devote its time and attention to literary pursuits. It is with a feeling of relief that one hurries on, passing over several minor names, to the first author of real importance. A giant as compared with his contemporaries in intellectual matters, and possessing also the virtues of a more civilised state of society, Alfonso is the first to win a place among Spanish authors above that occupied by the rude gleeman who wrote the *Poema del Cid*.

With the formation of Spanish prose two names are specially connected. Both belong to royal persons. Alfonso el Sabio was uncle to the Infante Don Juan Manuel. As eldest son of San Fernando the Conqueror, he succeeded to the throne of Castile in 1252. Unfitted by his scholarly tastes for the stirring life around him, his life was a long series of misfortunes. The monarch who at one time had claimed the title of Emperor, and who was actually elected, though his election was afterwards annulled, found himself, towards the end of his life, in the humiliating position of being forced to pledge his crown, and seek the protection of the Moslem king of Fez against the violence of his turbulent subjects led by his own son.   The most important legacy left by him to posterity consists of his legal works; he excelled, however, in every branch of knowledge as then understood, and in each was in advance of his age.   Even before his accession he took part in the translation of the *Fuero Juzgo* (Forum Judicum), the code promulgated by San Fernando for the government of those of his subjects who were streaming southward to settle in the districts of Andalucía recently won back from the Moors.   His greatest work is another code, called, from its division into seven parts, *Las Siete Partidas*.   It became the groundwork for all subsequent legislation in Spain, and was carried by the Spaniards to the New World, where traces of its influence may still be found.   Alfonso, on his accession, found the inherent difficulty of governing his restless and warlike subjects considerably increased by local privileges and customary rights that had been formally granted to, or had sprung up spontaneously among, the settlers who took possession of the land conquered by his father.   He attempted to reduce these conflicting elements to uniformity, and his scheme for the government of the newly-acquired territory is seen in his great work on legislation.   The *Siete Partidas* are not a mere collection of laws expressed in technical language; they are rather treatises on moral and political philosophy, giving proof of broad and liberal views rare even in a more enlightened age. The nature of justice is discussed, and the right of driving out tyrants is recognised.   Many also are the quaint passages in which the writer, departing from the tone and province of a jurist, condescends to discuss such details of private life as the duties of the governesses of princesses.

Connected with the first really great name in Spanish literature is a large body of verse, some of which is undoubtedly spurious.   The *Tesoro*, a very obscure treatise on the transmutation of metals, part of which is written in prose, undoubtedly belongs to the period of Alfonso the Wise, but it is unlikely that the king who in the *Partidas* spoke severely of the Alchemists as *engannadores* (cheats) should have himself pursued their studies, and written upon the methods of their art. The authenticity of the book of *Cántigas é Loores de Nuestra Señora* is scarcely disputed, but no really satisfactory explanation is given of the fact that Alfonso, who wrote his prose works and some of his poetry in Castilian, here made use of the Galician dialect (see p. 75), and ordered his hymns to be used in the Cathedral of Murcia, where they would be scarcely intelligible. The collection comprises about four hundred lyrics of a high order of merit, in a variety of metres, most of which the author probably learned from the Provençal poets who came to his court. Many well-known legends are here related, and among them the beautiful one of the nun, the portress of her convent, who, under strong temptation, escaped from the cloister, and for some time led a vicious life ; on her return, repentant and fearful of punishment, she finds that her absençe has passed unnoticed, for the Virgin herself, taking pity on one who had ever been her special devotee, has assumed her appearance and fulfilled her duties during her absence. A pathetic interest attaches to the poems known as the *Querellas* (Complaints) of King Don Alfonso, but their authenticity has been doubted. They are simple and noble in tone, and may well have been written by the king himself, if we may judge by the feeling with which they describe his misfortunes. The following passage may serve as a specimen of the *Querellas*, and also as an example of the *versos de arte mayor*, a metrical form which was at this time coming into use :—

[1] A tí Diego Perez Sarmiento, leal
　　Cormano é amigo é firme vasallo,

---

[1] " To thee Diego Perez Sarmiento the loyal—brother and friend and vassal

Lo que á mios omes de coita les callo
Entiendo dezir planniendo mi mal . . .
Como yaz solo el rey de Castiella
Emperador de Alemania que foé
Aquel que los reyes besaban el pie,
E reynas piden limosna é manciella ;
Aquel que de auxilio mantuvo en Sevilla
Diez mil de á caball y tres dobles peones ;
Aquel que acatado en lejanas naciones
Fué por sus Tablas é por su cuchilla.

During the reign and under the immediate superintendence
of the Wise King, if not by his own hand, were written two
great chronicles. This form of literature had already been
cultivated in Spain, as is shown by the *Crónicas* of Lucas de
Tuy and the *Historia Gótica* of the learned Rodrigo Jimenez
de Rada, who flourished during the first half of the thirteenth
century. The *Estoria de Espanna* and the *Grande é general
Estoria*, however, mark a distinct improvement in language,
style, and historical criticism. The former begins with the
Deluge, and brings the narrative down to the time of San
Fernando. The latter part is extremely interesting, for the
author is here describing events with which he is familiar,
either as an actual eyewitness, or from traditions and ballads
like those of the Cid and Pelayo. The *Grande é general
Estoria* is, as its name implies, a universal history. It is the
first work of its kind written in the vulgar tongue ; the amount
of research and learning it displays is extraordinary when we
consider the age in which it was produced, but it is less

true—That which for very grief I hide from my household—now would I tell
and mourn for my ills . . . How the king of Castile lies all alone—Emperor,
once of Germany—whose foot kings kissed—and queens sought from him alms
and favour :—he who to guard him maintained at Seville—Ten thousand horse
and three hosts of foot :—he who amongst far distant peoples—Gained reverence by his Tables * and his sword."

---

* The "Tables" here mentioned are the *Tablas Alfonsinas*, an astronomical
work celebrated throughout the Middle Ages, and still a subject of wonder to men of
science.

interesting than the *Estoria de Espanna*, for, beginning as it does with the Creation and ending with the first preaching of Christianity, its facts are drawn from the Bible and from other sources of which we are better able to judge than was its author. The style of both these works is simple and dignified, often quaintly pathetic, and bearing traces of the melancholy which misfortune had made a part of the Wise King's character. A good idea of it may be gained from the chapter called the Praises of Spain (*Los bienes que tiene Espanna*), a subject that earlier still had inspired beautiful passages in the writings of St. Isidor and the Arab El Makkari. The following is an extract from this poetical yet scarcely exaggerated description of the Peninsula :—

[1] Pues esta España que deximos tal es como el parayso de Dios : ca riégase con cinco rios cabdales que son Duero ed Ebro é Tajo é Guadalquevir é Guadiana : é cada uno dellos tiene entre sí é el otro grandes montañas é tierras : é los valles é los llanos son grandes é anchos : é por la bondad de la tierra y el humor de los rios llevan muchas frutas é son abondados. Otrosi en España la mayor parte se riega con arroyos é de fuentes ; é nunca le menguan pozos en cada logar que los han menester. É otrosi España es bien abondada de mieses é delectosa de frutas, valiosa de pescados, sabrosa de leche é de todas las cosas que se de ella facen, é llena de venados é de caza, cubierta de ganados, loçana de cavallos, provechosa de mulos é de mulas, é segura é abastecida de castiellos, alegre por buenos vinos, folgada de abondamiento de pan, rica de metales de plomo é de estaño, é de argen vivo é de fierro é de arambre é de plata é de oro é de piedras preciosas,

---

[1] " Now this land of Spain of which we spake is like unto the paradise of God : for it is watered by five full-flowing rivers, and these are Duero and Ebro and Tajo and Guadalquevir and Guadiana : and each hath betwixt it and its neighbour mighty mountains and lands : and the valleys and the plains are great and broad : and by reason of the goodness of the soil and the moisture of the rivers they bring forth much food and are fruitful. Moreover of Spain the greater part is watered by brooks and fountains : and wells are never lacking in every place that hath need of them. And moreover Spain abounds in crops of corn, in delicious fruits, in precious fishes, in sweet milk, and all such things as are made from it ; the deer roam far and wide, the flocks cover the earth, and the stately horses. The land is rich in mules, secure and well furnished with strong places, joyful with good wines, satisfied with abundance of bread, rich in metals, in lead, in tin, in quicksilver and in iron, in brass and silver, in gold and precious stones and in all kinds of

é de toda manera de piedra marmol, é de sales de mar, é de salinas de tierra, é de sal en peñas é de otros veneros muchos . . . de quantos se fallan en otras tierras. Briosa de sirgo, é de cuanto se falla de dulzor de miel é de azucar, alumbrada de cera, alumbrada de olio, alegre de azafrán. É España sobre todas las cosas es engeñosa é aun temida é mucho esforzada en lid, ligera en afán, leal al Señor, afirmada en el estudio, palanciana en palabra, complida en todo bien : é non ha tierra en el mundo quel semeje en bondad, nin se yguala ninguna á ella en fortaleza, é pocas ha en el mundo tan grandes como ella É sobre todas España es abondada en grandeza ; más que todas preciada por lealtad ; O España ! non ha ninguno que pueda contar tu bien.

During the latter part of the thirteenth century prose authors became more numerous. Their works may be divided roughly into two classes : didactic or moral treatises and collections of fables. These two categories, as will be seen from the examples mentioned below, frequently overlap. Among the most important books of the former class must be counted the *Setenario* of Alfonso the Wise, a treatise on the seven branches of learning, comprising the *trivio*, Grammar, Rhetoric, and Logic, and the *cuatrivio*, Music, Astronomy, Physics, and Metaphysics. The *Castigos y Documentos* (Warnings and Injunctions) of Don Sancho el Bravo, the son of Alfonso el Sabio, is a book of considerable learning drawn chiefly from the Bible, the early Christian writers, and some of the Latin classics. To the latter class—the fables—belong *Engannos é Assayamientos de las Mogieres* (The Deceits and Tricks of Women) and *Calila é Dimna*, fables translated directly from Eastern sources, as well as the collection known under the odd

marble, in salt of the sea and salt from the earth, salt in mountains and many other veins of metal . . . nay as many as are found in other lands. Her silk is her pride, and sweetest of honey and of sugar ; her wax gives her light and her oil gives her light, and the saffron gladdens her heart. And Spain, more than other lands, is cunning, yea and feared, and very mighty in battle, light-hearted in toil, loyal to her Lord, grounded in learning, courteous of speech and filled with all good things : and there is no land in all the world like unto her in goodness, none that is her equal in valour and few of all the world so great as she. And more than all others is she great and powerful, more than all others is she leal and true. O Spain, who is there that can tell thy praises ?"

name of *Libro de los Gatos* (Book of the Cats). Most of the books of this class are by unknown authors.

The second great Spanish prose writer, the Infante Don Juan Manuel, contributed to both of the two above-mentioned classes. Though playing a considerable part in the political troubles of his time as a turbulent and ambitious leader, he found time to compose a number of books, of which he gives a list in the introduction to the best known of his works, the *Conde Lucanor*, *Libro de los Enxemplos*, or *Libro de Patronio* as it is variously called. This is a book of fables consisting of fifty-one stories of varying length, some Oriental, some taken from Æsop, others local in character or derived from the common stock of traditions and legends of the Middle Ages. A good example of the style and character of the work is the *Story of what happened to a Dean of Santiago with Don Illán the great Magician who dwelt at Toledo*. A certain dean of Santiago wishes to learn the black art, and is attracted to Toledo by the fame of the magician Don Illán. He is hospitably entertained and explains his errand, making at the same time many promises of gratitude for the instruction he wishes to receive. The magician takes him to his underground study, having first ordered supper to be prepared. While the two are discussing, messengers enter and inform the dean that his uncle, the archbishop, is ill; a few days later, news comes that the archbishop is dead, and, presently, the dean is elected in his stead. The magician now begs the deanery for a relation of his own, but the new archbishop refuses the request. The two now set out for Santiago, where fresh honours are showered upon the former dean. On the occasion of each promotion Don Illán renews his demand to be allowed to share in his pupil's good fortune. Each time he meets with a rebuff. Finally the dean becomes Pope, and when his former instructor ventures to remind him of his promise he threatens to proceed against him as a heretic and enchanter, and dismisses him from Rome without even giving him the money necessary for his return to Toledo.   Don Illán retorts by declaring that, as His Holiness will not give him food, he must needs return to the supper which was ordered when the instruction began.   The dean now wakes up to find he has had a practical lesson in magic, having been himself bewitched.   All his honours are merely the illusions of an enchanted dream.   In order to punish him for his ingratitude, Don Illán dismisses him without even asking him to remain to sup.   The moral is contained in the quaint couplet—

> [1] *Al que mucho ayudares, et non te lo gradesciere,*
> *Menos ayuda habrás, desque á grant honra subiere.*

This story, like all the rest of the collection, is supposed to be told by Patronio the *consejero* (councillor) to Count Lucanor, his patron, who has asked advice as to his conduct with regard to a neighbour who has besought his aid, after having already on one occasion played him false in point of gratitude.   The tendency of all the stories is distinctly moral, and Don Juan Manuel carries out fully the purpose which he expresses in his preface in the following words :—

[2] Este libro fizo don Johan, fijo del muy noble infante don Manuel, deseando que los homes feciesen en este mundo tales obras que les fuesen aprovichamiento de las honras et de las faciendas et de sus estados, et fuesen más allegados á la carrera porque pudiesen salvar las ánimas.   Et puso en él los enxemplos más aprovechosos que el sopo de las cosas que acaescieron, porque los homes puedan facer esto que dicho es.   Et será maravilla si de cualquier cosa que acaezca á cualquier home, non fallare en este libro su

---

[1] " He who shows no gratitude for great benefits, will show still less when exalted to great honours."

[2] " This book was composed by Don Johan son of the very noble prince Don Manuel, in the desire that men should do in this world such deeds as might be profitable to their reputations and affairs and estates, and might more closely follow such courses as should enable them to save their souls. And he placed in it the most profitable examples that he knew of things that have happened, so that men may do as has already been set forth.   And it will be strange should any matter befall any person of such a kind that he

semejanza que acaesció á otro. . . . Et por las menguas que en sus libros fallaren no pongan la culpa á su entención, mas pónganla á la mengua de su entendimiento porque se atrevió á se entremeter et fablar en tales cosas. Pero Dios sabe que lo fizo por intención que se aprovechasen de lo quel diría á[1] las gentes que non fuesen muy letrados nin muy sabidores. Et por ende fizo todos los sus libros en romance ; et esto es señal cierto que los fizo para los legos et de non muy grand saber, que non fuesen para leerlos. Et daquí comienza el prólogo del Libro de los Enxemplos del conde Lucanor et de Patronio, et el prólogo comienza así.

Among the purely didactic works of Don Juan Manuel we may cite the *Book of the Knight and of the Squire*, relating in quaint and straightforward language the instruction in knightly virtues and graces given by a hermit, who had himself followed the profession of arms, to an aspirant to fame in a similar direction. Especially unfortunate is the loss of a *Book of Songs*, which the author himself tells us he composed and laid up with his other works in the monastery of Peñafiel, which he founded. The works of Don Juan Manuel are more than a mere literary curiosity : they mark a distinct progress in the development of the language, and it is to be regretted that his successors did not copy more closely the even and lucid style which lends a charm to these quaintly picturesque books that so well illustrate the aspirations and ideals cherished by the loftier spirits of the turbulent times among which their author's lot was cast.

cannot find in this book something like it that happened to another. . . . And for the defects that may be found in his books let the blame be given, not to the purpose he had in view, but to his want of wit, for that he made bold to meddle and speak of such matters. But God knows that he did it purposing that what he said might be profitable to such people as were not very learned nor very wise. And for this cause he made all his books in Romance,[2] which is a clear sign that he made them for the unlearned who would not (otherwise) be able to read them. And henceforth begins the prologue of the Book of Examples of the Count Lucanor and of Patronio, and the prologue begins thus."

---

[1] The text appears to be wrong here. Either *á* or the preceding *se* must be omitted.

[2] Spanish is frequently called Romance by the older writers.

Juan Ruiz, best known under the title of Archpriest of Hita, was born about the end of the thirteenth century in the neighbourhood of Madrid, which at that time was a mere village resorted to occasionally by the kings of Castile for hunting. We know little of his life except that which he tells us in his poems or *Libro de Cantares*, a collection of verse of about seven thousand lines, and the most original work of all the earlier period of Spanish literature. In it the Archpriest relates with the greatest vivacity and frankness, coupled only too frequently with the grossest indecency and profanity, the history of his love-adventures among the shepherd-folk and convents in the neighbourhood of his native place. His more than irregular life seems to have brought him into well-deserved trouble with his ecclesiastical superiors, and we know that he was for some time imprisoned in Toledo. In spite of their many blemishes his writings are very valuable as a curiously minute and highly-coloured picture of the manners of the time ; they have, moreover, distinct literary merit ; the author possesses an inexhaustible fund of imagination, and handles the heavy *cuaderna vía* with a freedom and fluency unknown elsewhere. As a story-teller he is unsurpassed, and he gives fresh point to the many fables which, as he himself admits, he drew from Latin sources. About eight hundred lines of the *cantares* are taken up with the spirited allegorical account of the *Battle between Sir Carnival and Lady Lent*, well known in early French. In the spring the Archpriest receives from the hand of Don Ayuno (Sir Fasting) letters from Santa Quaresma (Saint Lent) bidding him send a challenge in her name to Don Carnal (Sir Carnival), who for a year has been lording it far and wide. Don Carnal accepts the challenge and comes forth to battle with a noble array of capon, partridge, rabbit, bacon, beef, and hams. Their arms are copper cooking-pots, their shields are saucepans ; on their side fight the wild boar, the stag, and the hare. This goodly company, after a sumptuous banquet, is surprised at midnight by Doña Cuaresma accompanied by champions such as the tunny, the sardine, and the red lobster. After a desperate struggle the troops of Don Carnal are defeated, he himself is condemned to be imprisoned, whilst his allies, Lady Sausage and Sir Bacon, meet the harder fate of hanging. Don Carnal is visited in the prison, where he lies wounded and in evil case, by a confessor who brings him to a state of repentance. As he recovers his strength, however, Don Carnal's penitence disappears, and on Palm Sunday he escapes from church and communicates with his partisans, Sir Breakfast and Lady Lunch. He is now joined by a powerful ally, Don Amor, and the rebellion against the harsh rule of Doña Cuaresma breaks out on Easter Eve. The latter part of the poem describes the triumphant reception given by their subjects to Don Carnal and Don Amor on their return from captivity.

The book of *Cantares* ends with the death of *Trota-Conventos*, the Archpriest's go-between, and the conversion of her master from the error of his ways by a nun to whom he has made love. Throughout his more than questionable writings the vagabond priest stoutly maintains that his purpose is a moral one, and here and there he introduces edifying religious disquisitions and hymns, sometimes of great beauty and deep devotional feeling. If, however, his intentions were good, his way of carrying them out is the more extraordinary, for, as Menendez y Pelayo says, he most effectually concealed this ulterior purpose *sotto il velame degli versi strani.* He is the first writer in Castilian of the short lyric pieces, common in Provencal poetry, that describe the charms of shepherd-girls or milkmaids, and are consequently called *Serranillas* or *Vaqueiras.*[1] We are indebted to him for a very curious *Student's Song for asking Alms*, that serves to illustrate the condition of Spanish universities in the Middle Ages.

[1] For a specimen of this kind of composition, see extract, p. 74.

A writer of truly moral tendency is the Rabbi Don Sem Tob, who, as he tells us, was a Jew of Carrión. His book of maxims, many of which are derived from the Bible and the writings of Oriental moralists, is interesting in the extreme. His tone is manly and his standard high; it is curious that he was bold enough to address his teaching to Don Pedro the Cruel, whose humane treatment of the Jews provoked so much dissatisfaction among his Christian subjects. The seven-syllable lines in which he writes are graceful and well adapted to his subject, the treatment of which may be judged from the following extracts :—

> [1] Á tu algo non tocas
> Si non de lienços gruesos
> Algunas varas pocas
> Para enboluer tus huesos.
>
> .   .   .
>
> Honbre, tu te querellas
> Quando lo que te plase
> Non se cumple, y rreuellas
> A Dios porque non fase
> Todo lo que tu quieres,
> Y andas muy yrado ;
> ¿ Non te membras que eres
> De vil cosa criado ?
>
> .   .   .
>
> Por nasçer en espino
> La rrosa, yo non syento
> Que pierde, nin el buen vino
> Por salir del sarmiento.
>
> Nyn vale el açor menos
> Por que en vil nido syga.
> Nin los enxemplos buenos
> Por que judio los diga.

---

[1] "Of thy goods thou touchest nought,—except of coarse cloth—some few ells—which envelope thy bones. . . . Man thou complainest—when that which pleaseth thee—comes not to pass, and rebellest—against God because he does not—all that thou wouldst,—and walkest in anger.—Rememberest thou not that thou art—of vile matter created ? . . .

"For that it springs from the thorny shrub—the rose, to my mind,—is not the worse ; nor good wine—for coming from the wine-stock ;—neither is the falcon less precious—for that it abides in a foul nest,—nor wise admonitions—because they come from the mouth of a Jew."

For the last time in early Spanish poetry the free and martial spirit that inspired the *Poem of My Cid* is to be found in passages of the *Poem of Alfonso XI.*, discovered in 1573 by Diego Hurtado de Mendoza, and supposed at first to be the work of the champion whose victories it celebrates. Internal evidence, however, shows conclusively that its author was Rodrigo Yañez, who fought by Alfonso's side at the great battle of Salado which forms the central point of the poem and of the reign which the poem describes. Yañez is the first to use eight-syllable lines for the purpose of epic narrative; his system of rhyming every alternate line renders the metre tedious in his long rhymed chronicle, which rises to the level of poetry only in descriptions of battles like the following:—

> [1] Los moros perdían tierra
> Et por el monte sobían,
> Por el medio de la sierra
> Ondas de sangre corrían.
> Aquesto vió el rey moro,
> Más quisiera la su fin,
> El dió voces como un toro
> Llamando ¡ Benamarin !
>
> .   .   .   .
>
> Llamando iba ¡ Espanna !
> El rrey don Alonso, el bueno :
> Assy rronpió la montanna
> Como la piedra del trueno.
>
> .   .   .   .
>
> Cobiertos eran los puertos
> Fasta las aguas del mar :
> Atantos eran los muertos
> Que siempre avría que contar.
>
> .   .   .   .

---

[1] "The Moors were losing ground,—up the hill they were flying—in the midst of the mountains—streams of blood were flowing.—When the Moorish King saw this,—rather had he seen his end,—he roared aloud as does a bull—shouting, Benamarin ! Shouting his war-cry, Spain !—the king Don Alonso the bold—burst upon the mountain—as a bolt from a thundercloud—. . . The passes were covered with dead—down to the shores of the sea—So many

> Desían ; ¡ qué buen sennor !
> Et ¡ qué noble caballero !
> ¡ Val Dios, qué buen lidiador !
> ¡ Val Dios, qué real braçero !

The popular imagination of the Middle Ages created a fantastic allegory, known in France as the *Dance Macabre*, in which Death is represented as calling upon persons of all ages and all classes of society to join his gruesome revels. This subject was thoroughly suited to the grotesque and morbid taste of the period that preceded the Renaissance, and found favour equally with painters and with poets. A version of it appears in Spanish literature under the name of the *Danza de la Muerte*, in which the weirdness and horror of the subject are treated with great animation, and the interest is sustained by graphic touches and fluent verse.

At the end of the fourteenth century the influence of Provençal and Italian became strong, to the great detriment of Castilian poetry. There belongs, however, to this period one writer of note who followed the national traditions, and is therefore included in the present chapter. Pero Lopez de Ayala was a nobleman and courtier who lived during the reigns of Pedro I., Enrique II., and Juan I. Subsequently he was a member of the council appointed to administer the kingdom during the minority of Enrique III., under whom he rose to the dignity of Chancellor. Notwithstanding his lofty position he had some experience of the vicissitudes of life, being twice a prisoner of war, once in Portugal after the battle of Aljubarrota, and once in England after the battle of Nájera, in which he fought on

were the slain—that one might count for ever—. . . They said, How good a king—and noble knight is he !—Great God, how mighty in battle !—Great God, how royally he smites ! " *

---

* The above extract is composed of stanzas 1691, 1715, 1776, 1771 of the poem. They were selected for the purpose of illustration, together with others, by the late Don Francisco Sanchez de Castro, Professor of Literature at Madrid. I have altered some of the lines to the better readings of the edition of the *Autores Españoles*.

the side of Enrique de Trastamara. He wrote, as official chronicler, the history of his own times, with more detail and colouring than was usual with his predecessors (see p. 35); he translated, moreover, Boccaccio's *Fall of Princes*, and other Italian books, as well as some parts of Livy. But the work by which he is best known is the *Rimado de Palacio*, or *Libro de Palacio*, a poem of about four thousand lines. The body of the poem is written in *cuaderna vía*, but the *estrofa de arte mayor* is also occasionally used. The hymns and songs with which it is interspersed are in lines of eight syllables. After the introduction comes a version and explanation of the ten commandments, then follows the *Seven Mortal Sins* and the *Seven Works of Mercy*, the *Five Senses* and the *Seven Spiritual Works*. The poem now assumes a more secular tone, and speaks of the administration of the state, of war and of justice, with elaborate and amusing satires on merchants, lawyers, and tax-gatherers; after a long prayer we find the *Fechos del Palacio* (Affairs of the Palace) followed by chapters of *Advice to all Men*, *Admonitions for the Government of the Republic*, and the *Nine Matters by which the Power of the King may be recognised*. Prayers, hymns—often of considerable beauty—and moral lessons, supported by examples taken from the Bible, form the second and larger half of the book, which is interesting chiefly as a study of the social state of the country by a native, at the time of the stirring events for which Ayala's and Froissart's Chronicles form the principal authorities. Throughout this curious mixture of religious fervour and worldly wisdom runs a strong vein of satire. He who had seen so much of palaces and courts speaks thus of them in his old age :—

> [1] Grant tiempo de mi vida pasé mal despendiendo,
> Á sennores terrenales con grant cura syrviendo,

---

[1] "A great part of my life I badly spent and wasted,—serving with all diligence the lords of the earth ;—now do I see and am come to the under-

Agora ya lo veo é lo vo entendiendo,
Que quien y más trabaja más yrá perdiendo.
Las cortes de los reyes ¿ quién las podrá pensar ?
Quanto mal é trabajo el omne ha de pasar,
Perigros en el cuerpo é el alma condenar,
Los bienes é el algo siempre lo aventurar.
Si mill annos las syrvo é un día fallesco,
Disen que muchos males é penas les meresco.
Si por ellos en cuytas é cuydados padesco
Disen que como nesçio por mi culpa peresco.
Si por yr á mi casa liçençia les demando,
Despues á la tornada, nin sé como nin cuando,
Fallo mundo rebuelto, trastornado mi vando,
É más frio que nieve en su palacio ando.
Fallo porteros nueuos, que nunca conosçí,
Que todo el palacio quieren tener por sy :
Sy llego á la puerta disen ¿ Quién está y ?
Sennores digo, yo, que en mal día nasçy.

---

standing—that he who labours more in this will have the heavier loss.—Who can imagine the courts of kings?—All the suffering and labour that must be endured,—danger to the body and damnation to the soul,—goods and estate ever at stake.—If for a thousand years I serve, and one day come to die,—they say I have deserved harsh treatment and chastisement at their hands.—If for their sake I suffer grief and care,—they say I am a fool and my undoing is self-sought.—If I ask of them permission to visit my house,—when, afterwards, I return, even as it may hap,—I find affairs have changed, my influence broken up,—and colder than snow is my position in the palace.—New chamberlains I find, who are unknown to me,—who would have all the palace to themselves :—If I come to the gate, they cry out, 'Who is there?'—'Good Sirs,' say I, ''Tis I born in an unhappy hour.' . . . '

CHAPTER III

CHRONICLES AND ROMANCES OF CHIVALRY

In the *Partidas* of Alfonso the Wise (see p. 19) it is enjoined upon knights that they should listen, whilst at table, to the reading of the "histories of the great deeds of arms that others did." These are the chronicles, throughout which the personal greatly outweighs the political or the social element. Alfonso himself carefully brought down the history of his country to his own time. In spite of this good example and the noble model thereby furnished, many years were allowed to pass after his death before the history of his reign and that of the two succeeding ones was written. The account, moreover, of this period that has come down to us is probably untrustworthy, for the chronicler has, either willingly or of necessity, falsified the true aspect of affairs in order to palliate the undutiful conduct of the successor and other sons of the unfortunate Sage. The office of chronicler was, after Alfonso's time, regularly exercised by persons appointed by successive kings. These succeed one another without a break down to the reign of Fernando and Isabel, in which Hernando del Pulgar (the secretary, see p. 38), two years before the taking of Granada, abruptly closes his account of the stirring events of which he himself was an eye-witness. Even later, chroniclers were regularly appointed, but the slender merits of this class of writings are such as are possible only in an unsophisticated age; the "historiographi" of the seventeenth century are historians rather than chroniclers.

Few of the official chronicles deserve mention as literary works; they are generally merely bald relations of events and notable feats of arms, or, at most, are interspersed with inflated and improbable speeches modelled on those of the classical historians. The best are those of the reigns of Don Pedro the Cruel and his three immediate successors, composed by Lopez de Ayala, the author of the *Rimado de Palacio*, and that of Don Juan II., part of which is attributed to the court poet, Juan de Mena (see p. 75). The latter has been rated by competent authority as second only to certain of the Romances of Chivalry among the best ancient models of Castilian prose.

The following passage taken from the chronicle of Don Juan II., and describing the death of Don Álvaro de Luna, affords a fair specimen of the best narrative style of the period, and is not unworthy of its great central figure :—

¹ É otro día muy en amanesciendo, oyó misa muy devotamente é rescibió el cuerpo de Nuestro Señor, é demandó que le diesen alguna cosa que beviese, é traxéronle un plato de guindas, de las cuales comió muy pocas é bevió una taza de vino puro. É después que esto fué hecho, cavalgó en una mula, é Diego Destúñiga é muchos caballeros que le acompañaban, é iban los pregoneros pregonando en altas voces : "Ésta es la justicia que manda hacer el Rey nuestro Señor á este cruel tirano y usurpador de la corona real : en pena de sus maldades mándale degollar por ello." É así lo llevaron por la cal de Francos, é por la Costanilla, hasta que llegaron á la plaza donde estaba hecho un cadahalso alto de madera ; é todavía los Frayles iban juntos con él, esforzándole que muriese con Dios ; é desque

---

¹ "And on the next day so soon as it was dawn he heard mass very devoutly, and received the Body of Our Lord, and bid them give him something to drink; and they brought him a dish of plums of which he ate but few and drank a cup of unmixed wine. And after this was done, he mounted on a mule, as also did Diego Destúñiga and many gentlemen that bore him company ; and the criers went proclaiming loudly 'This is the justice that the King our lord commands to be done upon this cruel tyrant and usurper of the kingly crown : in punishment of his wickedness he commands that his throat be cut.' And thus they led him through the street of the Franks and up the Hillside until they came unto the market-place where was raised a lofty scaffold of wood ; and ever the Friars walked by his side exhorting him to die

llego al cadahalso, hiziéronle descavalgar, é desque subió encima, vidѳ un
tapete tendido, é una cruz delante, é ciertas antorchas encendidas, é un
garavato de fierro fincado en un madero ; é luego fincó las rodillas é adoró
la cruz, é despues levantóse en pie, y paseóse dos veces por el cadahalso.
É allí el Maestre dió á un page suyo llamado Morales, á quien había dado
la mula al tiempo que descavalgó, una sortija de sellar que en la mano
llevaba, é un sombrero, é le dixo : " Toma el postrimero bien que de mí
puedes recibir," el cual lo recibió con muy gran llanto. Y en la plaza y en
las ventanas había infinitas gentes que habían venido de todos los lugares
de aquella comarca á ver aquel acto : los cuales desque vieron al Maestre
andar paseando comenzaron de hacer muy gran llanto ; é todavía los Frayles
estaban juntos con él diciéndole que no se acordase de su gran estado é
señorío é muriese como buen christiano. Él les respondió que así lo hacía,
é que fuesen ciertos que en la fe parescía á los Santos Mártires. É hablando
en estas cosas, alzó los ojos é vido á Barrasa, caballerizo del Príncipe é
llamóle é díxole : " Ven acá, Barrasa ; tu estás aquí mirando la muerte que
me dan ; yo te ruego que digas al Príncipe mi señor que dé mejor gualardón
á sus criados quel Rey, mi señor, mandó dar á mí." É ya el verdugo
sacaba un cordel para le atar las manos, é el Maestre le preguntó : "¿ Qué
quieres hacer ?" El verdugo le dixo : " Quiero, Señor, ataros las manos con
este cordel." El Maestre le dixo : " No hagas así," é diciéndole esto quitóse
una cintilla de los pechos, é diógela, é díxole : " Átame con ésta, é yo te

---

reconciled to God ; so when he reached the scaffold they made him dismount,
and when he was come up upon it, he beheld a carpet spread and a cross
before his eyes and certain torches alight and an iron hook fixed in a beam ;
and straightway he knelt him down and made obeisance to the cross and rose
again to his feet and paced twice across the scaffold. And there the Master
gave to one of his pages named Morales, the same to whom he had given the
mule when he dismounted, a signet-ring that he wore on his hand, and a hat,
and said to him ' Take the last favour that thou canst receive of me,' and he
received it with much weeping. And in the market-place and in the windows
were much people that had come from all the hamlets of that district to see
the deed done : and these when they saw the Master pace up and down, began
to wail aloud ; and ever the Friars were at his side bidding him not to remember his great estate and lordship but to die as a good Christian. And he
answered them that even thus he was doing, assuring them that his faith was
like to that of the Holy Martyrs. And speaking still of these matters he
raised his eyes and beheld Barrasa, the equerry of the prince, and he called to
him and said : ' Come hither, Barrasa : thou art here looking on at my death :
I beg thee that thou bid the Prince my lord that he give unto his servants a
better reward than the King my lord hath commanded to be given to me.'
And already the headsman was drawing forth a cord to bind his hands, and
the Master asked him ' What wouldst thou do ? ' And the headsman said
' Sir, I would bind your hands with this cord.' The Master said to him ' Do
not thus,' and as he said this, he took off a ribbon from his breast and gave
it to him and said ' Bind me with this ; and I beg thee to see that thou

ruego que mires si traes buen puñal afilado, porque prestamente me despaches." Otrosí le dixo : " Dime : aquel garavato que está en aquel madero ¿para qué está allí puesto ? " El verdugo le dixo que era para que despues que fuese degollado, pusiesen allí su cabeza. El Maestre dixo : " Despues que yo fuere degollado, hagan del cuerpo y de la cabeza lo que querrán." Y esto hecho, comenzó á desabrocharse el collar del jubón, é aderezarse la ropa que traía vestida, que era larga, de chamelote azul, forrada en raposos ferreros ; é como el Maestre fué tendido en el estrado, luego llegó a él el verdugo é demandóle perdón, é dióle paz, é pasó el puñal por su garganta é cortóle la cabeza, e púsola en el garavato. Y estuvo la cabeza allí nueve días, y el cuerpo tres días ; é puso un bacín de plata á la cabecera donde el Maestre estaba degollado, para que allí echasen el dinero los que quisiesen dar limosna para con que le enterrasen : Y en aquel bacín fué echado asaz dinero.

The close relation existing between the chronicles and ballads may be studied by comparing the passages in which they severally treat of the incidents connected with the death of Don Álvaro de Luna, or in their respective accounts of Bernardo del Carpio and of the Cid.

More interesting from an artistic point of view than the official chronicles, though still falling within the province of the antiquary rather than that of the student of literature, are the chronicles of particular events and persons. One of the earliest is that of the Cid. This chronicle is probably founded on the *Estoria de Espanna* of Alfonso el Sabio, which furnishes the earliest version of the legendary stories of Bernardo del Carpio (see p. 46) and of the Siete Infantes de Lara (Seven

bearest a dagger well-sharpened so that thou rid me the sooner.' Moreover he said to him ' Tell me, the hook that is in that beam, wherefore is it there placed ? ' The headsman told him that it was in order that his head might be placed thereupon after that his throat were cut. The Master said ' When my throat is cut, let them do with the body and the head as they will.' And when he had said this he began to unfasten the collar of his doublet and to make ready the robes that he wore and these were long, of blue camlet lined with russet fox-skins ; and when the Master had laid him down on the scaffold the headsman straightway drew near and begged his forgiveness, and kissed him, and thrust the dagger through his neck, and cut off his head, and placed it on the hook. And the head remained there nine days and the body three days ; and he placed a silver basin at the place where lay the head of the Master when his throat was cut, that into it such as would give an alms for his burial might cast it ; and into that basin was cast much money."

Princes of Lara), as well as the germs of almost all the myths that so rapidly obscured the personality of the Conqueror of Valencia.

Among the more graphic and picturesque of these chronicles of particular persons must be cited that of Don Pero Niño, who died in 1453, and whose manifold adventures, both in Europe and on the coasts of Northern Africa, are recorded by his *alférez* or standard-bearer, Gutierre Diez de Games. Its description of the life of a nobleman and soldier both in public and in private is strikingly realistic. One of the most curious passages of the book is that which tells the story of the Count's roving expedition to England, in which he appears to have carried out most successfully his purpose of plundering the southern coast. The chapter also on " How the English differ from and are opposed to all other Christian nations " is interesting to those concerned. The rugged and quaint style of the faithful man-at-arms lends additional colour to the exploits of his beloved leader.

The *Chronicle of Don Álvaro de Luna* was evidently written by some one who bore him a deep affection and knew him well. This circumstance gives a pathetic interest and singular charm to the tragic history of this really great and, in some respects, noble and generous man ; for Álvaro de Luna's reputation has probably suffered greatly from the fact that his history was written after his fall.

The last of the chronicles of great men is that of Gonzalo de Córdova, the Great Captain, a short history of whom was written by his fellow-soldier and admirer Hernán Perez del Pulgar, who must not be confounded with the official chronicler of the same name. The soldier is distinguished by the honourable title of *El de las Hazañas* (He of the Exploits) and he it was who, during the siege of Granada, entered the city and nailed the *Ave Maria* to the door of the great mosque— a deed commemorated by certain privileges conferred on him at the taking of the city, and enjoyed by his descendants to this day.

Other curious works of the fifteenth century are the *Chronicle of the Paso Honroso* and the *Itinerary of Ruy Gonzalez de Clavijo*, who went on an embassy to Samarcand in 1403 to carry presents from Enrique III., King of Castile, to the famous Timur Beg. His account of his adventures was published in the fifteenth century under the odd title of *Life of the great Tamorlán*. The former book recounts with minute detail what is probably the greatest passage of arms of a purely chivalrous character on record. It took place in 1434. We are told how Suero de Quiñones, a famous knight, had made a vow to wear for the love of his lady an iron chain on every Thursday, and how, grown weary of his vow, he accepts as the condition of release from it an engagement to keep the bridge of Orbigo with certain companions for thirty days against all comers. In this enterprise he and his nine companions prove successful, tilting many times with seventy-eight knights and breaking many lances. The *Chronicle of the Paso Honroso* is scarcely a literary work, but giving in plain and simple language the account of an eye-witness of this extraordinary event, it helps us to realise how, to those who knew such things to have taken place in their own time, the extravagant absurdities of the Romances of Chivalry would not be so entirely incredible as to preclude interest. So popular were the Chronicles that imagination was drawn upon for facts which were however usually associated with some famous name. Examples of fabulous histories such as these are the *Chronicle of Don Rodrigo and the Destruction of Spain*, in which fact and fancy are inextricably mingled, and historical personages are found side by side with others of a purely mythical character. The *Crónica Troyana* gives an account of the Trojan war materially different from that of Homer. In both of these books the principal parts are played by knights-errant of the most accomplished type of the *libros de caballerías*. From heroes of this character to the Ámadises and Palmerines the transition is short and natural.

The Romances of Chivalry, though not peculiar to the country, attained, like the chronicles and ballads, an extraordinary popularity and development in Spain during the fifteenth and sixteenth centuries. They probably owe their origin to the taste for chronicles. Imagination stepped in to supply the place of history, and real persons and events paled before its fantastic creations and their superhuman adventures. To men who were familiar with the many absurdities that sprang from the codes of chivalry, the typical knight-errant of fiction was scarcely an extravagant character. Urganda the Unknown and the rest of the tribe of enchanters are indispensable when, as often happens, the exuberant fancy of authors brings the heroes into situations from which nothing less than supernatural intervention can release them. When once a taste for such literature had been created, and when, through the invention of printing, it reached a lower class of society, it is scarcely to be wondered at that imagination, unchecked by knowledge of foreign countries, of history, and of the physical laws that govern the universe, ran riot. Authors attempted to surpass one another in the wild improbability of the exploits of their heroes, and the result is a cold and repulsive picture in which sickly sentimentality has taken the place of chivalrous love, and the invariable successes of the heroes effectually stamp out the spark of interest that may have been kindled by the harrowing tales of their dangers and difficulties. Well might Juan de Valdés regret the ten years that he spent in reading "these lying fables" (*mentiras*). Happily one only of the books of this class calls for special mention.

The French romances of chivalry, the earliest of which date from the thirteenth century, may be divided into two classes : those connected with the legend of Charles the Great, and those connected with the legend of King Arthur and the Round Table. Both of these legendary stories have some shadow of historical foundation. Not so the earlier Spanish romances, which deal with purely imaginary personages, though their authors were no doubt familiar with the French and Celtic legends. The first Romance of Chivalry printed in Spain (*Tirant lo Blanch*) is written in the Valencian dialect, thus marking the foreign origin of the class.

The source of the *Amadis de Gaula*, the first and best of these books in Castilian, is somewhat uncertain. In its present form it is a translation, made by Ordoñez de Montalvo about the end of the fifteenth century, of the now lost work of Vasco de Lobeyra, a Portuguese who lived about a hundred years earlier. Whether the *Amadis* of Lobeyra was an original work or not we cannot know, but it is beyond doubt that some form of the Ámadis story existed still earlier in Spain, for Lopez de Ayala, the author of the *Rimado de Palacio* (see p. 31), who died at an advanced age in 1407, says, speaking of his youth, that he "wasted much time in listening to the false and vain stories of Ámadis and Lancelot." However this may be, *Amadis* deserves more than the negative praise bestowed upon him by Cervantes, the avowed enemy of his innumerable tribe. In the famous scrutiny of Don Quixote's books the priest, speaking with the book in his hand, says, " This was the first book of chivalry printed in Spain and deserves condemnation to the flames as the propagandist of so evil a sect."—" No," says the barber, " for I have also heard say that it is the best of all the books of the kind that have been composed, and thus it should be pardoned on account of its unique position."—" True," says the priest, " and for that reason its life is spared for the present." The learned author of *The Dialogue on Languages* (see p. 135), and Torcuato Tasso, regarded the *Amadis* from very different points of view, yet they agree in praising it in no measured terms : the former says it should be read by all who wish to learn Spanish; the latter, that it is the most beautiful and perhaps the most profitable story of its kind that can be read. This praise is well deserved. Throughout the book the interest is fairly sustained; it contains a real plot, and is no mere rambling series of adventures; the characters are admirably drawn, and it abounds in passages of true feeling. The chronology and geography are wild in the extreme, yet they are enough for the purposes of a book the object of which is to represent the perfect knight, loyal and true, tender and brave. The events are supposed to happen "between the time of the founding of Christianity and the time of King Arthur." The scene is mostly laid in England. "Gaula" is undoubtedly Wales; Windsor and Bristol are mentioned; but no attempt is made by the author to represent the manners of a definite bygone time or of foreign lands. The principal personages of the story are Ámadis, his lady Oriana, his brother Galaor, and his father Perión, but the host of minor characters who throng the pages are well and clearly drawn. The subject is the loves of Ámadis and Oriana, and the troubles and trials through which they have to pass before they are at last happily married. The supernatural is made use of to a large extent, but not so as to diminish the interest of the story. Ámadis is really a hero and not, like his descendants, a feeble creature bolstered up by enchanters.

Little or none of this praise can be bestowed on the imitations and successors of this most famous and popular book; "the goodness of the father must not stand the sons in stead," says Cervantes, and he is right. Each of them, beginning with the *Sergas de Esplandián* written by Montalvo himself, is worse than the last. The earlier editions of these romances are much prized by book-collectors on account of their rarity, but they are seldom read. Florisando, Lisuarte, Ámadis of Greece, Florisel, Felixmarte, and Primaleón, differ only in the size of the giants they slay and the degree of improbability of their colourless adventures and loves. It is hard to understand the extravagant praise bestowed by Cervantes on the *Palmerín of England*, of which he makes a notable exception; unless indeed his words are ironical. So popular was this form of fiction, until Don Quixote slew the monster at a single blow, that it was used for the purpose of religious allegory in such books as the *Celestial Chivalry* and the *Conqueror of Heaven*. It is evident that when the knight of La Mancha smote these feeble creatures they were already on the point of a natural death from inanition.

CHAPTER IV

THE BALLADS

THE Spanish word *romance*, which in earlier times signified the vernacular as opposed to Latin, has come to be restricted in meaning to short heroic poems or ballads of a particular form and to the metre in which they are composed. The *romances* are written in lines which may be regarded as consisting either of eight syllables with rhyme only in every second line, or of sixteen syllables with a strong cæsura after the eighth and with continuous rhyme. The analogy of the other octosyllabic metres, so popular with Castilian authors, and the invariable practice of earlier writers, go to favour the former view, in spite of the arguments brought forward by critics of authority on the other side. The system of rhyme common to all the ballads is called *asonante ;* it existed in the old French *chansons* till displaced by full rhyme in the twelfth and thirteenth centuries. Account is taken of the vowels only that bear and follow the last tonic accent in the line. Vowels should be identical in the syllables rhymed, but custom sanctions the rhyming of diphthongs containing the strong vowels *a, e, o,* with these vowels standing alone. Thus *hallando* is assonant to *cristianos ; decía* to *la villa ; y señor* to *prometió ; cambio* to *marcos ; van* to *dar.* Such a system of rhyme is possible only in a language in which the vowels are as strongly marked and as pure as they are in Spanish. The same *asonante* is frequently made use of throughout a whole ballad. To foreign ears this, the most popular of Spanish metres (see observations on popular poetry, p. 268), is not always at first agreeable ; but when once familiar, the rhythmical beat of the vowels will usually be preferred to the jingle of rhyme in ballads and dramatic dialogue (see p. 167), for as Juan de Valdés truly remarks, " the perfection of Castilian verse consists in its similarity to prose."

Some of the earliest extant ballads are apparently rhymed versions of the chronicles, whilst some of the chronicles are prose versions of the ballads. In other instances both have probably been drawn from some common source. This form of composition is very easy in Spanish, and about two thousand ballads of widely different dates go to form the great collection known as the *Romancero General*. Many of these, especially the oldest ones, possess great beauty and interest, but they are often, unfortunately, much degraded from their original simplicity, partly by the wearing-down process undergone in passing from mouth to mouth during centuries, and partly by arbitrary alterations and additions, and the so-called improvements introduced by those who collected and wrote them down in the sixteenth and seventeenth centuries. At first the ballads were to the ignorant what the chronicles were to the more educated : they related the great deeds of national heroes, historical or fabulous ; they furnished examples of valour and piety, and celebrated the legends of saints so dear to the popular imagination. That they were recited in public is certain. Alfonso the Wise speaks of the *juglares*, the gleemen, who are roughly divided into two classes : those who wrote or composed the ballads (*juglares de péñola*), and those who recited them (*juglares de boca*). Later on frequent mention is made of these more picturesque and dignified predecessors of the blind-men (*ciegos*) who have nowadays inherited their functions. The earliest printed *romances* appear in the *Cancionero General* of 1511. These are anonymous, and it is not until the middle of the sixteenth century that in the early *Romanceros* (ballad-books) ballads by known authors are found. The best modern collection is that of Durán (Madrid, 1861). The ballads, of which the vast majority are comparatively modern, are here divided according as they treat of Moorish legends, legends of the fabulous history of chivalry, sacred history, histories of Rome and Greece, Spanish history, lives of saints, and other subjects. The most valuable in every way are those relating to episodes in the national history and to the exploits of the national heroes. Three great Spanish legends were especially popular with the ballad-makers : that of Bernardo del Carpio ; that of the Seven Princes (*Infantes*) of Lara ; and that of the Cid. The word legends is used advisedly, for the Cid of the ballads is a very different person from the rough champion of the *Poema ;* and though Bernardo himself is historical, his exploits are certainly fabulous. Bernardo is represented as the son of a secret marriage between Jimena, the sister of Alfonso the Chaste, and the Count of Saldaña, a nobleman of the court. His parents fell under the royal displeasure for having married without permission ; his mother retired into a convent and his father was cast into prison. Bernardo was brought up at his uncle's court, where his noble qualities made him a general favourite. But the king, his uncle, in spite of the love he bore him, allowed him to suppose that he was a bastard. When already a grown man, Bernardo learns the secret of his birth, and immediately demands the liberation of his father. His request is roughly refused, but he nevertheless remains loyal ; he fights the king's battles, and on more than one occasion saves his life. Finally he is driven to despair, and revolts on hearing that his uncle intends to leave the kingdom of Castile by will to his powerful neighbour, Charles the Great. Bernardo now enters into an alliance with the Moors of Aragón and appears as victor in the great legendary battle at Roncesvalles, where he kills Roland with his own hand and delivers the country from the French. Alfonso now promises to give up his father to him, but acting with his usual bad faith, he first avenges his family honour by killing the Count in his prison. The body is placed on horseback, and so handed over in mockery to Bernardo. The series of ballads ends with Bernardo's vows of vengeance. The following beautiful lines contain the lamentations of Count Saldaña in prison :—

[1] Bañando está las prisiones
Con lágrimas que derrama
El conde don Sancho Diaz
Ese señor de Saldaña.
Y entre el llanto y soledad,
D'esta suerte se quejaba
De Don Bernardo, su hijo,
Del rey Alfonso y su hermana.
—Los años de mi prisión
Tan aborrecida y larga,
Por momentos me lo dicen
Aquestas mis tristes canas.
Cuando entré en este castillo
Apenas entré con barbas,
Y agora por mis pecados
La veo crecida y blanca.
¿ Qué descuido es este, hijo?
¿ Cómo á voces no te llama
La sangre que tienes mía
Á socorrer donde falta ?

Sin duda que te detiene
La que de tu madre alcanzas
Que por ser de la del Rey
Juzgarás mal de mi causa.
Todos tres sois mis contrarios,
Que á un desdichado no basta
Que sus contrarios lo sean
Sino sus propias entrañas.
Todos los que aquí me tienen
Me cuentan de tus hazañas,
Si para tu padre no,
Dime ¿ para quién las guardas ?
Aquí estoy en estos hierros
Y, pues d'ellos no me sacas,
Mal padre debo de ser,
O tu mal hijo, me faltas.
Perdóname si te ofendo,
Que descanso en las palabras,
Que yo como viejo lloro,
Y tu como ausente callas.

---

[1] " He is bathing his fetters—with the tears which he sheds—the Count Don Sancho Diaz,—the lord of Saldaña.—And amidst his solitary weeping—this was his complaint—against Don Bernardo, his son,—against the king Don Alfonso and his sister.—'The years of my captivity—so hateful and so long—are every moment told to me—by these sad gray hairs of mine.—When I came into this castle—I scarce wore beard on chin—and now for my sins—I see it long and white.—What indifference is this, my son?—How does it not cry aloud—that blood thou hast of mine—to succour where need is?—Doubtless thou art restrained—by the blood thy mother gave,—and since that is the blood of the king,—thou wilt ill judge my cause.—My enemies are ye all three,—for to the luckless it is not enough—that his foes should treat him ill,—his very heart's blood is against him.—All they who hold me here—tell me of thy exploits,—if it be not for thy father,—for whom dost thou keep them ?—Here am I in these chains—and since thou dost not deliver me,—a bad father must I be,—or thou, a bad son, failest me,—Pardon me if I wrong thee,—for in words I find relief,—for I like an old man weep,—and thou like the absent art silent.' "

The legend of the Seven Princes of Lara and the Bastard Mudarra does not contain quite so many inherent improbabilities as the foregoing. The outlines of this story are as follows : Ruy Velazquez or Rodrigo, a nobleman of the great house of Lara, marries Doña Lambra, a lady of high position. His nephews, the *infantes*, come to the wedding, but are advised not to attend the festivities for fear of quarrels. During the jousts a dispute breaks out between the bride and Doña Sancha, the mother of the *infantes*, as to whose kinsmen are the better knights. The *infantes* hear of it through their tutor, Nuño Salido. The youngest comes into the lists and with the first throw of his lance hurls to the ground the *tablado*, or hoarding, of which the other knights have only succeeded in breaking a few planks. The *infantes* are set upon by the opposite party, and a relation of the bride is slain in the melee. Doña Lambra now determines on vengeance and, during a hunting party, induces one of her servants to insult the Laras, who kill him, thus making the quarrel worse. Ruy Velazquez is led by his wife to betray his nephews to the Moors. He sends their father, Don Gonzalo Bustos, on a pretended embassy to Almanzor, king of Córdova, with orders that he is to be kept in captivity. Subsequently he treacherously leads the seven princes into an ambuscade, and they all die fighting bravely together with Nuño Salido their tutor. Their heads are presented to their father by Almanzor. Whilst Don Bustos is in prison a son is born to him by the sister of the Moorish king, who secretly loves him. Don Bustos is at length released, and his bastard son, the famous Mudarra, learning the secret of his birth, avenges the death of his half-brothers by burning Doña Lambra, and bringing the head of Ruy Velazquez to Don Gonzalo Bustos, who is now an old man, but still pines for the vengeance which lies beyond his power. Mudarra becomes a Christian, and his resemblance to one of her sons causes him to be greatly beloved by his father's wife.

The following spirited passage describes the first outbreak of the feud:—

[1] Tiran unos, tiran otros,
Ninguno bien bohordaba.
Allí salió un caballero
De los de Córdoba la llana,
Bohordó hacia el tablado
Y una vara bien tirara.
Allí hablara la novia,
D'esta manera hablara.
    Amad, señoras, amad
Cada una en su lugar,
Que más vale un caballero
De los de Córdoba la llana,
Que no veinte ni treinta
De los de casa de Lara.—
Oídolo había Doña Sancha
D'esta manera hablara :
    No digáis eso, señora,
No digades tal palabra,
Porque hoy os desposaron
Con don Rodrigo de Lara.—
    ¡ Callad, Doña Sancha ! vos
No debeis ser escuchada,
Que siete hijos paristes
Como puerca encenagada.—

Oídolo había el ayo
Que á los Infantes criaba :
De allí se había salido,
Triste se fué á su posada :
Halló que estaban jugando
Los Infantes á las tablas,
Si no era el menor d'ellos,
Gonzalo Gonzalez se llama ;
Recostado lo halló
De pechos á una baranda,
    ¿ Cómo venís triste, ayo ?
Decí ¿ quíen os enojara ?—
Tanto le rogó Gonzalo
Que el ayo se lo contara :
    Mas mucho os ruego, mi hijo,
Que no salgáis a la plaza.—
No lo quiso hacer Gonzalo,
Mas antes tomó una lanza,
Caballero en un caballo
Vase derecho á la plaza :
Vido estar allí el tablado
Que nadie lo derribara.
Enderezóse en la silla
Con él en el suelo daba.

---

[1] "One tries and then another—but none could hurl aright.—Then came forth a knight—of those of Córdova of the plain,—he hurled towards the hoarding,—well did he cast his lance.—Then the bride spoke out—in this wise did she speak.—'Bestow your love, my ladies,—each one as likes her best,—for better is a single knight—of those of Córdova of the plain,—than twenty or thirty knights—of the noble house of Lara.'—Doña Sancha heard her words,—in this wise did she speak—'Speak not so, lady,—say not such words as those,—for this day were you wedded—to Don Rodrigo de Lara.'— 'Hold thy peace, Doña Sancha ;—thou oughtest not have a hearing—seven sons hast thou borne—like a sow that wallows in mud.'—These words the tutor heard—who had the Princes in his charge :—straightway he left the place,—sadly he withdrew to his lodging,—and there he found the Princes,—at tables they were playing, —except the youngest of them —whose name is Gonzalo Gonzalez ;—him he found leaning out—with his arms on the window-sill.—'How come you so sad, dear master ?'—Say, who has injured you ?'— So earnestly begged Gonzalo—that the master told his tale :—'But I beg from my heart, my son,—that ye go not forth to the lists'—Gonzalo would not give heed—but he seized his lance in hand—and he mounted on his horse,—forth to the lists he went :—there he saw the hoarding stand,—for none had cast it down,—he straightened himself in the saddle,—and hurled it to the ground.''

The Cid of the *Romancero* differs but little from the Cid of the special Chronicle devoted to his exploits. He is the son of Diego Lainez, a knight oi Burgos. His father in his old age has been grievously insulted by the Conde Lozano, a proud and wealthy nobleman. Brooding over his affront he determines to make trial of the spirit of his sons. This he does by the barbarous but effective method of biting their fingers, which, at his bidding, they place in his mouth. The elder sons cry out and beg him to desist, but Rodrigo, the youngest, shows his spirit by threatening him, and thus is chosen as his father's avenger. Rodrigo challenges and slays the Conde Lozano. Jimena, the daughter of the Count, loudly demands justice of the king, and a marriage is brought about between her and Rodrigo in order to stay the feud. Rodrigo now begins his military exploits by the famous battle in which, by conquering five Moorish kings, he is supposed to have gained the title of "my Cid" (Arab. *seid* = lord). He now undertakes a pilgrimage to Santiago ; on his journey Saint Lazarus appears to him in the form of a leper to whom he has shown great humanity, and promises him a prosperous career. Chosen as champion of Castile to contest the possession of Calahorra with an Aragonese knight, he comes out of the lists victorious. Many expeditions against the Moors are mentioned or described, and in these the Cid is uniformly successful. When the Emperor claims recognition of his over-lordship from the King of Castile, the Cid encourages his master to refuse the demand. The parties are cited to appear before the Pope ; the Cid accompanies the king Don Fernando, and, finding the throne of the King of France placed in a more dignified position that than of his sovereign, he hurls it down and claims for Castile the highest place. For this outrage he is excommunicated ; but, of course, like a good Catholic submits and is readily pardoned. Jimena writes a letter complaining of the continual absence of her husband, and is wittily answered by the king to whom it was addressed. King Fernando dies after dividing his kingdom among his three sons, and leaving the town of Zamora to his daughter Urraca, who cherishes a romantic affection for the Cid. On the outbreak of war between the three brothers, Rodrigo takes the part of Don Sancho the eldest, who is consequently successful. He is afterwards sent by the king Don Sancho to request Doña Urraca to exchange or sell Zamora. She refuses, and bitterly reproaches him for the ingratitude with which he requites her love. The people of Zamora, led by Arías Gonzalo, determine to resist the king, who, unjustly attributing their conduct to the instigation of the Cid, drives him into exile and lays siege to the city. Arías Gonzalo, the defender of Zamora, warns the besiegers to beware of Bellido Dolfos, the traitor, who has gone forth from the walls; the king nevertheless, putting faith in his promise to deliver up the city, puts himself in his power and is treacherously slain by him. The Cid, who has by this time returned to favour and is present in the king's camp, though not taking an active part in the siege, pursues the traitor to the gates of the city and, failing to come up with him, pronounces his curse on all knights who ride without spurs. Diego Ordoñez challenges the Zamorans, accusing them of having taken part in the treacherous act by which Don Sancho met his death. The challenge is accepted by Arías Gonzalo and his sons, three of whom are slain by Ordoñez. The ordeal of battle, however, proves the goodness of their cause, and Zamora is freed from reproach of treachery by the challenger's horse accidentally carrying him outside the limits prescribed by the judges, thus leaving the victory undecided. Alfonso, the brother of Don Sancho, escapes from his captivity among the Moors and succeeds to the throne. He outlaws the Cid, who has offended him by exacting from him an oath "on an iron bolt and a wooden crossbow" that he had no part in Don Sancho's death. The Cid submits to his sentence, though powerful enough to have resisted it, and sets forth to win for himself a kingdom from the Moors. When successful, he recognises the overlordship of Don Alfonso who, finding himself unable to dispense with his services, recalls him. The Cid now conquers Valencia, and dwells there in semi-independent state, sending rich presents to the king, who in return arranges the marriage of his vassal's daughters, Doña Elvira and Doña Sol, with the Counts of Carrión. Some time after the wedding, the Counts of Carrión avenge themselves by maltreating their wives for insults brought upon them through their own cowardice. They are summoned before the king to defend their cause by arms, and, being defeated by the champions of the ladies, are condemned to pay compensation to their father-in-law, who now marries his daughters to the princes of Navarre and Aragón. The Cid returns to Valencia, and there he dies. The prophecy that he should be victorious after death is fulfilled by the rout of the Moors, who are besieging Valencia, and are put to flight by the sight of the hero's corpse mounted on his horse, lance in hand, according to his own dying instructions. The body of the Cid is finally carried to San Pedro de Cardeña, where it is laid in the monastery. Even the dead body of the champion is able to defend itself. It starts into life again when insulted by a Jew, who attempts to pluck the beard,[1] and such is the terror it inspires in the wretched infidel that he at once becomes a good Christian.

The ballads of this series, and throughout the whole of the *Romancero*, vary greatly in date, in interest, and in literary merit. Some of the most beautiful of them, unconnected with the heroes of romance and of history, are purely imaginative or pastoral in character; others are deeply infected with the artificial and euphuistic taste of the seventeenth century, in which the greater part of them were composed. The ballads

---

[1] Numerous interesting references to the superstitious reverence in which the beard was held are to be found in the *Poema de Myo Cid.*

were at that time ceasing to be really popular, and were becoming, greatly to their loss, the property of literary men. The tone, even of the later ones,[1] is however generally manly, for the more artificial and pretentious writers despised this simple form, and throughout them ring the keynotes of the Spanish inspiration, catholicism, loyalty, and the same intense sensitiveness as to the point of honour which appears again in an exaggerated form as the almost invariable theme of the drama of a later age.

[1] Among these some of the best are those that refer to the famous feud between the two great families of the Abencerrages and the Zegries at Granada.

CHAPTER V

CATALÁN LITERATURE

BEFORE passing on to the history of the novel and of the drama, a few words must be said about the writers who, before the union of Castile and Aragón under the Catholic monarchs, flourished in the north-east of Spain, and used their native Lemosin or Valencian tongue. It is true that these writers belong rather to Provence than to Spain, and were connected by race, language, and literary tradition with France and Italy rather than with Castile; still to Spain, as it now exists, belongs the honour of having produced them, and thus they come within the province of a history of Spanish literature. They have left behind them a large body of writings, consisting chiefly of amatory verse of the kind cultivated by the troubadours. Very few names deserve special mention among the long list of victors in the Floral Games and Courts of Love.

The troubadours are sharply distinguished from their Castilian contemporaries by both the matter and the form of their work; throughout their poetry, except that of a purely religious kind, a light and frivolous tone is noticeable, of which we have no example in Castilian until the time of Juan II., when it was introduced by the Provençal poets who were encouraged to take up their residence at court. The older Castilian poetry was written for the people and depended for its interest chiefly upon its subject; the Catalán poetry was written by a special class for a special class, and sought to shine chiefly by its form. Castilian is rich in ballads, but exceedingly poor in the metrical combination in which the Provençal, like the Galician poetry, excelled. The distinction above noticed originated probably in the strongly marked ethnological characteristics which, up to the present, have hindered all real sympathy between two nations thus unevenly yoked under one crown. Those who look to poetry for the general expression of the sentiments of an individual or of a people will ever prefer the rough and manly verses of the men of the uplands of Central Spain to the polished but vapid lyrics of the descendants of the troubadours who inhabited the north-eastern provinces.

In spite of altered times and changed ideals, the works of Ausias March are still read by his compatriots. He was a Valencian, and flourished in the fifteenth century. A devoted admirer and imitator of Petrarch, he addressed his somewhat fantastical and metaphysical verses to a shadowy lady, whose real existence has been doubted. However this may be, we cannot believe in the genuineness of his affection for her, expressed as it is in the stately but somewhat hollow-sounding *Songs of Love and Death*, where passion is set forth with most elaborate accompaniment of abstruse similes and metaphors. To Ausías March belongs the glory of being the greatest master of his native tongue; to him is also due the credit of avoiding the extravagant hyperbole that distinguishes the school of which he forms the chief ornament. The Marqués de Santillana, in the brief account of the Provençal school contained in his letter to the constable of Portugal, rates him highly, saying, "Mosen Ausías March, who is still alive, is a great troubadour, and a man of very lofty mind" (*gran trovador é hombre de asaz elevado espíritu*). This verdict agrees with that of the most learned of modern Spanish critics,[1] who treats him as a philosopher who happened to write in verse.

[1] Menendez y Pelayo, *Historia de las Ideas estéticas en España*, vol. i.

Jaume Roig wrote the *Ladies' Book* in short and lively verse in his native Valencian language. It is one of the many satires on women, which form so large a part of the literary stock of the Middle Ages, and is somewhat more worthy of attention than most books of the class by reason of the many quaint local details that it introduces. Its faults are its obscurity and licentiousness, as well as the unsuitability of its measure to so long a composition.[1]

Catalonia produced a celebrated Romance of Chivalry, *Tirant lo Blanch*, the work of Joanot Martorell. Though highly praised by Cervantes, in the scrutiny of Don Quixote's books, it has little merit as a book of entertainment. That which most favourably distinguishes it from others of the same kind is the almost unique quality of an entire absence of the supernatural element, the abuse of which forms one of the worst features of the class.

The Catalán chronicles are superior to the Castilian in literary execution and dramatic interest. Two of them deserve special notice. The first is the *Chronicle of En Jaime of Aragón*, surnamed *el Conquistador*. It was composed by the monarch himself, and continued up to a period immediately preceding his death in 1276. Written with frank and manly simplicity, and abounding in interesting details, it brings out with great vividness the striking personality of its author who is at the same time its central figure. The candour with which the great prince describes his public and private life is truly charming. The value of these memoirs as a historical document is very great. The second conqueror of Valencia is almost as interesting as the Cid, who was the first to successfully carry out the great exploit which gave En Jaime his surname.

The second chronicle to which reference has been made above is, like that of En Jaime, the work of a man of action.

---

[1] The author of the *Pelegrino Curioso* (sixteenth cent.) remarks on this peculiarity, likening Roig's verse to "feet of moles, club-footed men or hedgehogs."

Its author, Ramón de Muntaner, was of noble birth, and fought valiantly in the wars waged by the successors of En Jaime. He tells of the great men of his time, of courts and camps, feasting and fighting, and his chapters pass before us like some gorgeous pageant of the chivalrous times and sunny land in which he lived. The whole breathes the spirit of the faithful soldier, loyal gentleman, and good Christian, whose lance was not the less sharp because his pen was ready.[1]

The celebrated Raimundus Lullius, or Ramón Lull, "the knight-errant of philosophy, ascetic and troubadour, novelist and missionary,"[2] was born in 1235, in the island of Majorca, and in youth he led a gay and thoughtless life. Having one day followed into a church a lady whose beauty had attracted his attention, she ridded herself of his importunities by suddenly uncovering before him her bosom, disfigured by a hideous cancer. The revulsion of feeling was so violent that the young gallant forthwith turned his mind to serious thoughts; he travelled through Europe and the Holy Land, studying wherever he went, and ended his life as a martyr at the hands of the Moorish pirates. His philosophical works were originally written in Latin, but were afterwards translated. His literary works consist chiefly of religious poems. The best known of these is *Lo Desconort* (Despair), a long and monotonous work in heavy verse, which takes the form of a dialogue between the poet and a hermit. He also wrote a kind of allegorical novel called *Blanquerna*, from the name of its hero, which is meant to portray the ideal of Christian virtue at every period of life and in all classes of society.

Had it not been for the union with Castile, which took place shortly after the Renaissance, there is little doubt that

---

[1] An early version of this celebrated saying, which Cervantes quotes in a somewhat different form, is to be found in the preface to the Proverbs of the Marqués de Santillana ; it is as follows : *La sciencia no embota el fierro de la lanza ni face floxa el espada en la mano del caballero.*

[2] Menendez y Pelayo, *Historia de las Ideas estéticas en España.*

the influence of Italy, with which the Cataláns were closely connected, would have developed their national literature into something more truly worthy of the name; but with the unification of Spain, their language ceased to be a literary one. A revival of late years has done something to restore to it its former dignity, but the movement is rather erudite than popular, and savours somewhat of the "provincialism" that forms a distinguishing feature of the Catalán character.

CHAPTER VI

ORIGIN OF THE DRAMA

ONE of the oldest literary documents in Spanish is a fragment
of the *Misterio de los Reyes Magos*, a miracle play. Besides
the existence of this piece, there is enough proof to warrant the
belief that some form of dramatic representation had been from
classical times continually practised in Spain, although the
classical tradition as represented by Seneca had been utterly
lost. Alfonso the Wise refers to the subject in his *Partidas*,
and draws a marked distinction between religious and profane
representations, ordaining that in the latter, which he calls
juegos por escarnio (scurrilous plays), the clergy must not take
part either as actors or as spectators, because of the indecent
nature of such performances. With regard to the representations of religious subjects, such as the Nativity and the
Resurrection (see p. 186), he forbids them to be played in
small villages or for hire, and places them under the superintendence of the Bishops. The Chronicle of Don Álvaro de
Luna mentions *entremeses* (interludes), a name afterwards given
to short pieces of a comic character, but here referring apparently to dramatic allegories. The Chronicle of Juan II.
mentions *acciones cómicas*, and Don Alonso de Cartagena, a
bishop of the same century, in his *Doctrinal de Caballeros*
(Ordinances of Knighthood) declares it to be unsuited to the
dignity of a knight to take part in *momos* (farces). No specimen

of the compositions referred to under the above names has come down to us, but, judging from those of a later date, we may be sure they were of a very rough and primitive character.

The fifteenth century produced several works in dialogue, mostly allegorical, which, though unfitted for acting, may well have suggested it, and certainly had considerable influence in developing the theatre from its rude condition.

The name *comedia* or *comedieta* occurs in the title of a short poetical composition in dialogue by the Marqués de Santillana, which cannot fairly be considered as a drama and was probably never represented, but forms a kind of landmark in the literary history of this obscure period. The subject of the *Comedieta de Ponza* is the defeat and capture of the kings of Navarre and Aragón and the *infante* of Castile by the Genoese in 1435. The wives of these potentates are the speakers, together with Santillana himself and Boccaccio, who is naturally well versed in such matters as the *Downfall of Princes*. The disastrous news of the battle is discussed, and the "comedy" ends with the apparition of Fortune, who promises future glories that shall compensate for the present reverse.

The most important of such dialogues, excepting the *Celestina* (see p. 81), are the *Coplas de Mingo Revulgo*, and the *Dialogue between an Old Man and Love*, both of which are written in spirited verse and are ascribed to Rodrigo Cota, the author of the first part of the *Celestina*. The transition from such compositions to the regular drama is very gradual.

Contemporary authors are agreed in dating the definite rise of the national drama from the eventful year which saw the conquest of Granada and the discovery of the New World. The honour of being the first dramatist is assigned to Juan del Encina, a graduate of Salamanca, and famous poet and musician,[1] who enjoyed the protection of the first Duke of Alva. He subsequently took orders, made a pilgrimage to

[1] See the *Cancionero Musical de los Siglos XV. y XVI.* Madrid, 1890.

Jerusalem, and, after holding the position of musical director of the Pope's chapel, returned to die in his native country. His dramatic pieces were represented on festal occasions in the houses of grandees. He himself calls them *Églogas* in imitation of Vergil, whom he greatly admired and whose Bucolics he had translated. Of the twelve *Églogas* that have come down to us, six are religious, and are intended to celebrate the festivals of the Church, in accordance with the ancient custom. The other six are secular in character. They are written in lively *redondillas*, lines of eight syllables, rhymed A.B.B.A., sometimes in the more artificial form A.B.B.A.A.C.C.A. ; they contain carols (*villancicos*) of lyric form. The secular pieces are merely scenes from everyday life, and none of them show any comprehension of the classic methods of dramatic composition.

The *Aucto del Repelón* [1] represents, as its name implies, a street scuffle in Salamanca. Two shepherds, Piernicurto and Johan Paramas, whilst selling their cheeses in the market, are hustled and insulted by students. In order to escape they take different directions. Paramas takes refuge in a gentleman's house, and is beginning to relate his misadventure when Piernicurto interrupts him by entering and informing him that all the flock is lost. A student unwisely makes his appearance alone, and attempts to continue the horse-play. He is roughly thrust out by the shepherds, who, together with two of their companions, sing a *villancico*, which concludes the piece.

In *Plácida y Victoriano* mythological elements are introduced, probably in imitation of the Italian theatre with which Encina must have been familiar. The very titles of some of his pieces, such as *The Esquire who became a Shepherd*, and *The Shepherds who became Courtiers*, tell the simple incidents

---

[1] The word *aucto* or *auto* (Latin *actum*, cf. *auto de fe*) used in connection with the drama, at first signified any kind of dramatic composition. The name was subsequently restricted to those of a religious character, and particularly to the *autos sacramentales*.

on which Encina composed his pretty verses in praise of a country life.

Contemporary with Encina were Gil Vicente, a Portuguese, and Lucas Fernandez, whose works have recently come to light. The former, a close imitator of Encina, wrote some of his works entirely in his native language, some partly in Portuguese and partly in Castilian. Of this peculiarity we have other examples; a writer of the next century introduces into the same play Latin, Italian, Castilian, and Valencian; in the *Comedieta de Ponza* (p. 60) Boccaccio speaks in his native language. Vicente cultivated both religious and profane subjects; his idea of the art was almost as rude as that of his master, as may be seen from the plot of his *Viudo* (Widower), which turns on the inability of a gallant to make up his mind which he shall marry of two sisters for each of whom he entertains an evenly balanced affection. Lucas Fernandez brought little that is new to the stage, except the name *comedia* now first applied to dramas. It is worth while, however, to give a brief sketch of one of his *autos* in honour of the Nativity, in order to serve as a specimen of the condition at this time of that form of drama which Calderón afterwards cultivated with so much success. Four shepherds come on to the stage complaining, after the manner of their kind, of the weather and the crops. One of them, who is particularly bitter in his lamentations, consoles himself by lunching, and afterwards rouses a sleeping companion to play with him. Whilst the two are engaged in their game another shepherd rushes in announcing the Saviour's birth, of which he has been informed by the songs of the angels. The shepherds now recall to memory and relate one to another the prophecies of the event, and, singing a carol, they start for Bethlehem to adore the new-born Christ.

Dramatic poets now become more numerous, and their works more worthy of attention. Torres Naharro had known Encina in Rome; he had been a captive in Algiers, and, like so many of the Spanish literary men of his own and of a subsequent time, he became a priest before his death. He published his poetical works at Naples in 1517, under the high-sounding title of *Propaladia, or the First-fruits of Genius.* Amongst them are to be found eight plays which mark an important improvement in the dramatic art. Naharro draws a distinction between historical dramas and those of which the plot is drawn from imagination. His plays are divided into five acts (*jornadas*), and each opens with an argument and prologue (*intróito*). Of the eight plays, the historical ones are the best in form and execution, but most interest undoubtedly attaches to the *Comedia Tinelaria* and the *Comedia Soldadesca* Of these the characters are, as might be expected, more natural than either the carol-singing shepherds of the earlier dramatists, or the author's own historical personages.

The scene of the *Comedia Soldadesca* is laid in Rome. Guzmán, a Spaniard, complains of his bad fortune ; he meets a captain who is known to him, and who has a commission to raise troops for the army of the Pope. The captain offers him a place as lieutenant which he accepts. A drummer is enlisted and announces the terms of service to various recruits, to whom the captain afterwards makes a short speech explaining their future duties. A quarrel breaks out between two of the would-be soldiers, but is settled by the captain. A runaway friar enlists, and goes off with his fellows to the house of a farmer who speaks only Italian, thus giving rise to a good deal of misapprehension. The soldiers behave in a high-handed way, making love to the servant girl, and ordering the household about ; the farmer, aided by a friend, proposes to chastise them. Two of the soldiers discuss a plan of desertion and robbery. The farmer complains to the captain of the ill-treatment he has received. The captain pacifies him, and persuades him and his friend to enlist. They accept, and the whole company marches off singing a carol. From the above analysis, it will be seen that this piece cannot claim to fulfil any of the requirements of the drama ; it is merely a series of disconnected scenes reproduced on the stage. Its merit consists in the fact that the persons introduced are lifelike and true to nature, and speak in simple and unaffected terms.

Among the primitive dramatists, Lope de Rueda occupies a unique and important place. He was by trade a gold-beater of Seville, but became a dramatic *autor*, a word which signifies a writer of plays who is, at the same time, an actor and manager of a company—a combination of functions usual in the early days of the theatre. He travelled over the south of Spain, and is known to have played at Seville, Córdova, Granada, and Valencia. He is praised by both Cervantes and Antonio Perez, who had seen him act. He died about 1567. Lope de Rueda has left us *comedias, coloquios pastoriles*, after the fashion of those of Encina, and twenty *pasos*, or short pieces of a farcical kind, without real plot, some in prose and some in verse. These latter form the most valuable and important part of his work. The situations are often really comic, and are developed in natural and animated dialogue. An idea of the character of these compositions can be gathered from the plot of one of them, entitled *The Olives* (*Las Aceitunas*). Torrubio, an old farmer, comes on to the stage, which represents his house, bearing a load of wood ; his wife, Agueda, asks him if he has replanted the olive garden ; he says that he has done so, and forthwith the pair begin to discuss the probable amount of the produce, and the manner in which it is to be disposed of; their daughter, Mencigüela, is called in, and her mother gives her instructions to sell the olives at a certain price, her father all the while protesting that the price named is excessive ; Mencigüela tries to satisfy both parties by promising to each in turn to do as she is bid ; this only exasperates her parents, who fall upon her and beat her ; finally a neighbour comes in, attracted by the noise, and persuades the distracted family that it is somewhat premature to quarrel about the price of fruit that cannot be grown before the lapse of five years at the least.

The *comedias* of Lope de Rueda, four in number, mark a distinct improvement upon the work of the earlier writers ; one at least of them is imitated from the Italian. They are divided into scenes, but not into acts. In their plots we already get a trace of the intricacy which subsequently forms so marked a feature of the Spanish drama. Here also may be found the poor dramatic expedient, so dear to Spanish writers, of the two persons so extremely alike that they are continually mistaken by their friends ; sometimes, also, by the spectators.

Juan de Timoneda, a bookseller of Valencia, was a close friend of Lope de Rueda, whose works he published. He composed *Pasos*, Farces, Comedies, *Entremeses*, and an *Auto* or mystery, called the *Lost Sheep*, which is somewhat less worthless than the rest of his works. The incidents on which his plays are founded are often wildly extravagant ; his language is coarse ; almost all his pieces end with a scuffle on the stage ; neither in form nor in matter did he contribute to the improvement of the drama, and he deserves mention only by reason of the popularity which he undoubtedly enjoyed, and which gives a clue to the taste of his time.

Such were the writers who laid the foundation of a national drama destined to become both important and voluminous. The above-mentioned playwrights consulted the popular taste, which, under Lope de Vega, became supreme arbiter in matters dramatic (see p. 166) ; others of more bookish mind wrote somewhat more correctly, imitating classical models. Of such are Lupercio de Argensola (see p. 122) and Cristóbal de Virues (see p. 225), but their works are of slight merit, and do not bear the stamp of the forms peculiar to the Spanish drama in after-times.

Side by side with the secular flourished the Religious Drama, which will be treated in the chapter on Calderón, its greatest exponent. Of early religious plays many specimens

F

have been preserved. One of the most interesting is the *Comedia Pródiga*, by Luís de Miranda, which illustrates the favourite story of the Prodigal Son, with many graphic details drawn rather from its author's imagination than from sacred writ.

To complete this brief sketch of the early drama, it will be well to touch on the position of actors, their way of life, and the primitive costumes, scenes, and "property" at their disposal. On these particulars abundant information is contained in the works of contemporary writers. Cervantes,[1] in the preface to his own plays, speaking of his immediate predecessor Lope de Rueda, says :—

[2] In the time of this celebrated Spanish actor, the whole apparatus of an *autor* (see p. 64) was contained in a sack, and consisted of four white sheepskins trimmed with gilt leather, together with four false beards and wigs, and four shepherd's crooks, more or less. . . . There were no figures to come popping up from the centre of the earth, or the space beneath the stage. The stage itself was composed of four benches, forming a square, with four or six planks placed upon them, so as to be raised about four handsbreadths from the ground. Much less did clouds containing angels or spirits come down from the sky. The back scene of the theatre consisted of an old blanket which could be pulled by cords to one side or the other, and this formed the green-room, behind which stood the musicians singing some old ballad, without even a guitar to accompany them. . . . After Lope de Rueda came Naharro, a native of Toledo, who was famous in the part of cowardly bully. He somewhat raised the standard of theatrical adornment, exchang-

---

[1] *Comedias y Entremeses de Miguel de Cervantes.* Marín, Madrid, 1749. Vol. i. *Prólogo al Lector.*
[2] " En el tiempo de este célebre Español, todos los aparatos de un Autor de Comedias se encerraban en un costal, y se cifraban en cuatro pellicos blancos guarnecidos de guadamecí dorado ; y en cuatro barbas y cabelleras, y quatro cayados, poco más ó menos. . . . No havía figura que saliesse ó pareciesse salir del centro de la tierra por lo hueco del Theatro, al qual componían quatro bancos en quadro y quatro ó seis tablas encima, con que se levantaba del suelo quatro palmos ; ni menos baxaban del Cielo nubes con Angeles, ó con almas. El adorno del Theatro era una manta vieja, tirada con dos cordeles de una parte á otra, que hacía lo que llaman vestuario, detras de la qual estaban los Músicos cantando sin guitarra algun romance antiguo. . . . Succedió á Lope de Rueda, Naharro, natural de Toledo, el qual fué famoso en hacer la figura de un rufián cobarde. Este levantó algún tanto más el adorno de las Comedias,

ing the sack which used to contain the dresses, for chests and trunks. He brought out the musicians who formerly sang behind the blanket, to the public gaze; he also abolished the beards of the comic actors, for, up to that time, nobody played without a false beard, and he made them all play without preliminary adjustment; except those who had to represent old men, or other parts which required a change of features. He it was who introduced machinery, clouds, thunder and lightning, duels, and battles, but all this had not yet come to the pitch of perfection which it has reached nowadays.

At first no women appeared on the stage, the female parts being taken by boys. The simplicity of the secular drama must not, however, be taken as the standard by which to judge of the religious performances, for documents still existing in the archives of Seville mention silken dresses provided for Lope de Rueda, who had gained the prize offered for the best *auto* wherewith to celebrate the festival of Corpus Christi. Actors were considered as outcasts till a much later period, nor is this to be wondered at, if there is any truth in the memorial presented to the king in 1645, begging him to remedy the scandals and outrages caused by forty wandering companies of actors, comprising no less than one thousand persons, among them men of abandoned lives, and even escaped convicts. The representations of religious dramas often took place in churches and convents; secular pieces were played in the open air on Sundays or holidays, in inns or in places specially set apart for the purpose. These were merely quadrangles (*corrales*) open to the sky and surrounded by houses, the windows of which formed the most costly seats for the spectators. Such quadrangles were, in Madrid at least, the property of religious and charitable associations, which exercised the privilege allowed

y mudó el costal de vestidos en cofres y en baules : sacó la música, que antes cantaba detras de la manta, al Theatro público : quitó las barbas de los Farsantes, que hasta entonces ninguno representaba sin barba postiza ; y hizo que todos representassen á cureña rasa, sino era los que havían de representar los viejos, ú otras figuras que pidiessen mudanza de rostro : inventó tramoyas, nubes, truenos y relámpagos, desaflos y batallas ; pero esto no llegó al sublime punto en que está abora."

by law of heavily taxing for pious purposes the meagre receipts of the actors. The sites of two of the most celebrated of these quadrangles are now marked by two of the principal theatres of the Spanish capital.

In spite of these many disadvantages, and notwithstanding occasional persecution at the hands of the religious authorities, the actors seem to have led a free and joyous, though squalid and hard life. Augustín de Rojas, himself an actor, gives in his *Viage Entretenido* (Diverting Journey)—1603—a graphic and amusing account of the various kinds of dramatic companies, distinguished by slang names according to the number of actors they contained, and their higher or lower status in the profession. This is how he describes the *Carambaleo*, which stood midway in the order of importance :—

[1] Carambaleo consists of one woman who sings, and five men who weep ; their baggage comprises one play, two *autos*, three or four *entremeses*, and a bundle of clothes which a spider might carry ; sometimes they carry the woman on their backs, sometimes in a chair : they give representations at homesteads for a loaf of bread, bunch of grapes, and a cabbage stew ; in villages they charge six farthings, or a piece of sausage, a hank of flax, or whatever else may happen to be offered, counting everything as fish that comes to their net. In hamlets they stay four or six days ; they hire a bed for the woman, and, if the landlady takes a fancy to any of them she gives him a sackful of straw, and a blanket, and he sleeps in the kitchen. In winter the straw-loft is their constant abode. At midday they eat their *olla* of beef and six platefuls of broth apiece ; they all sit at the same table, or sometimes on the bed ; the woman portions out the dinner,

[1] " Carambaleo es una mujer que canta y cinco hombres que lloran : estos traen una comedia, dos autos, tres ó cuatro entremeses, un lío de ropa, que lo puede llevar una araña : llevan á ratos á la mujer á cuestas y otras en silla de manos ; representan en los cortijos por hogaza de pan, racimo de uvas y olla de berzas ; cobran en los pueblos á seis maravedises, pedazo de longaniza, cerro de lino y todo lo demas que viene aventurero, sin que se deseche ripio ; están en los lugares cuatro ó seis días ; alquilan para la mujer una cama, y el que tiene amistad con la huéspeda dale un costal de paja, una manta y duerme en la cocina : y en invierno, el pajar es su habitación eterna ; éstos á mediodía comen su olla de vaca, y cada uno seis escudillas de caldo ; siéntanse todos á una mesa, y otras veces sobre la cama ; reparte la mujer la

gives each his due share of bread, and measures out to each the wine and water ; each one wipes his hands and mouth with whatever comes handy, for they have only one napkin between the lot, and the tablecloth is so scanty that it falls short by several inches of covering the table.

comida, dales el pan por tasa, el vino aguado y por medida, y cada uno se limpia donde halla, porque entre todos tienen una servilleta, ó los manteles estan an desviados que no alcanzan á la mesa con diez dedos."

CHAPTER VII

In treating of the ballads and of the romances of chivalry, it
has been necessary to go far beyond the period represented by
Don Juan Manuel and the Archpriest of Hita in the other
branches of literature. It is true that many of the ballads were
collected and printed, and that romances of chivalry were still
produced during the seventeenth century, but to have placed
them alongside the great works of the Golden Age might have
led to a wrong impression as to their true position in the
general scheme of literature. When the ballads were petrified
by printing they were rapidly ceasing to be truly popular; the
later romances of chivalry are the weakest of their kind.

Turning to poetry, we find that foreign influence has become
all-powerful during the fifteenth century. The series of the
old Spanish heroic and religious epic ends with the *Poem of
Alfonso XI*. Provençal, Italian, and classical models begin to
be studied and imitated, and the general tone is less grave and
earnest. Lyric forms have taken the place of the old *versos de
arte mayor*, and love-songs of an artificial kind have ousted
the rough but glowing accounts of battles spiritual or physical.
The celebrated *Cancionero de Baena*, compiled during the
reign and by order of Juan II. of Castile, gives a very correct
idea of the taste of this time, during which the court was the

centre of literary activity, the elegant and feeble king himself and his favourite, Don Álvaro de Luna, both being poets. Juan Alfonso de Baena, from whom the collection takes its name, was himself a writer of verse ; his book contains five hundred and seventy-six compositions by sixty-two poets, consisting chiefly of love-songs, but interspersed with hymns and satires. This *Cancionero* marks a great advance in the mechanical part of verse-making, but the general effect is artificial and frigid. The purely formal ideal of art entertained by the school is expressed in Baena's Introduction :—

Poetry and the Gay Science (he says) is possessed, received, and attained by the in-breathed grace of our Lord God who grants and sends it, working upon those who, well and wisely, cunningly and aright, know how to make, order, and compose it, and to polish, scan, and measure it by its feet and pauses, and by its rhymes and syllables and accents, by cunning arts variously and strangely named : and moreover this art belongs to such intellect and such subtile wit that it cannot be learned or well and properly known save by the man of very deep and subtle invention, and of very lofty and pure discretion, and of very healthy and unerring judgment, and such a one must have seen and heard and read many and diverse books and writings, and know all languages, and have frequented king's courts, and associated with great men, and beheld and taken part in worldly affairs, and finally he must be of gentle birth, courteous and sedate, polished, humorous, polite, and witty, and have in his composition honey and sugar and salt, and a good presence and witty manner of reasoning ; moreover he must be also a lover and ever make a show and pretence of it, for many wise men have considered and affirmed that every man who is in love, that is to say who loves whom he ought and as he ought and where he ought, is endowed with all good doctrine.[1]

It is, however, necessary to mention the names of some of the authors whose works make up the *Cancionero*, both on account of the popularity that they enjoyed even long after their own time, and also because of the influence which they exercised on the poetry of a later age.

Alfonso Álvarez de Villasandino was a mercenary verse-maker, much appreciated during the reigns of Juan II. and his

[1] *Cancionero de Baena*, p. 9. Rivadeneyra, Madrid, 1851.

immediate predecessors. He composed for hire sonnets and other complimentary verses to ladies whose rich and powerful admirers were diffident as to the adequacy of their poetic genius to worthily celebrate so great a subject. He also wrote a series of satires on persons about the court. The point of many of the latter is lost, but they are cleverly turned and must undoubtedly have afforded amusement to those for whom they were written. Villasandino is, however, at his best in the hymns to the Virgin, in which he, like other secular poets of the age, frequently gives proof of a strong religious spirit underlying the artificial exterior of courtly life.

Micer Francisco Imperial was a Genoese by birth and an admirer of Dante, whom he attempted to imitate both in subject and in form, without attaining great success in either. He was, however, highly esteemed by his contemporaries ; Santillana speaking of him says, " I would not call him bard (*decidor*) or minstrel (*trovador*) but poet, for it is certain that, if any in this western region hath merited the reward of the triumphal garland it is he."

The name of Enrique de Aragón, Marqués de Villena, is more deserving of mention. This great nobleman gave himself up from his earliest years to study ; so great was his knowledge that during his lifetime he was looked upon with suspicion as a student of the black art, and after his death his collection of priceless books was burned, without examination, for fear of the evil they might contain. His literary sympathies were wide ; he translated parts of Vergil and Cicero into his native tongue, and wrote a heavy and pedantic allegory called the *Labours of Hercules*, as well as an *Art of Carving*. The work which gives him his best title to a place in the history of the poetry of his country is his *Arte de Trovar*, a brief treatise on poetry, addressed in the form of a letter to his nephew, the celebrated Marqués de Santillana. The fragment that is preserved contains some curious information about the Consistory of the Gay Science which the author was mainly instrumental in founding at Barcelona. This academy was carefully modelled after the more celebrated one that had its seat at Toulouse, and it succeeded in bringing together the Provençal troubadours who had taken refuge in Catalonia in order to avoid the persecution of the Albigenses.

Macías, surnamed *el Enamorado*, a Galician retainer of the Marqués of Villena, was himself a verse-writer, but he is known rather as a subject for poetry than as a poet. Remaining faithful to the lady of his affections, even after her marriage to another, he was put into prison. Confinement did not extinguish his ardent passion; he continued to sing his love in his native Galician tongue. Exasperated by his persistence, his successful rival slew him in his cell by hurling a javelin through the window. Few only of his verses have been preserved, and, judging by them, the faithful lover was an indifferent poet, but his fate inspired poets as widely separated in date as Villena his master in the fifteenth and Góngora in the seventeenth century. His name became proverbial, his story is alluded to by almost all the great Spanish writers, and formed the theme of Larra's (see p. 249) novel, *El doncel de Don Enrique el Doliente*, in the present century.

A poet more worthy of the name is the Marqués of Santillana, whom we have mentioned in connection with the early history of the drama, and must mention again in connection with proverbs. After taking an important part in the military and political life of his time, he found leisure in his old age to compose a large number of books of uneven merit, among which is a poem in praise of Villena, and one on the crowning of Mossen Jordi, the troubadour. To him and to Alfonso el Sabio is owed the introduction of the sonnet into Spanish, but he handles this form in an uncouth and incorrect fashion. His didactic works, both his *Centiloquio*, or one hundred proverbial precepts, addressed to the Infante Don Enrique, and his

Doctrinal de Privados (Warnings to Court Favourites), are dignified and correct in tone ; they contain the wide experience of a man of the world. The latter is probably inspired by the fate of Álvaro de Luna, whom Santillana had always strongly opposed. It is, however, in poetry of a lighter kind that the Marqués de Santillana attains his highest claim to fame. His *Serranilla* (see p. 28), addressed to a milkmaid (*vaquera*) of La Finojosa, is the best that exists in the language. While closely imitating Provençal models, it has a simplicity and charm of its own, which entitles it to a place in every Spanish anthology.

[1] Moza tan fermosa
Non vi en la frontera
Como una vaquera
De la Finojosa.
Faciendo la vía
De Calateveño
Á Santa María
Vencido del sueño,
Por tierra fragosa
Perdí la carrera
Do vi la vaquera
De la Finojosa.
En un verde prado
De rosas é flores
Guardando ganado
Con otros pastores,
La vi tan fermosa
Que apenas creyera

Que fuese vaquera
De la Finojosa.
Non creo las rosas
De la primavera
Sean tan fermosas
Nin de tal manera.
Fablando sin glosa
Si antes supiera
Daquella vaquera
De la Finojosa,
Non tanto mirara
Su mucha beldad,
Porque me dejara
En mi libertad.
Mas dixe, donosa,
Por saber quién era
Aquella vaquera
De la Finojosa.

---

[1] " So pretty a girl—on the border ne'er saw I,—as a milkmaid—of la Fino-josa.—Journeying along—from Calateveño to Santa María—weighed down with sleep,—in the rocky land—I lost my way,—there saw I the milkmaid—of la Finojosa—In a meadow green—of roses and flowers—tending the herd —with other shepherds,—so pretty was she—that scarce could I believe— that she was a milkmaid—of la Finojosa.—I cannot believe—that the roses— of spring—are so beautiful (as she)—nor her equals.—I speak not in jest,— had I known beforehand—of that milkmaid—of la Finojosa,*—I had not gazed so much—on her great beauty,—and so she had left me—my liberty. —But I said ' My pretty maid,'—that I might learn who was—that milk-maid—of la Finojosa."

---

* I have found myself obliged to alter the punctuation here. With the full stop as placed by Sanchez the passage does not make sense.

Santillana has also left one of the most important literary documents of his time, in his *Letter to the Constable of Portugal.* This brief treatise accompanied a copy of its author's poems sent by request to the young Prince Don Pedro about the year 1445. In it Santillana gives an interesting account of several of the poets who were his contemporaries or predecessors. It is to be noticed that he ascribes much importance to Galician and Portuguese influences. Speaking of this district of the Peninsula, he says, "It is certain that here the practice of this (poetical) science was more general than in any other region or province of Spain ; so much so that, until lately, all bards (*decidores*) and minstrels (*trovadores*) of our country, whether Castilians, Andalucians, or natives of Extremadura, composed all their works in the Galician tongue."

Juan de Mena was an erudite court poet of the time of Juan II. In his youth he had studied in the Italian universities, and his works contain little or nothing that is distinctively Spanish. It is difficult to understand the wide popularity which they enjoyed for more than two hundred years. The king himself was Mena's friend and patron, and is said to have habitually kept his *Laberinto*, or *Trescientas*, by his bedside. This work takes the first of its two names from its enigmatical obscurity ; the second from the fact that it originally contained three hundred stanzas ; to these sixty-five were afterwards added by the king's request in order to make the number equal to that of the days of the year, a whim well suited to the astrological conceits in which the poem deals. It is written in the form of a dream ; the poet is transported in a magic car into space, where he beholds three circles representing severally the Present, the Past, and the Future. This vision affords an opportunity for commenting in mysterious and pedantic style upon various historical personages, who are classed according to the " seven orders of the planets," and their supposed influences. So obscure, indeed, are the verses that a lengthy commentary on them was published shortly after their appearance by the celebrated scholar, Fernan Nuñez, surnamed the *Comendador Griego*. Juan de Mena makes his style still more heavy and pedantic by the wholesale introduction of Latin words, and of constructions entirely foreign to the genius of the Castilian language. In this particular he is not the first offender, but his great reputation undoubtedly did much to promote the vicious habit.

Besides the *Trescientas*, Mena wrote a panegyric or *Coronación de Santillana*, a poem on the Seven Mortal Sins, and some songs. The following is a specimen of the least obscure of his verses, a *Canción* to his lady :—

> [1] Oiga tu merced y crea,
> ¡ Ay de quien nunca te vido !
> Hombre que tu gesto vea
> Nunca puede ser perdido.
> Ya la tu sola virtud,
> Fermosura sin medida,
> Es mi todo bien y vida
> Con esfuerço de salud :
> Quien tu vista ver dessea
> Fablará no en fingido,
> Hombre que tu gesto vea
> Nunca puede ser perdido.
> Pues tu vista me saluó,
> Cesse tu saña tan fuerte ;
> Pues que, señora, de muerte
> Tu figura me libró,
> Bien dirá qualquier que sea,
> Sin temor de ser vencido
> Hombre que tu gesto vea
> Nunca puede ser perdido.

---

[1] " Listen I beg thee, and believe ;—alas for him who never saw thee !—the man that once thy face beholds—can never be undone.—Thy wondrous properties alone,—Oh beauty without peer !—form my whole wealth and life—and all my strenuous health ;—he who would see thy countenance—will say in sober earnest,—the man that once thy face beholds—can never be undone.—Since it was thy countenance that redeemed me,—let thy fierce anger cease ;—since, lady mine, from death—thy face hath freed me,—well can men say, whoever they be,—and fear no contradiction,—the man that once thy face beholds—can never be undone."

Standing out boldly amidst the artificial style and hollow sentiment of the poets of this time, it is a relief to meet with one simple, natural, and dignified composition. This is the celebrated elegy of Jorge Manrique on the death of his father, known as the *Coplas de Manrique.* Its tone contrasts as strongly with that of the other works of its author, as with that of his contemporaries. It has always been admired in Spain, and has been many times translated, but still stands as an abiding proof of the superiority of Spanish to other languages as an instrument for poetry of a grave and lofty character. Camoens imitated it; Lope de Vega speaks of it with the highest praise; even the severe Mariana waxes eloquent over its beauties. Jorge Manrique was the last scion of a noble house, distinguished in arms, in politics, and in literature. Like so many of the greatest writers of his country, he was a soldier: he died fighting heroically in 1479. The *Coplas* convey the reflections of a simple and noble mind upon the vanity of human affairs and upon death. The first part is full of the sadness caused by the recollection of past grandeur and delights. Gradually the tone becomes more submissive, and finally the writer turns his eyes to the abiding life beyond the grave, with feelings of hope and longing. The versification and language correspond admirably with the tone of the poem. The former has been well compared to the tolling of a deep-toned bell.

The *Coplas de Manrique* deserve a place amongst the finest verses, not only of the author's native land, but of the world. As an elegy they are unsurpassed. Space allows only eight out of the stanzas of which the poem consists to be given here.

[1] Recuerde el alma dormida,   Cómo se passa la vida
    Avive el seso y despierte   Cómo se viene la muerte
      Contemplando   Tan callando;

---

[1] "Thou slumbering soul, take heed,—lethargic mind, awake—and contemplate—how life is passing by—how death is creeping on—silently.—How

Quán presto se va el placer,
Cómo despues de acordado
      Da dolor;
Cómo á nuestro parecer
Cualquiera tiempo passado
      Fué mejor.

Nuestras vidas son los ríos
Que van á dar en la mar
      Que es el morir;
Allí van los señoríos
Derechos á se acabar
      Y consumir.
Allí los ríos caudales,
Allí los otros medianos
      Y más chicos.
Allegados son iguales
Los que viven por sus manos
      Y los ricos.

Este mundo es el camino
Para el otro, que es morada
      Sin pesar:
Mas cumple tener buen tino
Para andar esta jornada
      Sin errar.
Partimos quando nacemos
Andamos quando vivimos
      Y allegamos

Al tiempo que fenecemos:
Así que quando morimos
      Descansamos.

Aquel de buenos abrigo.
Amado por virtuoso
      De la gente,
El maestre don Rodrigo
Manrrique tan famoso
      Y tan valiente,
Sus grandes hechos y claros
No cumple que los alabe,
      Pues los vieron;
Ni los quiero hazer caros,
Pues el mundo todo sabe
      Quáles fueron.

Después que puso la vida
Tantas veces por su ley
      Al tablero,
Después que tan bien servida
La corona de su rey
      Verdadero:
Después de tanta hazaña
En que no puede bastar
      Cuenta cierta,
En la su villa de Ocaña
Vino la muerte á llamar
      A su puerta,

---

quickly pleasure flies,—how, afterwards, the thought of it—is pain ;—how to our seeming,—any of the years that are gone—was more sweet.—Our lives are as the rivers—that flow into the sea—which is death ;—thither go the lordly ones—straight to be ended—and swallowed up.—Thither the mighty streams—others of smaller size—and the rills.—There all are equal—those who labour with their hands,—and the rich.—This world is but a road—towards the other, which is a home—free from grief ;—but good heed must he take— who would accomplish this journey—without fail.—Our birth is the setting forth,—in life we journey on,—and reach our goal—at the hour of our decease ;—so it is that when we die—we have rest. . . .—Protector of the good,—for virtue high esteemed—by his fellows,—the constable Rodrigo— Manrique of high fame,—valiant knight,—his mighty deeds renowned,—why should I praise them here?—they are known.—Nor would I extol their worth, —for every one knows well—of what sort they were.—When he had staked his life—so often for his creed—on a throw ;—after such faithful service—to the crown and to the king,—as of right :—so many mighty deeds,—they cannot all be told—without fail,—in Ocaña his own town—came death to him

Diciendo : buen cavallero,
Dexad al mundo engañoso
   Con halago,
Vuestro corazón de acero
Muestre su esfuerzo famoso
   En este trago.
Pues que de vida y salud
Tan poca cuenta hicistis
   Por la fama,
Esfuérceos la virtud
Para sufrir esta afrenta
   Que vos llama.

El vivir, que es perdurable,
No se gana con estados
   Mundanales,
Ni con vida deleitable
Donde moran los pecados
   Infernales,

Mas los buenos religiosos
Gánanlo con oraciones
   Y con lloros,
Los cavalleros famosos
Con trabajos y afficciones
   Contra moros.

Así, con tal entender,
Todos sentidos humanos
   Conservados,
Cercado de su muger
De sus hijos y hermanos
   Y criados,
Dió el alma á quien se la dió,
El cual le ponga en el cielo
   Y en su gloria ;
Aunque á la vida murió,
Nos dexó harto consuelo
   Su memoria.

and knocked—on his gate—saying, brave knight,—leave this deceitful world
—and vain,—let not thy bold heart fail—to drink courageously—this bitter
cup—Since of thy life and health—so little store thou madest—for renown,—
let thy valour make thee bold—to endure the sentence harsh—and its claim.
. . .—The life which is eternal—is not gained with pomp or wealth—of
this world,—nor by the life of ease—where hideous sins abound—sprung
from hell ;—but the faithful anchorites—gain it by their prayers—and their
tears,—and the famous knights—by their labours and heaviness—against the
infidel. Thus, then, strong in such faith,—all his faculties—unimpaired,—
surrounded by his wife,—his sons and brethren,—and dependents,—he gave
his soul to him who gave it ;—may he place it in the heavens—and in glory ;
—though he died to mortal life—he left to banish vain regrets—his memory."

CHAPTER VIII

THE NOVEL

DURING the period that preceded the reign of the Catholic monarchs and the Golden Age of Spanish literature it is evident that, as the national horizon widens, the forms of literary composition hitherto cultivated are becoming less and less adequate to supply the increasing demand for something new. Poetry has become erudite and metaphysical in tone, and the imitation of classical and Italian models has rendered it uncongenial to the popular taste ; books of chivalry are still written and continue to be widely read, but their heroes are becoming less and less like human beings, and the world in which they live is ever less like that inhabited by mortals unendowed with superhuman strength, and unaided by the all-powerful enchanters who in each new volume play a larger part in these extravagant histories of monstrous exploits. The sixteenth century is justly counted as the period which saw the rise both of the novel and of the drama in Spain ; traces, however, of either form may be found earlier, and these must be briefly examined in order to understand their later developments.

In the novel, as almost everywhere in the literature of the fifteenth and sixteenth centuries, Italian influence is distinctly traceable in the beginning, and it continues so throughout the large class of fantastic books known as pastoral novels. But the Spaniards created a kind of story peculiar in its origin to the Peninsula, though afterwards imitated with great success by writers of other nationalities, and notably by Le Sage. This is the *novela picaresca* or "rogue story."

The earliest Spanish novels, if we except the books of chivalry, are allegorical in form; they belong to neither of the above-mentioned classes, but are a kind of offshoot of the romance of chivalry. One of the first is the *Siervo libre de Amor* (The Free Slave of Love), by Rodriguez del Padrón, a troubadour who ended his life as a hermit in the Holy Land. It is a work of little merit and of less originality. In imitation of Dante it is written in the form of a dream, in which abstractions such as *Understanding* and *Discretion* play an important part; but it launches out into a regular romance of chivalry, of which the plot is formed by the ill-starred loves and supernatural adventures of Ardanlier and Liesa. The book is arbitrarily divided into three periods, according as the author's love is reciprocated, disregarded, and extinguished. Finally he is roused from his trance, and verses in the style of the more purely pastoral novels of later times, expressive of a lover's despair, conclude this tedious and ill-told story.

Another book of a like character is the *Cárcel de Amor* (Prison of Love), by Diego de San Pedro, a poet of the fifteenth century. Here, by means of the usual vision, Love is represented as a tyrant who employs his minister Desire in torturing his votaries. In the affairs of one of these the author in person intervenes; the lover is restored to the upper world, and, after a series of fantastic adventures, meets at last an unhappy end, being slain by the coldness of his lady, whose honour has most unjustly been called in question.

In 1492 was published a book of real originality, important alike in the history of the novel and of the drama. This is the celebrated *Celestina* or *Tragicomedia de Calisto y Melibea*. It is said to have been begun by Rodrigo de Cota and finished by Fernando de Rojas, but, in spite of the opinion of Juan de Valdés, who says that the wit of the first author is superior to that of him who wrote the latter part, the evenness of its very distinctive style, and the thorough consistency of the characters throughout, make it difficult to believe that it is the work of more than one person. Fernando de Rojas, whose name appears in an acrostic at the end, may well have wished to make some one else responsible, in part at least, for the questionable incidents in which the work abounds. The plot is developed entirely in dialogue, and the word *Tragicomedia*, which appears in the title, is justified by the author, who declares the book to be a comedy with an unhappy ending. In spite of its dramatic form, the work is not well adapted for theatrical representation, especially with the scanty stage .appliances of the time. The great length, moreover, of its twenty-one acts, as well as the long tirades which occur, and the moral reflections with which it ends, make it improbable that it was written with such a purpose. It is however unsafe, as will be seen later, to gauge the tastes of a Spanish audience by the rules which would apply to a French or English one.

In the first chapter Calisto is scornfully rejected by Melibea, the lady of his love, who is somewhat his superior in social position ; he is comforted by his servant Sempronio, who advises him to apply to Celestina, an old woman, half witch, half go-between, whose agency has often before been success-fully employed by lovers. Celestina undertakes the affair, and makes a hard bargain for her services. She subsequently contrives to introduce herself into the house of Pleberio, the rich father of Melibea, but is dismissed somewhat harshly by the lady. Concealing her want of success, she presents to Calisto a love-token purporting to come from Melibea. On repeating her visit, she is more successful, and obtains from Melibea a confession of her love for Calisto. A meeting is arranged between the lovers, and Melibea's virtue yields with an extraordinary facility that unhappily is not rare in Spanish stories. But swift retribution is at hand. Celestina is murdered by her associates, with whom she has quarrelled over the spoil. Calisto is surprised during an interview with his mistress, and is killed by falling from the ladder by which he is attempting to make his escape. Melibea commits suicide by leaping from a lofty tower before the eyes of her father.

The following dialogue which passes between Sempronio and Parmeno, the two serving gentlemen (*escuderos*) of Calisto, while awaiting their master outside Pleberio's house, bears a striking likeness to those which enliven similar situations in the 'cloak and sword plays' of the seventeenth century.

[1] *Semp.* Ya no temas, Parmeno, que harto desviados estamos, y en sintiendo bullicio, el buen huir nos ha de valer. Déjale hacer que, si mal hace, él lo pagará.

Parm. Bien hablas, en mi corazón estás; así se haga, huyamos la muerte, que somos mozos: que no querer morir ni matar no es cobardía, sino buen natural. Estos escuderos de Pleberio son locos; no desean tanto comer ni dormir como cuestiones y ruidos: pues más locura sería esperar pelea con enemigos que no aman tanto la victoria y vencimiento como la contínua guerra y contienda; ¡Oh si me vieses, hermano, como estoy, placer habrías! A medio lado, abiertas las piernas, el pie izquierdo adelante en huida, las haldas en cinta, la adarga arrollada y so el sobaco, porque no me empache: que por Dios creo que fuese como un gamo según el temor que tengo de estar aquí.

---

[1] "*Semp.* Thou needest fear no longer, Parmeno, for we are well out of the way and, if we hear any uproar, the swiftness of our heels will stand us in good stead. Let him be, for if he does ill, 'tis he who will pay for it.

Parm. Wise words indeed, and after my own heart; so be it; let us flee from death, for we are still young: unwillingness to kill or to be killed is not cowardice but springs rather from a kindly disposition. These serving gentlemen of Pleberio are madmen; eating and drinking are less dear to them than quarrels and strife; we should be even more mad than they, were we to await a struggle with enemies whose object is rather continual war and opposition than victory and the discomfiture of their adversaries. Oh, gossip, it would do thy heart good to see my attitude! Facing half round; legs well apart; left foot forward to run; my skirts in my belt; my target rolled up and tucked under my arm so that it may not hinder me; by heaven, I should go off like a buck, such is the fear I have of remaining here.

Semp. Mejor estoy yo, que tengo liado el broquel y el espada con la correas porque no se cayga al correr, y el caxquete en la capilla.

Parm. ¿Y las piedras que traías en ella?

Semp. Todas las vertí por ir mas liviano, que harto tengo que llevar en estas corazas que me heciste vestir por importunidad; que bien las rehusaba de traer, porque me parescían para huir muy pesadas. Escucha, escucha ¿oyes, Parmeno? A malas andan; muertos somos. Bota presto; echa hacia casa de Celestina, no nos atajen por nuestra casa.

Parm. Huye, huye, que corres poco; ¡Oh, pecador de mí! si nos han de alcanzar; deja el broquel y todo.

Semp. ¿Si han muerto á nuestro amo?

Parm. No sé, no digas nada: corre y calla; que el menor cuidado mío es ese.

Semp. Ce, ce, Parmeno; torna, torna callando, que no es sino la gente del alguacil que pasaba haciendo estruendo por otra calle.

Parm. Míralo bien: no te fies en los ojos que se les antoja muchas veces uno por otro. No me habían dejado gota de sangre: tragada tenía ya la muerte, que me parescía que me iban dando en estas espaldas golpes. En mi vida me acuerdo haber tan gran temor, ni verme en tal afrenta aunque he andado casas agenas harto tiempo, y en lugares de harto trabajo; que nueve años serví á los frayles de Guadalupe, que mil veces nos apuñeábamos yo y otros; pero nunca como esta vez hube miedo de morir.

Semp. I am even better prepared, for I have tied my buckler and sword together with the straps so that they may not fall as I run: I have got my steel cap in the hood of my cloak.

Parm. What of the stones that thou broughtest in it?

Semp. I threw them all away so that I might go the lighter. As it is I have too much to carry with this buff coat that thou madest me wear by thy obstinacy; how right I was to object to bring it, for it seemed to me very heavy for running away in! Hark, hark! Dost thou not hear, Parmeno? Something untoward is taking place; we are dead men. Throw quickly: make for Celestina's house lest they cut us off from our own.

Parm. Flee, flee, for thou runnest but poorly. Ah! sinner that I am! think if they were to catch us! Drop thy buckler and everything.

Semp. I wonder if they have slain our master.

Parm. I know not: do not speak; run, and hold thy tongue, for that is the least of my cares.

Semp. Hist! hist! Parmeno, turn thee about in silence, for it is nought but the watch that was tramping noisily along the other end of the street.

Parm. Look well. Trust not thine eyes for often do they take one thing for another. Not a drop of blood was left in me; I had already swallowed the bitter draught of death: it seemed to me that they were already pummelling this back of mine. Never in my life do I remember to have been thus afraid, nor to have been in so much danger, though for long I have dwelt in others' houses and in situations most laborious. Nine years I served the friars of Guadalupe; a thousand times I came to fisticuffs with my companions, but never, as now, was I in peril of my life.

Semp. ¿Y yo no serví al cura de san Miguel, y al mesonero de la plaza, y á Mollejas el hortelano? Y tambien yo tenía mis cuestiones con los que tiraban piedras á los pájaros que se asentaban en un álamo grande que tenía, porque dañaban la hortaliza. Pero guárdete Dios de verte con armas, que aquel es el verdadero temor; no en balde dicen *cargado de hierro, cargado de miedo.* Vuelve, vuelve, que el alguacil es cierto.

Such is the outline of the plot of this remarkable book, but the incidents and episodes, the loves and quarrels of the servants, and the low life surrounding Celestina generally, form a wonderfully vigorous picture of manners, and constitute its most valuable part. Cervantes speaks of it somewhat enigmatically in the verses prefixed to Don Quixote, calling it "a book that in my opinion were divine, did it conceal more carefully the human element."[1] Yet it is just this human tone, and the bold step taken by the author in cutting himself off from tradition and seeking his subject in the everyday life of his time, that gives the book its special worth. The style is animated, lucid, correct, and idiomatic, and is mentioned with the highest praise by almost all the best Spanish critics.

The *Celestina* aided the development of the drama by giving the Spaniards the first specimen in their own language of easy and natural dialogue in which a plot is worked out. In the servants' characters may be found distinct traces of the *gracioso* or *comic* character who plays so large a part on the Spanish stage, and afterwards becomes stereotyped in Calderon's plays.

The *Celestina* may also be looked on as the earliest example

---

Semp. And did I not serve the priest of San Miguel, and the tavern-keeper in the market-place, and Mollejas the gardener? I too had my differences with those who throw stones at the birds that were wont to settle in a great elm of his: for they used to damage the green-stuff. But heaven preserve us from bearing arms, for that is terrible indeed. Well does the proverb say 'A burden of steel is a burden of fears.' Come back, come back. It is without doubt the watch. . . ."

[1] "Libro en mi opinión divino,
Si encubriera más lo humano."

of the "picaresque" novel. Its popularity is proved by the innumerable editions, translations, imitations, and adaptations to which it gave rise.

The success of the *Celestina* did not destroy the popular taste for literary food of a milder and more insipid character. The origin of the pastoral novel is probably to be found in the late Greek writers, but the Spanish works of this class are inspired by, if not directly imitated from, the *Arcadia* of the Italian Sannazaro (sixteenth century). The first and most celebrated of these is the *Diana Enamorada*, by Jorge de Montemayor, a Portuguese. It is written partly in Castilian and partly in the author's native language, and was first published at Madrid in 1545. The scene is the banks of the river Esla in León, a region infested by troops of lackadaisical shepherd-lovers leading a most unnatural life. They speak in a courtly and affected style, entirely unbefitting their station and surroundings, and celebrate their successful love or lament their woes in very indifferent verse. These nerveless personages play a provoking game of cross-purposes until shuffled and re-arranged in pairs by "the wise Felicia," a benevolent old lady, possessing supernatural powers and inhabiting an enchanted palace in the neighbourhood. The chief merit of Montemayor's work lies in its correct though somewhat inflated prose. On the whole we may agree with the judgment of Cervantes, who says, speaking through the mouth of the priest, "Let all that treats of the wise Felicia and of the enchanted water be cut out, together with almost all the longer passages of verse, and let it retain, and welcome, the prose and the honour of being the first of the books of its class."

Two more *Dianas* speedily made their appearance, desirous of profiting by the great popularity of the first. Both were published in the year 1564. One of them is called the *Segunda del Salamantino*. It was written in accordance with the instructions of Montemayor, who had left his work unfinished, by Alonso Perez, a doctor of medicine of Salamanca. The other is the *Diana Enamorada* of Gil Polo. Both these works are carefully modelled on the first *Diana*. The verses of Polo are certainly better than those of Montemayor and Perez, but it is hard to understand why Cervantes draws such a marked distinction between the two, condemning one to the flames and recommending that the other should be preserved "as though it were the work of Apollo himself." He was probably pleading indirectly the cause of his own *Galatea*, of which special mention will be made in the chapter devoted to his writings. For both Cervantes himself and his great rival Lope de Vega published pastoral novels neither better nor worse than the other books of this class. It is curious to note that, speaking of another novel of this kind, the *Pastor de Fílida* by Montalvo, which Lope also greatly admired, Cervantes praises it for the very circumstance which would make a modern critic disposed to condemn it, namely, the incompatibility of the characters with their surroundings. He says, "This is no shepherd, but a very discreet courtier; let him be preserved like a precious jewel." It is, however, certain that Cervantes clearly saw the weakness of this artificial kind of composition, for elsewhere he (*Coloquio de los Perros*) contrasts the rustic songs and coarse manners of the shepherds of reality, who in Spain are sometimes little better than savages, with the airs and graces of the shepherds of the pastoral novels, and concludes by saying "that all these books are pure imagination, and are written for the amusement of the idle, but without a particle of truth in them." Other celebrated books of the kind are the *Arcadia* by Lope de Vega, *Constante Amarilis* by Suarez de Figueroa, and the *Siglo de Oro* by Balbuena.

Side by side with the novelists of the pastoral school grew up another class of writers of romance, whose conception of the art is so entirely different that, if the works of both are to be called novels, novel must mean little else than a work of imagination in prose. These were the writers of the picaresque stories. Cervantes cultivated both branches, and the comparative degree of interest possessed by either class at the present day may be best judged by those who have read both his *Galatea* and his *Rinconete y Cortadillo*. The reason for this is the same in both cases. The "rogue stories," equally with the pastoral romances, had a common source in one great work, and in both a great similarity may be traced among the books included under the name. But in the case of the *novela picaresca* the model was a genuinely national one, and the very form of the story gives rise to an infinite variety of episode.

The model referred to is the *Lazarillo de Tormés*, ascribed, though seemingly without proof of any kind, to Diego Hurtado de Mendoza, a soldier, statesman, historian, and poet of the good old Spanish type, who flourished during the reign of Charles V. He is said to have written during his university career (1520-23) the novel which, if really his, would constitute his chief title to fame. It was first published anonymously thirty years later at Antwerp. Lazarillo, like the *pícaros* (rogues) whose exploits are celebrated in the other books of the kind, is a poor boy of disreputable parentage, who successively enters the service of persons of all classes of society, and manages, partly by adroit cheating and partly by flattering the vices of his masters, to live in positions that would, to persons of less resource and nicer sense of honour, be intolerable. He finally becomes town-crier of Toledo, and it is in that honourable position that the unfinished story leaves him. The most amusing characters in the book are Lazarillo himself; the blind beggar, his first master; the "pardoner," the amusing description of whose unscrupulous proceedings brought down on the book the wrath of the Inquisition; and the *escudero*, or poor gentleman, a type which, though modified by altered surroundings, is not yet wholly extinct in Spain. Its most

distinctive features are admirably summed up in the following
passage :—

[1] Un día que habíamos comido razonablemente y estaba algo contento,
contóme su hacienda, y díjome ser de Castilla la Vieja, y que había dejado
su tierra no más de por no quitar el bonete á un caballero, su vecino.
" Señor " dije yo " si él era lo que decís y tenía más que vos no errábades
en quitárselo primero, pues decís que él tambien os lo quitába."—" Sí es, y
sí tiene, y tambien me lo quitaba él á mí ; mas de cuantas veces yo se le
quitaba primero, no fuera malo comedirse él alguna y ganarme por la mano
. . . no sientes las cosas de la honra en que, el día de hoy, es todo el
caudal de los hombres de bien . . . Mayormente no soy tan pobre que no
tengo en mi tierra un solar de casas, que á estar ellas en pie y bien labradas
. . . valdrían más de doscientos mil maravedís, según se podrían hacer
grandes y buenas. Y tengo un palomar que á no estar derribado, como
está, daría cadá año más de doscientos palominos, y otras cosas que me callo
que dejé por lo que tocaba á mi honra : y vine á esta ciudad pensando que
hallaría un buen asiento . . . Ya cuando asienta un hombre con un señor
de título todavía pasa su lacería ; pues por ventura no hay en mi habilidad
para servir y contentar á éstos ? Por Dios si con él topase muy gran privado
suyo pienso que fuese, y que mil servicios le hiciese ; porque yo sabría men-
tille tan bien como otro, y agradalle á las mil maravillas ; reillehía mucho
sus donaires y costumbres, aunque no fuesen las mejores del mundo : nunca

---

[1] " One day that we had dined reasonably well and he was in good spirits,
he told me his story, saying that he was a native of Old Castile and that he
had left his country only so as not to take off his cap to a gentleman, his
neighbour. ' Sir ' said I ' if he was, as you say, a gentleman, and richer
than you, you were not doing wrong in taking it off to him first, for you admit
that he used to take his hat off to you.'—' He is and has more than I, and
moreover he used to take off his hat to me ; but, with all the times I took it
off to him first, it would have been well for him to have sometimes been so
polite as to forestall me . . . you know nought of these matters of honour
which nowadays make up the whole resources of honourable men . . . Moreover I am not so poor but that I have in my own country a site for houses,
and, if they were erected and well built . . . they would be worth more than
200,000 maravedis, so large and good could they be made. And I have a
dovecote which, if it had not been pulled down, would produce yearly more
than 200 pigeons ; besides other matters that I do not mention. All this I
abandoned out of consideration for my honour ; and I came to this city
thinking that I should find a good position. . . . When a man takes service
with a gentleman of title he may stomach his hardships : What say you ? Am
I not fitted to serve and to delight such persons ? By heaven, if I were to
find such a one, I would make myself his prime favourite and render him a
thousand services ; for I could tell him lies as well as another, and please him
amazingly. I would laugh at his quips and his habits, though they might not
be the best in the world ; I would never say anything that might displease him,

decille cosa que le pesase, aunque mucho le cumpliese ; ser muy diligente en su persona en dicho y hecho ; no me matar por no hacer bien las cosas que él no había de ver ; y ponerme á reñir con la gente de servicio porque pareciese gran cuidado de lo que a él tocaba . . . y muchas galas de esta calidad, que hoy se usan en Palacio y á los señores de él parecen bien."

The whole story, consisting of only nine short chapters, is lively and interesting in the extreme. It at once found favour with the general public, and produced a host of imitators eager to avail themselves of the wide field for imagination and satire afforded by its simple form.

In 1555 a continuation of the Lazarillo by an anonymous writer, who takes up the story where it had been left by its original author, appeared at Antwerp. He entirely fails to understand the character of the book he professes to continue, and gives an absurd and dull account of the hero's submarine adventures in the shape of a tunny fish. A teacher of the Spanish language in Paris named Luna produced a *Second Part of Lazarillo de Tormés* in 1620. This is a book of considerably more merit than the last named ; its style is correct and idio matic ; some of the stories which it contains are amusing and well told, but it lacks the brisk and natural tone of the original, and is, in parts, coarsely indecent.

Mateo Alemán, who was employed in the finance depart-ment in the time of Felipe II., attempted in his *Guzmán de Alfarache* (Madrid, 1599) to make the *pícaro* serve a moral purpose. In this he was not fully successful. His hero is a prosy and contemptible personage who relates with much relish and unction his own more than questionable adventures, with the avowed object of dissuading others from following his evil courses. When he gives play to his moralising tendencies he

though it were to his great advantage to do so ; I would be very diligent about his person in word and deed, and would not trouble myself to do too well the things that he would not see : and I would scold his servants that I might appear very careful of all that concerned him . . . and exhibit many accom-plishments of the kind, such as are now customary in great houses and are esteemed by their owners.' "

is always intolerably dull, as also in the episodical stories which
he frequently introduces. His attempts to be amusing often
produce disgust. Guzmán is no gay scamp like Lazarillo, but a
canting scoundrel of very low tastes. If, however, the sermons
with which the book is interlarded are cut out, it cannot fail
to interest as a somewhat exaggerated and highly - coloured
account of the life of the author's contemporaries in their own
country and in Italy. Properly used it may serve to illustrate
the 'cloak and sword drama' of the succeeding century.

Alemán, like Cervantes in his *Don Quixote*, promised a
second part of his book, and like him he was forestalled ; like
him also he held up the author of the spurious second part to
contempt in his own continuation. Of these two continuations
of the worn-out story it is enough to say that Alemán, in his
Second Part of Guzmán de Alfarache, exaggerates the faults and
minimises the scanty merits of his first attempt ; and that the
work of Mateo Luján de Saavedra, as the forger calls himself,
is the worse of the two.

During the seventeenth century a whole series of stories of this
kind was published. Among them the most worthy of notice are
La Pícara Justina, by Lopez de Úbeda, which relates the story
of a daughter of Celestina ; *Lazarillo de Manzanares*, a base
imitation of the original Lazarillo, by Juan Cortés de Tolosa ;
Marcos de Obregón, a well-written and readable book, by Vicente
Espinel (1618), in which the author gives a witty account of
many of the adventures of his own chequered career as a soldier
in Flanders and vagabond in Spain. Espinel, who subsequently
became a priest, is the reputed inventor of the metrical form
called *decimas* or *espinelas*. *El Donado Hablador* by Gerónimo
de Alcalá, *La Garduña de Sevilla* by Salorzano (1654), and the
Gran Tacaño of Quevedo, all belong to this class ; the latter,
as well as the *Rinconete y Cortadillo*, and the "novels of adventure" of Cervantes, will be specially mentioned in the chapters
devoted to their authors. To the student of the social history

of the age which produced them, these books are invaluable; as works of imagination they are generally tame and lacking in interest; their popularity died out, never to return, on the first appearance of the modern novel.

While speaking of the novel, mention must be made of two curious attempts at, or rather forerunners of, the historical novel. The first is the short and well-written *Story of the Abencerraje and the beautiful Jarifa*, by Antonio de Villegas (1565). This is the legend, known to us by the *Romancero*, and probably founded on fact, of how a Moorish knight of the noble family of the Abencerrages, while on his way to pay a nightly visit to his lady, was captured by Rodrigo de Narvaez, the chivalrous *alcaide* or governor of the fortress of Antiquera. Taking pity on his distress, the alcaide generously releases his prisoner on parole; the Moor shows himself worthy of the confidence placed in his honour by returning to captivity, bringing with him the lady; after which the pair are happily married.

The second is the *Wars of Granada*, by Gines Perez de Hita (*First Part Saragossa*, 1595), consisting of two books of entirely different character. The first is an almost purely imaginary account of the internal troubles at Granada during the period preceding its conquest (1492). The doughty single-handed fights in the *vega* or fertile plain outside the city between the chivalrous Moslem and Christian champions, the loves of the Moorish knights and ladies, and the gallant shows and tournaments celebrated in the city, are described with great detail as to costume and manners, but apparently with total ignorance of Oriental customs and disregard for historical accuracy. The second part treats of the celebrated rebellion of the oppressed *Moriscos* (subject Moors) against the harsh rule of Felipe II. In the suppression of this rising the author took part; but even here he draws largely upon his imagination for his facts, and serving as he did in an inferior capácity, he is often obliged merely to repeat the rumour of the camp as to movements and events which he did not fully understand. It is interesting to compare his account of the last struggle of the Moors with those by Diego Hurtado de Mendoza and Luís de Carvajal, the historians of this cruel and bloody war of extermination. Hita's style is elegant and natural, and by its modern tone and artless simplicity recalls that of Santa Teresa.

The "novel of adventures" is but poorly represented in Spanish. Cervantes' *Novelas ejemplares* are by far the best representatives of the class, unless indeed *Marcos de Obregón* be reckoned as belonging to it rather than to the "rogue stories." Wearisome and colourless as are the stories of Francisco Santos, Gonzalo de Céspedes, and María de Zayas in the seventeenth century, they are utterly outdone in absurdity by the *Various Prodigies of Love*, published by Isidro de Robles, and containing five stories, the chief distinction of which is that in each of them severally one of the five vowels does not anywhere appear.

CHAPTER IX

MYSTIC AND RELIGIOUS WRITERS

MYSTICISM in some of its forms is as old as the religions of the East; it appears in Plato, in St. Thomas Aquinas, and above all in the *De Imitatione Christi*. In Germany it was cultivated at an early date, and previous to the authors we are about to mention Spain had produced Ramón Lull, in whose writings distinct traces of this spirit may be found. Mysticism, standing "half-way between belief and understanding, between faith and science," [1] is the direct outcome of asceticism and the contemplative life. Its details vary considerably in different ages and different countries, but its characteristic feature is always a belief in the direct communication of the purified soul with its ideal, or with its God. This is regarded by the mystic not as a supernatural state, but as the sure reward of a certain degree of perfection. As the soul becomes more and more detached from the things of this world, so does its intercourse with the Divine Love become more and more immediate. Santa Teresa, by means of the following allegory, in which the grace of God is compared to water in a dry land, describes the three degrees or stages of prayer which must be passed through before the highest state can be reached.

[1] Menendez y Pelayo, *Historia de las Ideas estéticas en España.*

¹ Pues veamos ahora de la manera que se puede regar para que entenda-
mos lo que hemos de hacer y el trabajo que nos ha de costar, si es mayor la
ganancia, ú hasta qué tanto tiempo se ha de tener. Paréceme a mí que se
puede regar de cuatro maneras ; ú con sacar el agua de un pozo, que es á
nuestro gran trabajo ; ú con noria y arcaduces, que se saca con un torno
(yo la he sacado algunas veces), es á menos trabajo que estotro y sácase más
agua ; ú de un río ú arroyo, esto se riega muy mijor, que queda mas harta
la tierra de agua, y no se ha menster regar tan á menudo, y es menos trabajo
mucho del hortelano ; ú con llover mucho, que lo riega el Señor sin trabajo
ninguno nuestro, y es muy sin comparación mijor que todo lo que queda
dicho. Ahora pues, aplicadas estas cuatro maneras de agua, de que se ha
de sustentar este huerto, porque sin ella perderse ha, es lo que á mí me
hace al caso, y ha parecido que se podrá declarar algo de cuatro grados de
oración en que el Señor por su bondad ha puesto algunas veces mi alma.
Plega á su bondad atine á decirlo, de manera que aproveche á uno de las
personas que esto me mandaron escribir, que la ha traido el Señor en cuatro
meses harto más adelante que yo estaba en diez y siete años : hase dispuesto
mijor y ansi sin trabajo suyo riega este verjel con todas estas cuatro aguas ;
aunque la postrera aun no se le da sino a gotas, mas va de suerte que pronto
se engolfará en ella con ayuda del Señor ; y gustaré que se ría, si le pare-
ciere desatino la manera de el declárar.

The spirit of mysticism, as might be expected, reveals itself
most frequently in persons of nervous and somewhat morbid

¹ "So then let us now see what are the manners of watering in order to
understand how we must act, and what amount of labour it will cost us,
whether the gain be greater, or how long it will be ours. To me it appears
that watering may be done in four ways ; either by drawing the water from a
well which is heavy toil to us ; or by the water-wheel and cups which draws
it with a windlass (I have drawn it thus myself more than once), this is less
toilsome than the other way and more water is thereby drawn ; or from a
river or stream (by channels), thus the watering is better done, the earth is
more saturated with water, and it is not needful to do it so often, and the
labour of the gardener is greatly lightened ; or by abundant rain which the
Lord sends to water the earth without any toil of ours, and which is incomparably better than all that we have said. Applying then these four manners
of giving water wherewith this garden must be refreshed, for otherwise it will
be lost, my purpose is and my hope that something may be learned of
the four degrees of prayer in which the Lord of His bounty has sometimes
placed my soul. May it please His goodness that I succeed in declaring it in
such wise that it be profitable to one of those who bid me write this book, and
whom the Lord has brought in four months to greater advancement than I
gained in seventeen years : He hath ordained better, and thus without labour
of the possessor He waters this garden in all the four manners ; but the fourth
until now is only vouchsafed in drops, yet such is the progress that soon it will
be drenched with it by the help of the Lord : and I shall rejoice if that person
smiles at my manner of explanation, if it seems to him absurd."

disposition, with bodies worn down by fasting and penance. The fervid and passionate temperament, characteristic of the great body of the Spanish nation, influenced by the political exigencies which made it the champion of the Catholic religion, offered a suitable soil for a growth of this kind, and during the sixteenth and seventeenth centuries there sprung up a series of mystic writers so remarkable that mysticism of a certain kind may almost be regarded as a peculiarly Spanish development. At first the attitude of the Church towards the persons, many of them entirely illiterate, who claimed direct inspiration was hesitating. Some were stated to have worked miracles or to have had miracles manifested in their bodies while in a state of ecstatic trance. Such supernatural pretensions were discouraged by the authorities, and searching inquiries were set on foot by the Inquisition. These generally resulted in the submission and recantation of the person under examination. Even the miracles of Santa Teresa were not allowed to pass unchallenged. She incurred much suspicion, and it was only during the last years of her life that her claims to sanctity were fully acknowledged.

It is a remarkable feature of Spanish mysticism that from Ramón Lull onward its devotees, even the most favoured of them, were not mere dreamers, but had a strong practical element in their character. Almost all of them worked hard for the advancement of the religious congregation to which they severally belonged, and for the initiation or perfecting of charitable schemes. Some even proved themselves shrewd diplomatists in the negotiations they conducted with persons in authority, skilfully disarming or rendering ineffective the hatred and jealousy with which they were often regarded by the members of rival orders. The Jesuits more especially looked with suspicion upon them and upon their indirect claims to superior sanctity. Another quality possessed in common by the adherents of this school is an extraordinary gift of expression and command over their native language. At a time when pedantry and classical affectation were rife, the mystics are almost the only class of writers who keep themselves free from these faults and preserve a simple and natural tone, expressing by striking and often beautiful allegories transcendental feelings and ecstatic states of mind which ordinary language is inadequate to describe. It was in the seventeenth century and in the writings of the mystics that Spanish prose reached its highest development as a literary instrument; and so little has the language changed since then, that a novelist and critic of the present day,[1] whose style is universally and justly admired, points proudly to the religious writers of this period as his models.

The first of the series is Juan de Ávila, the friend and religious adviser of Santa Teresa. From his youth upwards he showed extraordinary religious fervour. He withdrew from the University of Salamanca, whither he had been sent to study law, in order to undergo a self-inflicted penance of three years. He afterwards took orders, divided his goods among the poor, and dedicating himself to preaching met with extraordinary success. His perfect disinterestedness was shown by his refusal of all the high positions offered to him in the Church; the saintliness of his life was well known, but even this did not disarm his enemies, and he suffered much wilful misrepresentation and actual persecution at their hands. He is the author of several moral and theological treatises, the most remarkable of which is the *Cartas Espirituales*, a collection of letters divided into four parts, and addressed respectively to the clergy and religious orders, to nuns and young women, to married women, and to noblemen. They contain rules for the conduct of life based entirely on religious considerations; this world is but a place of probation, and the only happiness that can be attained in it results from the communion of the soul with God,

---

[1] See preface to *Pepita Jimenez* by Juan Valera.

which presupposes all the virtues and gives a foretaste of the better and eternal life. Juan de Ávila's book is in perfect keeping with the portraits of the man himself. These represent a sweet grave face, too delicate to contain any strong lines, and with dreamy contemplative eyes, whose gaze seems lost in another world. His easy and fluent style is here and there allowed to become careless and loose, for he cared nothing for the form of his works ; his only thought is to persuade others tó seek happiness where he himself had found it.

Santa Teresa de Jesus was born in the city of Ávila in Old Castile in the year 1515. Her history is told with admirable simplicity in the *Libro de su Vida* (Book of her Life), which she wrote by command of her spiritual advisers. Her parents were persons of good family, severe, frigid, and exceedingly punctilious in the discharge of all religious duties. The somewhat harsh and formal character of her surroundings produced in early youth a reaction and spirit of rebellion in the heart of the passionate girl. In later life she never ceases to reproach herself for the apparently innocent vagaries of this period of her life, among which she reckons the writing of a romance of chivalry at the age of fourteen years. It was not long, however, before the serious and deeply religious groundwork of her character became apparent, and when only sixteen years of age she entered with many misgivings the Augustine convent in her native place. Three years later she took the life-long vows, and shortly afterwards she entered upon her great task, the reform and extension of the Carmelite order. Her health was delicate, but throughout long periods of acute suffering she showed heroic fortitude and unflinching resolution. In the discharge of what she considered to be her duty she allowed herself to be interrupted neither by her physical ailments nor by the many and bitter persecutions resulting from the jealousies she had provoked and the prejudices she had attacked. In spite of the cruel misconstruction put upon her actions by those to whom she might reasonably have looked for help, and in spite of coolness and even direct opposition from the highest quarters, she succeeded in her object by sheer force of character and business-like activity. In twelve years she reformed the order to which she belonged, and founded seventeen convents under the new regulations drawn up by herself and her friends. Immediately after her death, which occurred in 1582, her admirers, among whom were now reckoned many of her former enemies, agreed that a great saint had passed away, and they applied to Rome for the recognition which her merits had so thoroughly deserved. Her beatification was succeeded by her canonisation in 1622. A curious testimony to the esteem in which she was held is furnished by the attempt to make her joint patron of Spain along with Santiago (see p. 181).

Santa Teresa's moral and mystic works gained almost immediately after her death a world-wide reputation, which they have preserved in Roman Catholic countries down to the present day. Without pretensions to learning or literary prejudices of any kind, she describes in language, admirable for its simplicity and clearness, the ardent aspirations of her soul, and urges others to follow in the path by which she herself obtained such singular favour from on high. The wonderful directness and evident good faith with which she recounts the miracles of which she believed herself to be the object, and which she published only when commanded to do so, preclude all suspicions of fraud, and went straight to the hearts of the pious folk for whom her writings were intended. The rules which she drew up for the government and administration of the convents under her charge, as well as many anecdotes concerning her life, show the shrewd and practical side of her character, which acted as a check on what would otherwise probably have become a consuming madness. Her poetical works will be mentioned in another chapter.

A contemporary of the two above-mentioned writers and also of Luis de León, with whose name this short notice of a most interesting and important class ends, was Fray Luís de Granada. Twelve years after its conquest he was born in the city from which he took his name. His mother was a widow, so poor that she was obliged to beg her bread at the doors of the newly-founded convents which made the needy their special charge. He owed his education to the liberality of the Marqués de Mondéjar, the father of Diego Hurtado de Mendoza, who was at that time governor of the city. Joining the Dominican order, Luís de Granada soon won the reputation of a great preacher. After a long and active life, a large part of which was spent in an attempt to convert and to better the lot of the unfortunate Moriscos of his native land, he finally became provincial of his order in Lisbon, where he died at the age of eighty-three. Luís de Grarfada was a theologian, but it is not on subtle arguments that he relies for winning souls to God. In burning and eloquent phrases of great sweetness and power he deplores the miseries of the present world, contrasting the fleeting joys of even its most fortunate votaries with the rewards of the true believer on this side of the grave as well as on the other. With passionate earnestness he points to the figure of the Redeemer, exhorting mankind by an appeal to the loftiest and noblest feelings of the human heart to follow Him. In the pursuit of his great object he rises to the highest pitch of inspiration, expressing himself in flowing, graceful, and correct language. His writings are still widely read and, as devotional books, his *Guide of Sinners* and *Prayer and Meditation* are surpassed only by the unrivalled *Imitation of Christ*.

Of the life of Luís de León and his qualities as a poet mention will be made elsewhere (see p. 126). Remarkable as is his verse, his prose is equal to it in merit. He is a more thorough scholar and theologian than the other mystics already mentioned. This may be seen in his treatise on the *Names of*

Christ, in which he interprets and comments on the symbolic Biblical titles of Bridegroom, Prince of Peace, and Shepherd. His learning is, however, far removed from pedantry and minute quibbling. The reflections to which these names give rise in his mind are often truly sublime. In the translation of the Song of Solomon, which brought upon him such bitter persecution, he finds scope for his luxuriant style, full of oriental imagery, but never bombastic. With the exception of his poetical works, the book by which he is best known is his *Perfecta Casada* (Perfect Wife), in which, taking for his text the thirty-first chapter of the Book of Proverbs, he sketches in grave and forcible language his somewhat severe but admirably pure conception of the strong woman. So true is his picture, and so accurately did he gauge the feelings of his countrymen in this respect, that a Spanish authoress of great talent (Emilia Pardo Bazán) has lately expressed an opinion that his book still represents the national ideal of the Perfect Wife.

The list of Religious and Mystic writers of real importance might be prolonged to greater length, but their general characteristics may be gleaned from a few examples. The beauty of their style belongs to their age and literary surroundings, and has no relation to their theological opinions, for Juan de Valdés and C. de Valera write with the same perfection and grace as the most orthodox of those mentioned above. Religion was an ever-present reality to Spaniards of all classes during the period of national glory, and their splendid language and powerful imaginations combined to make it one of the most important branches of their literature.

CHAPTER X

HISTORY

THE *Chronicle of the Catholic Sovereigns* by their secretary, Hernando del Pulgar, is the last of a series, and bears traces of the transition stage between chronicle and history. It is true that during the reign of Charles V. the compilation of a new *Crónica General de España* was entrusted to Florián de Ocampo, who brought his work down to the Roman period, where it was taken up by Morales, and afterwards by Sandoval, the author of a history of the reign of Charles V. But the scope and aims of this work are widely different from those of the earlier chronicles, and it is evident that historical science has already made considerable strides. Judged by the canons and compared with the methods of the present day, the works of Ocampo and later historians appear credulous and uncritical in the extreme, but they no longer content themselves with mere tales of battles and of the rise and fall of dynasties in chronological order.

In 1547 the General Assembly of the kingdom of Aragón first appointed an official chronicler, and their choice fell most happily upon the learned and industrious Gerónimo de Zurita. Leaving out the earlier period, which had cost his predecessors so much fruitless labour, and beginning his history at the Moorish invasion, Zurita brought it down to the year 1510, at which point it was, after his death, taken up by his successors and continued till the year 1705. Zurita's work marks a new epoch in the writing of history; painstaking and exact in the extreme, he cannot rest satisfied with mere tradition. Abandoning the practice of former historians, who had been satisfied to copy from their predecessors, he undertook more than one long journey for the sake of consulting original documents. His *Anales de la Corona de Aragón* is still by far the most useful and trustworthy authority on his subject and period; his judgment is correct and impartial, and his conception of history is broad and liberal. But Zurita was no artist; his account of the stirring and picturesque events which form the subject of his book is colourless and lacking in dramatic interest; his *Annals* form a splendid collection of material, but can scarcely be looked on as a literary work.

Very different in character is Juan de Mariana, the greatest of Spanish historians, who was Zurita's junior by one generation. He was a foundling, and owed his education at the University of Alcalá to the charity of one of the canons of Toledo. While still very young he became a member of the Society of Jesus, and later on taught theology and scholastic philosophy in Rome, and at the Sorbonne. In 1574 he returned to Spain and took up his abode in a religious house at Toledo, where he lived almost continuously till the time of his death, which took place in 1623, in extreme old age. Mariana's history of Spain was published in Latin at the end of the sixteenth century, but in 1609 he brought out a translation with many additions and corrections. This is the work with which we are chiefly concerned. The earlier part of it is somewhat uninteresting, for Mariana, according to the custom of his age, begins with the fabulous period at which Tubal, son of Japheth, settled in Spain. For the Roman period also, a vast increase in the number of documents, together with improved methods of criticism, have rendered Mariana's work obsolete. It is only when he reaches later times that we are able to appreciate to the full his great genius. His style is of the purest and most facile, his descriptions animated and brilliant, and in the painting of character he is probably unsurpassed. Even the apocryphal speeches which, in imitation of classical authors, he frequently puts into the mouth of historical persons have a real importance, resulting from their artistic value and the life-like effect thereby produced. In them, moreover, is revealed a great deal of their author's shrewd political views. Mariana has a wonderful gift of transferring himself in imagination to the times of which he wrote, and of realising the motives and views of contending parties. In spite, however, of his broad, and in many respects enlightened views, he is very uncritical, more particularly where religious matters are concerned. Above all he is a Christian historian, and legends and miracles of saints are related by him with the greatest good faith, side by side with historical facts resting on undoubted evidence. Even this peculiarity, rightly regarded, ceases to be a defect, for it helps toward the better understanding of the times of and for which he wrote, and in which such beliefs exercised a wide influence over conduct. As a historian, Mariana has to the full the defects and limitations of his age, country, and order; as a writer of Spanish prose, he is above criticism.

Besides his great history, Mariana published several tracts of great value on political and religious matters. These show how well qualified he was to be a judge of economic and political questions, and how conscientiously he worked when he had the necessary documents at hand. His memorial on the subject of public shows and dramatic representations is a thoughtful piece of work containing much valuable information. The following passage on the bull-fight would raise a smile among followers (*aficionados*) of what is still the national sport:—

[1] Pero esta costumbre nunca se quitó en España, ó con el tiempo se ha tornado á revocar, por ser nuestra nación muy aficionada á este espectáculo,

[1] "But this custom was either never lost in Spain, or has again been revived after a lapse of years, by reason of the affection of our people for such spectacles and the extraordinary ferocity of Spanish bulls, caused by the

siendo los toros en España mas bravos que en otras partes, á causa de la
sequedad de la tierra y de los pastos, por donde lo que más había de
apartar destos juegos, que es no ver despedazar á los hombres, eso los
enciende más á apetecellos, por ser, como son, aficionades á las armas y á
derramar sangre, de genio inquieto, tanto que cuanto mas bravos son
los toros y más hombres matan, tanto el juego da más contento : y si
ninguno hieren, el deleite y placer es muy liviano ó ninguno ; . . . en
nuestros juegos . . . todos los toreadores salen de su voluntad al coso, al
derredor del cual hay muchas barreras y escondrijos donde se recogen
seguramente, porque el toro no puede entrar dentro tras ellos, de suerte
que si algunos perecen, parece que no es culpa de los que gobiernan,
sino de los que locamente se atrevieron á ponerse en parte de donde no
pudiesen huir seguramente. Principalmente á los que torean á caballo
ningún peligro, á ló menos muy pequeño, les corre ; sólo la gente baja
tiene peligro, y por causa dellos se trata esta dificultad, si conviene que
este juego por el tal peligro se quite como los demás espectáculos, ó si
será mejor que se use con fin de deleitar el pueblo, y con estas peleas y
fiestas ejercitallc para las verdaderas peleas.

Considering the conditions under which he lived, Mariana
is a liberal-minded thinker and exceedingly bold in the expression of his views. In 1598 he published at Toledo a
tract, entitled *De Rege et Regis Institutione,* that created a storm
of controversy throughout Europe. In it he examines the
foundations of regal authority, and with a boldness unknown
in his age he justifies the slaughter of tyrants in extreme

dryness of the land, and of their pastures ; and so it comes about that that
which ought chiefly to repel in such sports, namely the sight of men torn to
pieces, is the very reason for which they are sought after. For the Spaniard
loves weapons and bloodshed and is restless by nature to such a degree that
the greater the ferocity of the bulls and the number of men that they slay, the
more he is pleased with the sport : and if nobody is wounded his pleasure and
enjoyment is but slight or disappears altogether ; . . . in our sports . . . all
the bull-fighters come into the ring of their own free will, and round about it
are abundance of barriers and lurking-places to which they withdraw in safety,
for thither the bull cannot pursue them ; so that, if any are slain, it seems not
to be through the fault of the rulers, but owing to the foolhardiness of those
who expose themselves in such positions that they cannot obtain safety by flight.
More especially those who fight on horseback are out of danger, or their risk is
but slight ; it is only the common people that are in danger, and for their sakes
we discuss the question whether it behoves that this sport should like other
public spectacles be abolished by reason of the aforesaid danger, or whether it
is better that it should continue for the delight of the vulgar and in order that
the people may be trained and exercised for real warfare by such fightings and
festivities."

cases. This work was burned at Paris by the hands of the executioner, and brought odium upon its author and upon his order. For his vigorous protest against the debasement of the coin of the realm, Mariana was imprisoned by the king. His review of the Society of Jesus, which we can scarcely suppose to have been intended for publication, met with the censure of his religious superiors and brought speedy punishment upon its author.

Diego Hurtado de Mendoza has already been mentioned as the supposed author of *Lazarillo de Tormés* (see p. 88). He was the son of the Marqués de Mondéjar, the first governor of the newly-conquered kingdom of Granada, and was born there in the year 1503. After studying at Salamanca he became a soldier and saw much active service in the wars of the Emperor. He rendered important services to the state as ambassador to the Republic of Venice, was made governor of Lima, and subsequently appointed to represent Spain at the Council of Trent, where he manfully defended the interests of his native land. When quite an old man he brought upon himself, by his hot temper, the displeasure of Felipe II. and was banished to Granada, where he spent the greater part of his latter days. As a man of letters and a scholar he associated with the great writers, both Spanish and Italian, of his time; he showed his interest in classical studies by obtaining from the Sultan, whom he had laid under an obligation, an important collection of Greek manuscripts, which, together with his collection of Arabic and Hebrew works, he presented to the library of the Escorial, where they are still preserved. While living in retirement at Granada (about 1571), he wrote, under the title of *History of the Rebellion and Chastisement of the Moriscos*, an account of events which occurred in the years 1568-70. In Mendoza's prose, as in his verse, his affection for the classics is clearly seen. Tacitus and Sallust are his models, and in certain passages his imitation of them is so close that it is hard to believe that he has not distorted historical facts for the sake of following more closely in the steps of his favourite authors. As a literary work the *Guerra de Granada* has been vastly overrated. It certainly contains a few brilliant descriptive passages, and some few vigorous apocryphal set speeches, but the style is laboured and pedantic, repetitions are frequent, and many passages are extremely obscure. For the latter fault the editors are undoubtedly in some degree accountable. Mendoza's book contained serious reflections upon the conduct of several important personages who had been engaged in the war, and this is probably the reason why it was not published until some years after his death. When it finally appeared, many mistakes had crept into the text, and incorrect punctuation, combined with an abrupt and epigrammatical style abounding in Latinisms, make it, with the exception of some of Quevedo's works, one of the most difficult prose books in the Spanish tongue.

As a historian, Mendoza has many good qualities ; he was thoroughly conversant with the people and events about which he wrote, and the picture he paints is a striking one though somewhat confused in its details. His greatest merit lies in his frankness and impartiality. He writes, not to celebrate the military glories of Don John of Austria and those who fought under him, but to give an unbiassed account of an event of great political importance. He is particularly distinguished by the fairness and humanity with which he speaks of the unhappy Moriscos whose last struggles he records. This is the more remarkable when we consider the exaggerated hatred and contempt with which writers of the succeeding generation, and even the liberal-minded Cervantes himself, treat the unfortunate remnant of a once powerful nation.

The conquest of the vast country of Mexico by Hernán Cortés and his small but devoted band of heroes was a subject well fitted to inspire Spanish writers. It found a historian worthy of it in Antonio de Solís, private secretary to Felipe IV., and afterwards chronicler of the Indies. Solís was also a poet and a dramatic author, but it is in history that he finds his true vocation. His book, in addition to giving an accurate and picturesque account of the events which it narrates, has, like that of Mariana, published nearly a century earlier, the advantage of being undoubtedly one of the great models of the language in which it was written. To say, as his fellow-countrymen do, of Solís' *Historia de la Conquista de Méjico*, that it is not surpassed by any of the great histories of antiquity, is certainly extravagant praise, but his merits, whether we regard him as a writer of prose or as a historian, are very great. From the latter point of view, relating as he did the events of a few years, it was easy for him to attain the dramatic unity which, by the nature of his subject, was denied to Mariana. But this consideration alone is far from being enough to account for the wide interval that separates the two. Solís continues the fashion of putting into the mouths of his heroes and of their adversaries the set speeches in which historians of the period delight. In spite of this and of other mannerisms, now quite out of date, his history is wonderfully modern in tone. It enters thoroughly into the spirit of the events it recounts, and is readable from end to end. Besides historical considerations that cannot fail to interest, Solís represents great passions at work and strongly marked characters brought into collision. These, in the setting of the magnificent and then all but unknown country which he describes in stately and glowing terms, combine to make his work a prose epic of great artistic perfection, and worthy to be compared with Schiller's *Thirty Years' War*.

In connection with the early history of America three books must be mentioned, as much on account of their intrinsic literary value as on account of their connection with the names of famous men of action. The first is the collection of

Letters and Memorials of Christopher Columbus. In spite of his foreign birth, Columbus handled the Castilian language with perfect facility, and in it he wrote the letters which best describe the hopes, fears, ambitions, and dreams that swayed his conduct and led him to undertake his great discovery. Pathetic indeed are the accounts of his dejection when he saw himself thwarted in his great enterprises by mutinous crews, petty jealousies, and the downright dishonesty of his unscrupulous enemies. His correspondence reveals a curious mystical and half-inspired side to his otherwise practical and business-like character. He believes himself to be a chosen instrument for fulfilling the prophecies of the Bible; he destines the wealth of the countries he had discovered to further the reconquest of the Holy Sepulchre; he sees visions, and, when he is on the point of despair, angels are sent to comfort him. The following well-known passage from one of his letters to Fernando and Isabel contains Columbus's own account of this miraculous intervention in his affairs :—

[1] Mi hermano y la otra gente toda estaban en un navío que quedó adentro ; yo muy solo de fuera en tan brava costa, con fuerte fiebre, en tanta fatiga ; la esperanza de escapar era muerta ; subí así trabajando lo más alto, llamando á voz temerosa, llorando y muy apriesa, los maestros de la guerra de vuestras Altezas, á todos cuatro los vientos, por socorro ; mas nunca me respondieron. Cansado me dormecí gimiendo ; una voz muy piadosa oí diciendo : "¡ O estulto y tardo á creer y á servir á tu Dios, Dios de todos ! ¿Qué hizo él mas por Moysés ó por David su siervo? Desque naciste, siempre él tuvo de tí muy grande cargo. Cuando te vido

---

[1] Navarrete, *Viages*, vol. i. p. 303. Madrid, 1825. I have slightly changed the punctuation and accentuation.

" My brother and all the rest of the company were in a ship that remained in port ; I, sore lonely, outside on that cruel coast, with a great fever and very weary ; my hopes of escape were gone ; and so it was that toilsomely I climbed to the highest part, calling in fear and with many tears to the captains of your Highnesses, towards the four quarters of heaven, for help ; but none answered me. Worn out I fell asleep sobbing ; I heard a voice of pity that said : ' Oh fool, and slow to believe and to serve thy God, the God of all. What more did He for Moses or for David His servant? From thy birth He ever had thee in peculiar care. When thou camest to the age that seemed

en edad de que él fue contento, maravillosamente hizo sonar tu nombre en la tierra. Las Indias que son parte de la tierra tan ricas, te las dió por tuyas : tú las repartiste adonde te plugo y te dió poder para ello. De los atamientos de la mar óceana que estaban cerrados con cadenas tan fuertes te dió las llaves y fuiste obedescido en tantas tierras, y de los cristianos cobraste tan honrada fama. . . . Tórnate á él y conoce ya tu yerro ; su misericordia es infinita : tu vejez no impedirá á toda cosa grande : muchas heredades tiene él grandísimas. . . . Tú llamas por socorro incierto : responde ¿ quién te ha afligido tanto y tantas veces, Dios ó el mundo ? Los privilegios y promesas que da Dios, no las quebranta. . . . él va al pie de la letra ; todo lo que él promete cumple con acrescentamiento : ¿ esto es uso ? Dicho tengo lo que tu Criador ha fecho por tí y hace con todos. Ahora medio muestra el galardón de estos afanes y peligros que has pasado sirviendo á otros." Yo así amortecido oí todo, mas no tuve yo respuesta á palabras tan ciertas, salvo llorar por mis yerros. Acabó él de fablar quien quiera que fuese diciendo : "No temas, confía : todas estas tribulaciones están escritas en piedra marmol, y no sin causa." Levantéme cuando pude, y al cabo de nueve días hizo bonanza. . . .

Another collection of almost equal interest is formed by the reports of Hernán Cortés to the Queen and to the Emperor. Cortés has no literary pretensions, his style is simple and direct ; in plain and soldierly language he narrates the great events in which he took a leading part.

Fray Bartolomé de las Casas, deservedly called the Apostle of the Indies, described in words glowing and eloquent,

good to Him, He made thy name to sound wondrously throughout the world. The Indies, the richest region of the earth, He gave thee for thy own ; thou didst portion them out according to thy pleasure, this power He granted thee. Of the confines of the ocean-sea which were closed with mighty chains, He gave to thee the keys, and thou wast obeyed in many lands and in Christendom thou didst win so honourable a name. . . . Turn thee to Him and admit thy fault : His mercy is infinite : thy old age shall not debar great deeds : many and great bequests are in God's hand. . . . Thou art calling for a vain help : say then, who hath afflicted thee thus and thus often,—God or the world ? The privileges and promises that God vouchsafes He does not transgress. . . . His fulfilment is strict ; all that He promises He fulfils with interest ; do others so ? I have told thee what thy Creator hath done for thee and doth for all. Even now He reveals to thee the reward of this toil and danger which have befallen thee as the servant of others.' Thus sunk in stupor I heard all, but had nought to answer to words so true, save that I bewailed my faults. And he who spake, whoever he were, finished thus : 'Fear not, but trust ; all these tribulations are writ on rock, and not in vain.'—I rose so soon I might, and after nine days there came a calm. . . ."

with honest indignation, the hideous cruelties to which the natives under his religious charge were subjected, showing at the same time how fatal to Spanish interests would be the extermination of the native races, and how rapidly it would be completed if the king did not interpose to prevent it. Besides his *Relación de la Destruición de las Indias*, he wrote a *General History of the Indies*, which, unfortunately, is still unpublished.

Antonio Perez is not, properly speaking, a writer of history, but his *Letters and Reports* are so interesting, both on account of their form and contents, that he ought not to be passed over. Good family connections, backed by a ready wit and unscrupulous audacity, early gained for him a place at the court of Felipe II. Holding the office of private secretary to the king, Perez was employed in some of the darkest operations of his master's tortuous policy, and there is little doubt that he was guilty of murdering at least one person who had made himself objectionable. Eager to rid himself of the possessor of dangerous secrets, the astute Felipe picked a quarrel with his former secretary, the immediate cause of which still remains a mystery.[1] It is, however, certain that the life of Perez was in danger when, after years of persecution, he suddenly fled to Aragón. Here the king attempted to reach him by means of the long arm of the Inquisition. This proceeding, however, provoked a rebellion among the people of Saragossa, who considered their privileges invaded by such interference. Antonio Perez fled first to the court of Béarn, then to Paris, and then to England, where he became the associate of Essex and of Bacon, living as a pensioner on the bounty of the enemies of his country. For years the king's hatred pursued him relentlessly, and Perez's cunning is amply proved by his numerous escapes from the emissaries who sought to entrap him. Finally he sank into obscurity, and

[1] See Professor Froude's Essay on Antonio Perez.

died at Paris in 1611.   His letters, written during his exile,
form a large collection, which he published in parts.   They
are addressed to persons in all stations of life, and are written
in all styles, from grave and dignified arraignments of the
author's former master, to familiar and affectionate gossip with
wife and children.   Their language is singularly clear and
appropriate to their subjects ; at times pathetic and again self-
assured in tone, now passionate and again calm, they are the
best models of epistolary writing in the Spanish language.   As
historical documents they are rendered almost worthless by
their author's evident bias and constitutional disregard of
truth.

Deserving of mention, by reason of its literary merit, is the
remarkable forgery of the seventeenth century [1] known as the
Centón Epistolario, and purporting to be the work of the
Bachiller Fernan Gomez de Cibdareal, the physician of Juan
II.   It consists of a hundred letters to great persons who lived
during the fifteenth century, and was considered one of the
greatest monuments of early Spanish prose until further inquiry
proved it to be a late production, compiled chiefly from the
chronicle of Juan II. for the purpose of magnifying the importance of a particular family and at a time when forgeries of the
kind were by no means uncommon.   It is sad indeed to find
in place of the old doctor, so faithfully attached to his royal
patient, and so full of worldly wisdom and good doctrine, the
wily scribe of an unscrupulous master, and to detect fraud in
the quaintly pathetic passages in which the *Centón* abounds.

[1] See Adolfo de Castro, *Sobre el Centón Epistolario.*   Sevilla, 1875.

CHAPTER XI

THE list of the poets who flourished during the fifty years that separate Jorge Manrique from Boscán and Garcilaso de la Vega (d. 1536) is a long one, but scarce one of the names contained in it is worthy of mention. Religious subjects are the only ones that furnished any real inspiration to the writers who lived in the midst of such great events as the taking of Granada and the discovery of the New World. The imitation of classical and Italian writers continues, and so stereotyped has poetry become that, on opening a volume of verse of the period, we straightway expect it to begin with a vision and to be crammed full of allegory and mythology. During the latter half of the reign of the Catholic Sovereigns, Spain for the first time enjoyed security and peace at home. Learning and culture greatly increased, but it seemed at first as though this was destined to redound to the disadvantage of literature, for the learning of the time took the form of pedantry and intentional obscurity, whilst culture showed a marked tendency to degenerate into false sentiment and affectation. It is only here and there among the voluminous works of second-rate authors that the genuine national spirit shines forth in some ballad or hymn. It is hard indeed to detect the first low notes that prelude the great outburst of inspired song of the crowning period of Spanish poetry.

Eleven-syllable verse and the sonnet had been occasionally cultivated by Spanish poets ever since the time of Alfonso the Wise, who was the first to attempt them : compositions in these exotic forms are found among the works of Francisco Imperial and the Marqués de Santillana.   To Juan Boscán, however, belongs the honour of having thoroughly naturalised the Italian measures, and of having been the first to make good use of blank verse.   Boscán was born at Barcelona about the beginning of the sixteenth century, and died at middle age. He left behind him a miscellaneous collection of poems, some in the short national measure, but most of them in the Italian style.   None of these are of great merit, and many are utterly worthless ; their tone is correct but frigid, and wholly lacking in inspiration.   Their author owes his place in the history of the literature of his country to the circumstances of having revived or introduced more elegant and elaborate forms of verse, and to his connection with a really great poet.

This was Garcilaso de la Vega, a member of a distinguished family, and contemporary and intimate friend of Boscán and of the learned Juan de Valdés.   A picturesque figure in a brilliant and courtly age, he was celebrated for his personal beauty and for the valour which he displayed in several of the campaigns of the Emperor Charles V.   He took part in the gallant struggle against the Turks on the Danube.   Banished from Naples in consequence of a private quarrel, he was for some time imprisoned on an island in that river.   Here it was that he wrote a considerable part of the small collection of verses which was to win him a place among the greatest poets of his country.   After distinguishing himself at the taking of La Goleta and at the battle of Turin, he was killed, while yet a young man, by a blow on the head from a stone during an assault on the castle of Fréjus.

His works, which were first published by Boscán's widow together with those of her husband, consist of three eclogues, two elegies, five odes (*canciones*), an epistle, and about forty sonnets, all in the Italian manner. Garcilaso is an imitator in the fullest sense of the word. Whole passages of his verse are translated almost directly from Latin and Italian authors, but he deserves the singular praise of having seldom fallen below the perfection of his models, an honour which belongs to few indeed of those who have ventured to vie with Vergil and with Petrarch. To those who would see to what pitch of grandeur the Castilian tongue can rise, when subject and verse alike are suited to it, no better example can be cited than Garcilaso's first eclogue, of which the following passage may serve as a specimen :—

> [1] ¿ Quién me dijera, Elisa, vida mía,
> Cuando en aqueste valle al fresco viento
> Andábamos cogiendo tiernas flores,
> Que había de ver con largo apartamiento
> Venir el triste y solitario día
> Que diese amargo fin á mis amores?
> El cielo en mis dolores
> Cargó la mano tanto
> Que á sempiterno llanto
> Y á triste soledad me ha condenado.
> Y lo que siento más es verme atado
> A la pesada vida y enojosa,
> Solo, desamparado,
> Ciego sin lumbre en cárcel tenebrosa
>   .   .   .   .   .
> Como al partir del sol la sombra crece,
> Y en cayendo su rayo se levanta
> La negra escuridad que el mundo cubre,
> De do viene el temor que nos espanta

---

[1] "Who could have told me, Elisa mine,—when in this valley in the fresh breeze,—we walked and gathered tender flowers,—that after long absence I should see—the coming of the sad and lonely day—which put a bitter end to all my love?—Heaven in filling my cup of woe—so charged it to the brim—that to never-ending tears—and mournful solitude it has condemned me.—But chief of all my griefs is to be bound—to life dreary and wearisome —alone, bereft of help,—blind and deprived of light in my dim prison-house. . . . As at the sun's departure shadows lengthen—and, as his beam declines, there rises up—black darkness covering the earth,—whence springs the fear by

Y la medrosa forma en que se ofrece
Aquello que la noche nos encubre,
Hasta que el sol descubre
Su luz pura y hermosa :
Tal es la tenebrosa
Noche de tu partir, en que he quedado
De sombra y de temor atormentado,
Hasta que muerte el tiempo determine
Que á ver el deseado
Sol de tu clara vista me encamine.
Cual suele el ruiseñor con triste canto
Quejarse, entre las hojas escondido,
Del duro labrador, que cautamente
Le despojó su caro y dulce nido
De los tiernos hijuelos entre tanto
Que del amado ramo estaba ausente ;
Y aquel dolor que siente
Con diferencia tanta
Por la dulce garganta
Despide y á su canto el aire suena,
Y la callada noche no refrena
Su lamentable oficio y sus querellas,
Trayendo de su pena
Al cielo por testigo y las estrellas :
Desta manera suelto yo la rienda
A mi dolor y así me quejo en vano
De la dureza de la muerte airada.

Cervantes, Lope, and the other great poets of his country, are agreed in calling Garcilaso "sublime," and well does he merit the name. Though a soldier, and living constantly in

which we are alarmed,—the awe-inspiring form in which appear—things shrouded by the night—until the sun reveals—his pure and beauteous light :— so in the gloomy—darkness of thy departure I too remain—by shadows and by fears tormented,—till death the hour decide—in which toward the longed-for —sun of thy radiant presence I set forth.—Even as the nightingale with plaintive song,—hiding among the leaves, complains—of the harsh rustic who treacherously—despoiled her sweet beloved nest—of all its tender brood meanwhile—she lingered absent from the well-loved bough;—and all the grief she feels—at her irreparable loss—from her sweet throat—pours out, and with her song the air resounds,—and the silent night does not refuse—her duteous sympathy and her complaint,—but calls to testify her grief—the heaven itself as witness and the stars,—so I do not restrain—my grief, so I lament in vain —the cruelty of unrelenting death."

camps and courts, his compositions are all pastoral or amorous, and show a deep love of nature and appreciation of its beauties. Still it is by the form rather than by the matter of his poems that he is chiefly distinguished, and it must be confessed that occasionally he gives way to the affectation and pedantry common among the writers of his time. Imitating artificial compositions such as the Eclogues of Vergil, it is scarcely to be expected that he should be perfectly natural in tone, but he thoroughly appreciated and faithfully rendered their delicacy and finish. The most beautiful passages of his *Églogas* take the form of *liras*, elegant combinations of lines of eleven and seven syllables (see passage quoted above).

A revolt against foreign influences in Castilian poetry was headed by Cristóbal de Castillejo, a writer of the first half of the sixteenth century, who at one time held the position of secretary to Ferdinand, King of Bohemia, brother of Charles V. He produced a violent poetical attack on foreign forms, making use principally of the lines of unequal length known as *estrofas de pie quebrado*, but also of *redondillas*, *quintillas*, and other national metres formed by various combinations of the octosyllabic line. But his adverse criticism of the poetry of his time apparently applies only to its form, for he himself in his amorous and satirical poems freely introduces the feeble mythology which was the bane of literature throughout Europe in the sixteenth and seventeenth centuries.

Francisco de Castilla, in the *Dialogue between Humanity and its Comforter*, employed successfully the *octosílabo de pie quebrado*, octosyllabic verse with every third line truncated to four syllables, which had already found its finest exponent in Manrique. His style, like that of most of his fellow-countrymen when writing on grave and religious subjects, is lofty and pure, and his language is remarkably free from affectation and pedantry. Castilla, as the eminent critic Sanchez de Castro justly remarks, has been unduly neglected by historians of the

literature of his country.   Among those who ranged themselves as the defenders of the traditional school none have
given better proof of what its methods are capable when
applied by a true poet.

Diego Hurtado de Mendoza, whose name has already
been mentioned in connection with *Lazarillo de Tormés*
(pp. 88, 106), and who has been again referred to as a
historian, was a friend of Boscán, and one of the principal
figures of the literary as well as of the political world during
the reigns of Carlos V. and Felipe II.   He cultivated both the
national and Italian forms of poetry without attaining any
marked success.   Mendoza's verse is generally erotic and
mythological in character; his scholarly tastes led him to
admire Horace, whose worldly philosophy is somewhat feebly
echoed in his Epistles and Odes.   He writes correctly and
sometimes with a certain degree of brilliancy, particularly in
the octosyllabic metres, but must be considered fortunate in
having something beside his verse on which to depend for his
reputation.

Among the greatest Spanish poets Fernando de Herrera
deserves a very high, if not the highest, place.   He was born
in Sevilla, and lived a retired and studious life in his native city.
A great admirer of Garcilaso de la Vega, he published an
elaborate commentary on his works, citing parallel passages
from Italian and classical authors.   Herrera was an ecclesiastic,
and though he is not, strictly speaking, a religious poet, he
drew most of his inspiration and all his wealth of imagery from
the Bible.   The works in which this is most evident are his
best.   When he imitates classical and Italian models the
result is hollow-sounding, commonplace, and declamatory.
Among the latter kind must be classed the numerous sonnets
and odes which he addressed to the Countess of Gelvés, whom he
seems to have chosen as the object of his verses in much the
same manner as Don Quixote chose Dulcinea as the object of

his affections. The knight-errant required a lady to whom to send the captives of his good right arm ; the poet required a lady to whom to address his odes. The sentiments expressed by either are seemingly equally unreal. It was not considered wrong in Herrera's time for a priest to address a lady in an amorous strain, but, had his religious superiors wished for any proof that he was not really in love with the lady to whom, under the names of *Leonora*, *Eliodora*, *Lumbre*, and *Luz*, he directs his verses, they had ready to their hands his poems in which the unreality of his affected passion may be everywhere detected. It is not in his treatment of subjects such as these that we get an insight into Herrera's real power. The great victory of Lepanto was sung by him in strains worthy of its importance, echoing in their grand and solemn cadence the books of the Old Testament. The *Canción á Lepanto* is the song of triumph for the victory of Spain and of Christendom over the infidel who for so many years had been a perpetual menace. Thoroughly Christian in spirit, and equally happy in conception and execution, it deserves to be placed side by side with the first eclogue of Garcilaso as one of the noblest monuments of the Spanish tongue. This, however, was not the work of Herrera which his contemporaries considered most deserving of praise. Lope de Vega, led astray by the bad taste which had in his time almost entirely gained the upper hand, speaks in almost enthusiastic terms of the *Canción de San Fernando*, a work somewhat frigid and artificial in tone, but bearing here and there the traces of a master hand. Once only did Herrera approach the standard he had created in his *Canción á Lepanto ;* this is in his *Pérdida del Rey Don Sebastián y su Ejército.* The great victory of the Christian arms battling against the Moslem had found a responsive echo in his verse, and once more its mighty tones went to swell the dirge that mourned the fate of the soldier of the Church and of the gallant army sacrificed in a fit of reckless religious enthusiasm.

The following extract, though short, will give better than any mere description some idea of Herrera's power :—

[1] ¡ Ay de los que pasaron confiados
En sus caballos y en la muchedumbre
De sus carros, en tí, Libia desierta,
Y en su vigor y fuerzas engañados,
No alzaron su esperanza á aquella cumbre
De eterna luz ; mas con soberbia cierta
Se ofrecieron la incierta
Vitoria, y sin volver á Dios sus ojos,
Con yerto cuello y corazón ufano,
Solo atendieron siempre á los despojos
Y el Santo de Israel abrió su mano
Y los dejó, y cayó en despeñadero
El carro, y el caballo y caballero.

. . . . .

¿ Son éstos por ventura los famosos,
Los fuertes los belígeros varones
Que conturbaron con furor la tierra,
Que sacudieron reinos poderosos,
Que domaron las hórridas naciones,
Que pusieron desierto en cruda guerra
Cuanto el mar indo encierra,
Y soberbias ciudades destruyeron?
¿ Do el corazón seguro y la osadía?
¿ Cómo así se acabaron y perdieron
Tanto heróico valor en solo un día;
Y lejos de su patria derribados,
No fueron justamente sepultados?

---

[1] "Alas for them who went forth confiding—in their horses and in the multitude—of their chariots, to thee, desert Africa,—and by their strength and might led astray,—raised not a prayer of hope to the pinnacle—of light eternal ; but with reckless pride—promised themselves the doubtful—victory, and turning not to God their eyes,—with stiffened necks and proud hearts,—thought only of the spoil !—And the Holy One of Israel opened his hand—and let them fall and down the steep they crashed—the chariot and the horse and the horseman . . . Can these be then the famous ones,—the mighty and the warriors,—whose fury overset the earth,—and shook mighty kingdoms,—who overcame savage nations,—and by harsh warfare laid waste—all that the Indian seas surround,—and spoiled stately cities?—What of their dauntless hearts and bravery?—How came it to be thus brought low and lost, —all this heroic courage in a day ;—and shattered, far off from their native land,—was it not right their graves should lie?—For these were even as the

Tales ya fueron éstos, cual hermoso
Cedro del alto Líbano vestido
De ramos, hojas, con excelsa alteza :
Las aguas lo criaron poderoso,
Sobre empiñados árboles crecido,
Y se multiplicaron en grandeza
Sus ramos con belleza :
Y extendiendo su sombra, se anidaron
Las aves que sustenta el grande cielo,
Y en sus hojas las fieras engendraron,
Y hizo á mucha gente umbroso velo ;
No igualó en celsitud y en hermosura
Jamás árbol alguno á su figura.
Pero elevóse con su verde cima,
Y sublimó la presunción su pecho,
Desvanecido todo y confiado,
Haciendo de su alteza sólo estima.
Por eso Dios lo derribó deshecho,
Á los impíos y ajenos entregado,
Por la raiz cortado.

Many historians of Spanish literature have sought to classify the lyric poets of the Golden Age, assigning some to the Sevillian school, others to the school of Salamanca, of Aragón, and so forth. Divisions such as these, founded more upon the accident of locality than upon any marked features common to the authors included under them, are useless if not misleading. Undoubtedly when a great author arose he collected round him a number of admirers, some of whom became imitators while others unconsciously reflected his manner. The class-names above mentioned are useful at most only in works the scope of which allows the consideration of a large

beauteous—cedar of lofty Lebanon, clothed about—with boughs and leaves, and towering on high ;—the waters fed it in its pride,—grown high above the tallest trees,—and in its strength it multiplied—its stately branches,—and, as its shadow widened, nests were built—by the birds whose home is heaven's vault, —and amidst its leaves the wild beasts bred,—and it made a shady covering to much folk ;—unequalled in loftiness and in beauty—of form by any other tree.—But as its green crown rose high,—pride swelled its heart,—boastful it was and overweening,—esteeming nothing but its own lordly height.—And thus God shattered it and cast it down—and gave it over to the infidel and the stranger,—cut off even to the root."

number of minor poets. For the purpose of the present study it is enough to continue to distinguish between authors who espoused the losing cause of the old national forms of metre, and those who belonged to the erudite and foreign school, warning the reader beforehand that not even here can a rigid line of demarcation be drawn, seeing that many writers essayed both methods. Before coming to the religious poets, to whom belongs so large a part of the finest verse in the Spanish language, one or two more secular ones must be mentioned.

A determined adherent of the old-fashioned school of verse wrote under the name of the Bachelor Francisco de la Torre. His works were published in 1631 by Quevedo, who professed to have found them accidentally. So little is known of his life that for long it was supposed that this name was an assumed one, and concealed the personality of the great satirist himself, who was also called Francisco, and bore the title of *Señor de la Torre de Juan Abad.* Recent investigations, however, have made it practically certain that Francisco de la Torre is no assumed name. Yet it is difficult to identify the author of the work in question with the friend of Boscán who fought in Italy and ended his life as a priest in the sixteenth century, leaving behind him in contemporary *cancioneros* only a few rough verses. The Bachelor's poems give proof of great skill in handling the forms of which he made himself the champion, but in spite of many graceful and tender passages, they lack the inspiration necessary to establish his claim to the name of poet; he moreover frequently devotes his talents to the production of feeble mythological compositions. It is hard to see how critics could persuade themselves that these simple and correct verses are the production of Quevedo, whose strongly-marked characteristics are laboured brilliancy and artificial antithesis.

The principal writers of the so-called Aragonese school were the brothers Lupercio and Leonardo de Argensola, who flourished during the latter part of the sixteenth and the beginning of the seventeenth centuries. They were gentlemen of good family. Lupercio, the elder, dedicated himself to public life; he became secretary to Felipe III. and afterwards occupied an important position in the government of Naples. Leonardo, the younger, who survived his brother, entered the Church at an early age and rose to the dignity of Canon of Saragossa and chronicler of his native kingdom of Aragón. Both brothers were scholars, and cultivated poetry merely as a pastime. The elder even attempted before his death to burn his verses, and did in fact destroy a large portion of them. The works of both are very similar in character; they are good translations and imitations of the odes, satires, and epistles of Horace, together with certain sonnets and elegies in the Italian style. They prove a very thorough appreciation of their model and a masterly knowledge of the Castilian language, but the highest praise they deserve is that of being neat and scholarly exercises by cultivated men. The elder brother, as has already been mentioned, wrote three tragedies, taking Seneca as his model; their tone is artificial and erudite, and they failed to obtain the popular favour, which indeed they probably never courted.

Poets of a similar character to the Argensolas, though somewhat less stiff and not so exclusively classical, are the Prince of Esquilache and Manuel de Villegas, the latter of whom produced some really pretty imitations of Anacreon in seven-syllable lines. But poets at this time are so numerous as to make it impossible, as well as unnecessary, to mention the minor ones; so close is the similarity between the works of many of them, both in matter and form, that the above brief descriptions might be applied to a considerable number of writers, who, neglecting the stirring themes afforded by their national history both during their own time and in the past, sought their heroes in Greek and Roman mythologies, the beauties of which they miserably travestied. The list, however, ends with a really great name, the bearer of which, partly through his own fault and partly through the irony of fortune, has become a synonym for all the bad tendencies that eventually brought about the decadence of Spanish literature. This is Luís de Góngora.

The stately Spanish language has a tendency, even in the best hands, to become bombastic and turgid ; its rich vocabulary and infinite resources give great facilities for the concealment of poverty of idea under high-sounding and sonorous periods. This tendency, together with an intentional seeking after obscurity and a laboured attempt at brilliancy, is already evident in the poems of the courtly school of the reign of Juan II. As time went on it became exaggerated and complicated with the extraordinary aberrations of the euphuistic school, which exercised its fatal influence during the sixteenth and seventeenth centuries over all but the greatest minds among the writers of Europe. In Spain the weed found a suitable soil, and sprung up and flourished with a growth so rank that under its shadow the old literature pined and finally died away.

When the euphuistic school perished by its own exaggerations the military glory of Spain had already waned, the great effort was over, the reaction had set in and left the country exhausted and without the power of producing great men in either politics or literature. For all the mischief which resulted from the false literary doctrine called in Spain *cult:ranismo* Góngora has been held responsible, and the word *gongorismo* has been coined to denote all that savours of the bad taste, affectation, abuse of metaphor, and violent and unnecessary departure from the ordinary form of the sentence, which are common to the school known in France as *précieuses*. For degrading his great talents to the service of a literary heresy of the worst kind, and exaggerating in his works the extravagances of its adherents, Góngora is no doubt accountable, as well as for the introduction of many of the foreign words and idioms that went to make up the barbarous jargon, the *latiniparla* so dear to the initiated. But he is not the first, perhaps not even the worst offender, and the origin of the movement in Spain lies deeper than the influence of any one author. Calderón and Quevedo are deeply infected with *gongorism*, and the great Cervantes himself is by no means free from it. Lope de Vega, who on several occasions vigorously attacked the *culto* school while himself giving way to its aberrations, speaks thus of it in his *Dorotea :*—

[1] *Ces.* Algunos grandes ingenios adornan y visten la lengua Castellana, hablando, y escriviendo, orando y enseñando, de nuevas frases y feguras Retóricas que la embellecen y esmaltan con admirable propiedad, á quien como á Maestros . . . se debe toda veneración porque la han honrado, acrecentado, ilustrado y enriquecido con hermosos y no bulgares términos, cuya riqueza aumento y hermosura reconoce el aplauso de los bien entendidos : pero la mala intensión de otros por quererse atrever con desordenada ambición á lo que no les es lícito, pare monstruos disformes y ridículos : . . .

Lud. Decid algo de este nombre *culto* que yo no entiendo su etimología.
Ces. Con deciros que lo fué Garcilaso queda entendido.
Lud. ¿ Garcilaso fué culto ?
Ces. Aquel poeta es culto que cultiva de suerte su poema, que no dexa cosa áspera ni obscura. . . .

Góngora was born in Córdova in 1561. He studied at Salamanca, took orders, and became Honorary Chaplain to

[1] " *Ces.* Certain great geniuses adorn and clothe the Castilian language in their speech and writings, in their pleadings and teaching, with new phrases and rhetorical figures which beautify and illuminate it with admirable nicety, and to such, as masters, . . . all respect is owed because they have honoured, increased, diversified and enriched it with stately and select terms ; these riches, increase and beauty have found their recognition in the approval of men of good understanding ; but others ill-advised, whose unchecked ambition has led them to dare that which is unlawful, have produced monstrous and ridiculous examples of deformity. . . .

Lud. Tell me something about this word *culto* for I do not understand how it got that meaning.
Ces. If I tell you that Garcilaso is included under the name, that will help you to understand it.
Lud. Garcilaso was *culto* ?
Ces. All poets are so who *cultivate* their verses in such a manner as to leave in them nothing harsh or obscure."

Felipe III. He returned in middle age to his native place, where his reputation was very great, and died there in 1627. His literary life may be marked off into two very distinct periods. No poet has better understood the capabilities and limitations of the short Spanish metres than the Góngora of the first period. His madrigals and lyrics (*letrillas*) are perfect in form and full of simplicity and grace. His ballads are among the finest of the later contributions to the *romancero*, and show a thorough comprehension and appreciation of the spirit which animated the earlier writers of this kind of verse. His many and notable merits, and his success in the use of national forms applied to national subjects, render the more inexplicable the sudden change by which he was led to prefer mere sound to sense, and to become the apostle of the affectation and obscurity which was afterwards systematised by Gracián. In Góngora's later works no trace can be found of the graceful and witty author of pieces such as *Los Dineros del Sacristán, Ande yo caliente, Milagros de Corte son*, and the amorous and somewhat risky lyrics which, though a priest, he did not disdain to write. His *Panegyric of the Duke of Lerma*, his *Fable of Polyphemus*, and his *Soledades* are lasting memorials of the depths to which a really good poet can sink when his judgment has once been thoroughly perverted. So intricate and obscure are they that, though received with applause by the select circle of the initiated, they were found incomprehensible even by the most cultivated; learned commentators at once set to work to explain the writings of the great master to his admiring disciples.

We now come to a series of four religious poets, two of whom have already been mentioned among the greatest prose writers of their country. The first, and undoubtedly the most famous, is Fray Luís de León. He was born in the year 1528. His father, a lawyer of good position, sent him to the University of Salamanca where he soon laid the foundation of a brilliant reputation. He obtained the chair of philosophy, and subsequently that of theology.   His success, however, had provoked the jealousy and hatred of those whom he had defeated in the public arguments and discussions appointed by statute for the purpose of deciding between the claims of rival candidates for university distinctions.   His frank and fearless character disregarded the pitfalls with which his path was beset ; in 1571 he was denounced to the Holy Office for having expressed an opinion that the translation of the Vulgate was in certain respects defective, and for having written a translation of the Song of Solomon, in which he departed from the doctrines of the Church by treating it as a poem of purely secular character. An attempt was at the same time made to place him in an odious light by showing that he had inherited Jewish blood. After many preliminary inquiries carried on with the secrecy customary to the Inquisition, he was cited to appear in person before a court formed of its familiars.   He immediately adopted an attitude of complete submission, declaring his absolute belief in all the doctrines of the Church, his regret that his translation of the Song of Solomon written at the request of a friend should have been made public by the treachery of his enemies, and his willingness to abide by the sentence of the tribunal before which he stood.   He was thrown into prison where he remained for four years, subject to continual and severe examinations and to persecutions of all kinds.   The documents relating to his trial are still extant, and we know that when in 1576 sentence was pronounced the majority of his judges were still in favour of torturing their prisoner for the purpose of obtaining further evidence.   This decision was fortunately quashed by the supreme tribunal at Madrid, and Luís de León was declared absolved from the charges brought against him ; he was, however, obliged to take an oath to be in future more circumspect as to the opinions he expressed, to observe strict silence as to the proceedings of the tribunal, and to bear no malice against his accusers.   During his long imprisonment his chair in the University had not been filled. On resuming his lectures crowds flocked to him, expecting to hear some bitter allusion to the sufferings he had undergone, but he simply rose in his place and began without preamble—"As we were saying yesterday . . ."

It would probably be difficult to find a better instance of true Catholic submission, and it is the more admirable when we consider the vast learning and resource he showed in his defence. The character of Fray Luís, as shown in the whole course of his life, forbids the belief that his concurrence in his sentence was either affected or wrung from him by suffering. Public opinion too was so strongly in his favour that he could easily have excited the greatest odium against the court which had heaped cruelties and indignities upon him. His long imprisonment seriously affected his health, and he spent the fourteen remaining years of his life in strict retirement.

The collection of lyrics which entitle Luís de León to rank as a great poet as well as a great prose writer was so lightly esteemed by its author that it would probably have perished had it not been for Quevedo, who published it. Many of the verses undoubtedly stand in need of the finishing touches of the master's hand. They are divided into three books, two of translations, one sacred and one profane, and one of original poems. All are instinct with feeling and beauty. They give expression to a contemplative and scholarly mind inspired by a deep love of nature and of solitude. The following lines illustrative of the author's manner are taken from the *Ode to Retirement* :—

> [1] ¡ Oh ya seguro puerto
> De mi tan luengo error ! Oh deseado
> Para reparo cierto
> Del grave mal pasado
> ¡ Reposo dulce, alegre, reposado !
>   Techo pajizo adonde

---

[1] "Oh port secure—after long wanderings ; and much desired—as refuge sure —from ills now past ;—sweet rest, and bright tranquillity !—Thatched roof,

> Jamás hizo morada el enemigo
> Cuidado, ni se esconde
> Invidia en rostro amigo,
> Ni voz perjura ni mortal testigo.
>   Sierra que vas al cielo
> Altísima, y que gozas del sosiego
> Que no conoce el suelo,
> Adonde el vulgo ciego
> Ama el morir ardiendo en vivo fuego,
>   Recíbeme en tu cumbre,
> Recíbeme ; que huyo perseguido
> La errada muchedumbre,
> El trabajar perdido,
> La falsa paz, el mal no merecido.
> .   .   .   .   .
>
>   ¡ Ay, otra vez y ciento
> Otras, seguro puerto deseado !
> No me falte tu asiento,
> Y falte cuanto amado,
> Cuanto del ciego error es cudiciado.

The *Ode to a Calm Night* may well bear comparison with Wordsworth's best passages. The magnificent *Ode to Music* has points of remarkable similarity to the *Intimations of Immortality;* that to the *Ascension of our Lord* is full of deep religious feeling combined with exquisite simplicity and grace. The translation of some of the Psalms and parts of the Book of Job show how thoroughly Fray Luís appreciated their sublime grandeur. A wonderfully spirited and impressive poem on a national subject is the *Prophecy of the Tagus;* the passage which describes the movement of the infidel hosts towards Spain to avenge the ill-starred love of Don Rodrigo carries away the reader by its irresistible and harmonious flow. This,

beneath whose shade—there never dwelt malicious—care ; nor lurking— envy in amicable guise,—nor lips forsworn, nor death-dealing treachery.— Mountains that rise to heaven—aloft, and taste such peace—as is unknown on earth,—where mankind blind—loves death and burns in living fire,—receive me to your heights,—receive the hard-pressed fugitive—from erring crowds,— from labour vain,—peace that is no peace, and evils undeserved.—Oh ! yet a hundred times—and then again,—my port secure and much desired—I pray thy resting-place be mine ;—so let all else be taken from me,—all that blind error loves and covets.''

like many of its author's best poems, is inspired directly by Horace, but even where he imitates most closely, or frankly translates, Luís de León may be read with pleasure for his stately versification, his sober yet splendid style, and the new and charming lights which he so often throws upon his models.

Of the life of Santa Teresa de Jesus an outline was given when we spoke of the prose works which form the most valuable part of her writings. As a poetess she devoted herself wholly to religious subjects, and her verse everywhere reveals the spirit of ardent devotion and mysticism which combined so strangely with homely mother-wit in the formation of her character. Her style is simple and unaffected to such a degree that at times it becomes almost childish. This attitude seems to be purposely assumed in her carols, which have the defects as well as the merits of rustic and popular songs. She is, however, at her best in the somewhat artificial *glosas*, a form of composition cultivated by most Spanish poets, and consisting of the amplification and application of some short rhymed motto, paradox, or proverb, with the introduction of the original lines at stated intervals. Even into such trifling compositions as these she breathes something of her fervent religious spirit and strong individuality. A good example is her gloss on the lines—

> [1] Vivo sin vivir en mí,
> Y tan alta vida espero
> Que muero porque no muero.

Here the last line forms the refrain of each verse.

San Juan de la Cruz, another saintly and mystic poet, was an imitator of Luís de León and a friend of Santa Teresa, to whom he lent important aid in carrying out her scheme of reforming the Carmelite order. It is in the works of this

[1] " I live a life beside myself,—The life I hope is life so high,—I die because I cannot die."

writer that mysticism reaches its extreme development, soaring to heights where language is powerless to express the feelings. The character of the saint himself and of his writings may be gathered from the title of *Doctor Extático*, which was conferred on him by his contemporaries. In common with the other mystics he possessed a wonderful command of his native tongue, and this he uses with great effect in tender and passionate descriptions of the transports of the devotee. His style is luxuriant with metaphors of oriental origin, imitated generally from the Song of Solomon. He handles with great skill and delicacy the allegory by which human love is made to portray the divine.

Contemporary with Juan de la Cruz and Santa Teresa was Malón de Chaide, a monk of the order of Saint Augustine. His principal work is the prose life of St. Mary Magdalene, into which most of his verses are introduced. Like other writers of the same school he imitated Luís de León, but his lines have often a hollow ring that is not heard in those of the masters already mentioned. His verse is correct, but seldom stirring; passages of real beauty and delicacy are often followed by others giving details of the life of the saint that are ill-chosen for the edifying purpose for which they were intended. Throughout the book can be traced a somewhat harsh and intolerant spirit, from which the other mystic writers are remarkably free.

CHAPTER XII

DIDACTIC WORKS AND COLLECTION OF PROVERBS

THE Spanish mind seems to have been at all times singularly averse to abstract thought, unless indeed sublime dreams springing from ecstatic religious contemplation can be counted as such. Even in this department it is noticeable that authors continually have recourse to concrete metaphors and anthropomorphic allegories in order to express their ideas. Scholastic philosophy and theology were earnestly studied in the universities, but, in the former at least, no Spaniard attained to any considerable and lasting reputation; works on such subjects, moreover, long continued to be written in Latin, and thus have no place in Spanish literature. Merely local are the reputations of Feyjoo, who during the last century, and of Jaime Balmés (see p. 247), who more recently, did something towards bringing up the knowledge of physical and mental philosophy among their fellow-countrymen to the level of that of other European nations. Spanish theologians have always commanded respect at Rome, but the greatest religious writers appeal rather to the heart than to the intellect; the fate of Luís de León and many others sufficed to check candid criticism in this direction, even by persons of orthodox opinions. To attribute solely to the baneful effects of the Inquisition the decay of Spanish literature, and the state of lethargy into which the country sank during the last century, is to ignore many other equally powerful causes of national decay ; but there can be little doubt that the terror it inspired did much to check philosophical inquiry. It was only within the last hundred years that the great discoveries of Bacon and Newton filtered through to Spain and modified the old-fashioned notions as to man and his relations to the outer world.

Besides the moral and political treatises of Quevedo, two works on statecraft and two on criticism may be mentioned as specimens of didactic writing during the Golden Age. To the former class belongs the *Reloj de Príncipes* (the Dial of Princes) by Antonio de Guevara, a member of the order of St. Francis who, for services rendered at the time of his accession, was raised to the see of Mondoñedo, and appointed official chronicler by the Emperor Charles V. This book furnishes a notable instance of the above-mentioned leaning to concrete examples for the sake of teaching. Guevara's purpose was to write a treatise for the guidance of monarchs ; this he does by singling out Marcus Aurelius as a model prince, and placing him in a variety of imaginary situations such as may serve to illustrate his own theories. By this means he succeeds both in describing a very perfect prince and in inculcating the many wise and practical principles of statecraft, which he had learned during his long experience of courts and diplomatic affairs. Nor does he limit himself to the public life of his imaginary prince ; marriage, old age, and the private duties of persons of high stations, are discussed with much practical wisdom. The most remarkable part of the book is that in which Guevara, who had seen the war of the *Comunidades*, and who lived during the most absolute period of Spanish monarchy, takes the popular side and warns monarchs against approaching too nearly the limit at which passive obedience, goaded by oppression, suddenly changes to active resistance and retaliation. In style the *Reloj de Príncipes*, like its author's novels, satires, and moral works, is affected ; it is spoiled by an unnecessary display of learning and a laboured effort to acquire brilliant effect.

Diego Saavedra Fajardo was, like Guevara, a churchman and a diplomatist. He flourished during the reign of Felipe IV. Entrusted with important missions to foreign courts, Fajardo travelled over a great part of Europe. His *Political Undertakings*, or *Ideal Christian Prince*, is defaced by the exceedingly artificial form in which he chose to write it. He says in his preface that he lacked time to polish it, but it would be considerably improved if written with greater simplicity. Taking as his text the arms and mottoes borne by well-known families, he proceeds to deduce from them the whole public and private duties of a prince. This is done with considerable ingenuity and freshness, for it is the form only of the book that is affected and unnatural; its style is pure and lofty, well fitted to express the really admirable precepts which it contains.

Fajardo is the author of several other works. In the *Policy and Statecraft of the Catholic King Don Fernando* he discourses wisely of the political body in health and in disease, taking as his example of the perfect ruler the astute Ferdinand, to whom he attributes broad and enlightened views for which historical evidence is wanting. In his *Literary Republic* Fajardo has recourse to the vision which was so popular a resource with Spanish writers. Here it is used with some skill as a means of introducing the author's conception of the arts and his witty judgments upon some of the great writers of his country. The following estimate of Góngora is brief and pointed :—

---

[1] En nuestros tiempos renació un Marcial cordobés en don Luís de Góngora, requiebro de las musas y corifeo de las gracias, gran artífice de la

---

[1] "In our days was born at Córdova a second Martial in don Luís de Góngora, the darling of the Muses and coryphæus of the Graces, a mighty artist in the Castilian tongue and, more than any other skilled in playing

lengua castellana, y quien mejor supo jugar con ella, y descubrir los donaires de sus equívocos con incomparable agudeza. Cuando en las veras deja correr su natural, es culto y puro, sin que la sutileza de su ingenio haga impenetrables sus conceptos, como le sucedió después queriendo retirarse del vulgo y afectar escuridad : error que se disculpa con que aun en esto mismo salió grande y nunca imitable. Tal vez tropezó por falta de luz su *Polifemo ;* pero ganó pasos de gloria. Si se perdió en sus *Soledades* se halló después tanto más estimado cuanto con mas cuidado le buscaron los ingenios y explicaron sus agudezas.

The *Corona Gótica* is, as its name implies, a narrative of a period of Spanish history. Valueless from a historical point of view, it is a charming model of easy narrative style.

In the sixteenth century the Spaniards began to work upon their own language, and Lebrija published his celebrated *Vocabulario.* The controversy between the champions of the new artificial and euphuistic and the simple and traditional school of literature was at its height. It was at this point that Juan de Valdés, the learned correspondent of Erasmus, wrote his *Diálogo de la Lengua*, a curious and interesting treatise upon the Castilian language. It was not published till last century when Gregorio Mayans y Siscar, the learned royal librarian, inserted it in his *Orígenes de la Lengua Castellana.* The *Diálogo* takes the form of a somewhat lengthy discussion, in which Valdés himself and two Italian friends are the interlocutors. It gives an informal account of its author's views as to the best literary style, condemning many vulgarisms and incorrect forms of expression, some of which, in spite of his protests, have since taken root in the language. The *Diálogo*

upon it and revealing its graceful mystifications with incomparable wit. When he allows his real nature to have full play, he is polished and pure, nor does the subtilty of his mind make his quips unintelligible, as happened to him afterward in his attempt to avoid triviality by intentional obscurity, faults in excuse of which he can plead that, even here he won the first place and his supremacy is unchallenged. We must admit that his *Polyphemus* stumbled from want of light ; but he was already on the high road to glory. When he went wandering in his *Wilderness* he found, on his return, that he was the more esteemed for the care with which men of genius had sought him out and explained his wit.''

has no pretensions to be exhaustive; it affects to be addressed, not to native Castilians, but to foreigners desirous of learning the language, warning them against certain errors of speech into which they are liable to be betrayed. Valdés, however, allowed himself a considerable amount of latitude, and the faults pointed out are by no means exclusively those to which foreigners only are liable. Not the least interesting part of the book is that in which he discusses the authors who best embody his views. In spite of the fact that modifications of usage have made many of its precepts inapplicable at the present day, the *Diálogo* is extremely valuable to those who would appreciate the best Castilian style of the best period; the clear and elegant language in which it is written shows that its author was well qualified to give a verdict on the matters which he discusses. The same sterling good sense, correct judgment, and pure style that characterise his essay on the language are to be found again in Valdés' *Diálogo de Mercurio y Carón*, a masterly review of some of the political, social, and religious questions that were uppermost in men's minds during the sixteenth century.

A writer very famous among his contemporaries of the first half of the seventeenth century, and one whose brilliancy must be admitted even by those who differ radically from him in opinions, was Baltasar Gracián. Backed by wide reading and considerable wit and ingenuity, he made himself the champion of *conceptismo*, reducing its methods to rule in his *Agudeza y Arte del Ingenio*. His doctrine is that the perfection of style consists in an even flow of ingenious antitheses, startling paradoxes, and elaborate metaphors. The object of writing is, from Gracián's point of view, to call forth the admiration of the reader for his author rather than to interest him in what he says. These heretical and subversive principles are set forth with great elaboration of classification in the most affected and pedantic language. The obscurity and laboured insipidity of

Gracián's poetical works ought to have warned his admirers as to the danger of putting his system into practice.

In another branch of literature Gracián attained greater success, thanks to the fact that he now and then forgets his literary canons and allows himself to be natural. His *Criticón* is a well studied allegory of human life, somewhat after the fashion of the *Pilgrim's Progress*, but lacking its noble simplicity. The hollow but sonorous maxims of his *Oráculo* found favour outside the author's native land. They were translated into many languages and long enjoyed much popularity in France, where their defects, as well as their merits, found a sympathetic echo, and Gracián was regarded as the greatest of Spanish writers and moralists.

Spanish is richer in proverbs than any other language. Among the lower orders conversation is continually adorned and arguments enforced by these "terse verdicts of the concentrated practical wisdom of ages." [1]   Sancho Panza's affection for *refranes*, as they are called, is by no means a caricature of the esteem in which they are held by his fellow-countrymen.   Not only in number, but also in point and directness, Spanish proverbs are superior to those of other nations.   The language itself is sententious, and the dry and somewhat peculiar wit of the natives finds its readiest expression in this form, which frequently adds to its other charms the quaintness of words and expressions of a bygone age.

Proverbs form the titles of many celebrated plays, and the works of most of the best Spanish writers are freely spiced with them.   The oldest collection of these "miniature gospels" (*evangelios en miñatura*), as they are called by Quevedo, is that of the Marqués de Santillana, made in the beginning of the fifteenth and published early in the following century; but long before this date the Infante Don Juan Manuel, in his *Conde Lucanor*, quoted the pithy "sayings of the old wives

[1] Cervantes, *Don Quixote*, cap. 39.

of Castile." Since then the interest in proverbs has grown apace, and various collections of them have been published. That of the Comendador Griego in the sixteenth century contains six thousand proverbs, and the number was brought up by Don Juan de Iriarte, during the last century, to the astonishing total of twenty-four thousand.[1] In view of these figures, it is scarcely to be wondered at that Garay was able in the sixteenth century to write three long letters consisting entirely of proverbs. Even yet the stock in the mouths of the people is probably by no means exhausted. Those who would study the peculiarities of the Castilian character from books cannot better employ their time than in the perusal of these proverbs, and of the popular poetry (*coplas*, see p. 267) which forms the pendant to them.

[1] For full information on the subject see Sbarbi (J. M.), *Monografía sobre los refranes y las obras que tratan de ellos.* 4to. Madrid, 1891.

CHAPTER XIII

CERVANTES

MIGUEL DE CERVANTES [1] was born at Alcalá de Henares and there baptized on the 9th of October 1547. Other cities have disputed the honour of being the birthplace of the most famous of Spaniards, but the entry in the baptismal register, together with the affection with which he always speaks of Alcalá and its "famous Henares," should suffice to decide the controversy. Cervantes' family was noble, tracing its pedigree back to the old kings and chieftains of the north, to whom Lope alludes in the well-known couplet—

> [2] Para noble nacimiento
> Hay en España tres partes ;
> Galicia, Vizcaya, Asturias,
> O ya montaña le llamen.

Some of the immediate ancestors of the great writer had held worthy positions in the state, or had been members of the noble military orders. His father was but a poor gentleman, and Miguel was the youngest of four children, two girls and two boys.

The legend that the young Cervantes, like most celebrated men of his time, studied at Salamanca rests on insufficient evidence. Of his early life and education we know little

---

[1] In after life Cervantes added the name of Saavedra to his own in order to distinguish himself from other members of the same family.

[2] "Birthplaces of noble families—there are three in Spain ;—Galicia, Biscay, Asturias, —or the mountain-region, as it is called."—*Premio del bien hablar.*

except that he was a pupil of Lopez de Hoyos, a school-master of some fame in Madrid, and that, like others of his schoolfellows, he contributed to the elegies published on the lamented death of Isabel of Valois, the third wife of Felipe II. Nor was this Cervantes' only youthful attempt at verse, for he himself makes mention of other pieces, among which was a pastoral poem called *Filena*, now lost.

At the age of twenty-two Cervantes commenced the wandering life which brought him into such strange adventures, and, by causing him to mix with all classes of society and to become, as he says, "versed in misfortune," widened his sympathies and gave the experience necessary for the production of one of the world's greatest books. In Cardinal Acquaviva, the Papal Legate, occupied at that time in Madrid on affairs of state, Cervantes found the patron then necessary to a young man in search of fortune. He subsequently accompanied the Legate to Rome in the capacity of chamberlain. But the idle life of a great churchman's household was ill-suited to his bold and enterprising spirit, and in 1570 we find him at Naples serving in the renowned regiment of Moncada, with which he fought as a private soldier at Lepanto in the October of the following year. In after life the part, humble as it was, that he had taken in the greatest victory of the age never ceased to be regarded by him with honest pride, in spite of the heavy price he paid for his glory. For, speaking of the battle in lines to which even the literary defects give pathos, he says :—

[1] At that sweet moment I, unfortunate, stood with sword grasped firmly in one hand, whilst from the other the blood ran down ; in my breast I felt a deep and cruel wound and my left hand was shattered into fragments.

---

[1] "A esta dulce sazón yo, triste, estaba
Con la una mano de la espada asida,
Y sangre de la otra derramaba.
El pecho mío de profunda herida
Sentía llagado y la siniestra mano
Estaba por mil partes ya rompida."
Letter to Mateo Vazquez.

The valour of Cervantes on this occasion is fully proved by the statements of his comrades. In the testimonials which the elder Cervantes caused to be drawn up in the hope of gaining some relief for his own pressing necessities, and aid in procuring the release of his sons from slavery, Miguel's shipmates speak in glowing terms of the way in which, heedless of the fever from which he was suffering, he boarded the ship of the Pasha of Alexandria, and won the wounds which gave him the nickname of *el manco de Lepanto* (the cripple of Lepanto). Notwithstanding the disablement of his left hand, and the slow recovery which kept him for long a prisoner in the hospital at Naples, he continued to serve as a soldier for four years more. He was present at the taking of la Goleta under Don Juan de Austria, the hero of Lepanto, and accompanied his old regiment to Sardinia and Lombardy. In 1575, accompanied by his brother, he set out for home with letters of recommendation to distinguished persons. The galley, *El Sol*, in which they sailed, when nearly at the end of her voyage, was taken by the Algerian corsairs, who, at that time and long after, infested the narrow seas. At the division of the booty Cervantes fell to the share of a bloodthirsty renegade Greek, Deli Mami by name. For five bitter years he remained a captive and a slave at Algiers. Of his life during this time, and of his valour and enterprise, we have contemporary testimony. Before he had acquired fame as a writer, he was already widely known for the strange part he played at Algiers. He eventually became the property of Hassan Pasha, a renegade whose barbarous cruelties provoked comment, even in a place where mutilations of defenceless captives and brutal outrages of all kinds were common. Cervantes was one of twenty-five thousand Christian slaves who worked in chains for their owners, while awaiting their ransom from their native land. The letters addressed to persons of high position that had been found upon him at the time of his capture produced an exaggerated idea of his

importance, and a larger sum was demanded for his liberation
than his worldly position warranted. He seems to have taken
from the first a prominent position among his fellow-captives,
and he it was who planned and attempted to carry out many
daring attempts at escape. It is from an impartial witness
that we have the statement that Hassan Pasha was wont to
declare that, but for the one-handed Spaniard, his prisoners, his
ships, and his city would be safe. It is difficult to understand why Hassan, who in *Don Quixote* is described as the
"murderer of the whole human race," did not cut short his
bold slave's career by a speedy execution ; we are told that he
was impressed by the bold bearing and clever answers of the
man ; and indeed Cervantes' qualities were such as to win
admiration even from the most brutal. In the story of the
captive, which forms one of the episodes of *Don Quixote*,
speaking of himself as "a certain Saavedra," he tells us that,
in spite of the notoriety of his attempts at escape, his master
never treated him harshly, and this notwithstanding the fact
that he was accustomed to assume the whole responsibility of
these daring enterprises that so often miscarried only through
the cowardice or treachery of accomplices.

Rodrigo de Cervantes, the elder brother of Miguel, was
ransomed after a comparatively short captivity, and it was
partly through his exertions that a sum, the payment of which
reduced still further the slight resources of the family, was at
last placed in the hands of the devoted Redemptionist Fathers,
in order to procure the younger brother's release. This took
place in 1580, and towards the end of the same year Cervantes
returned to Spain after an absence of ten years, little bettered
in fortune or prospects, but bringing with him a fund of experience of the characters and manners of the Algerian corsairs
which he afterwards turned to good account in many of his
writings. His services and sufferings gained him no promotion
—nay, on his release he had to defend himself against enemies

who accused him before the commission of the Inquisition, appointed to inquire into the purity of the faith of such prisoners as returned after long residence among Moslems. He again joined the Figueroa regiment, in which, as well as in the Moncada regiment, he had previously served, and during the next two years he saw much active service both by land, in the Portuguese campaign, and by sea, off the Azores. In the latter campaign his elder brother gained promotion, but no such good fortune fell to the lot of Miguel ; he never rose above the position of a private soldier. Whilst in Portugal Cervantes gained the affections of a lady of position. She became the mother of his natural daughter and only child, Isabel, who lived to comfort her father's old age, and afterwards became a nun.

The year 1584 brought two important events in our author's life—his marriage and the publication of his first book. Of his wife little is known, for Cervantes does not, like his great rival Lope de Vega, allude in his writings to the domestic happiness which we have reason to believe that he enjoyed. She was younger than her husband, she bore him no children, and shared his many trials to the end of his life. That she had a kindly character may perhaps be inferred from the fact that she allowed his natural daughter to live under the roof in Madrid that sheltered the struggling little family, consisting of herself, her husband, his daughter Isabel, his elder sister Andrea, and her young daughter. The little dower brought by the young wife was not sufficient to keep the wolf from the door when, as happened more than once, Cervantes' characteristic carelessness or the dishonesty of agents brought him into financial troubles.

The work to which we have referred above is the *Galatea*, a pastoral novel of the same character as the *Diana* mentioned in another chapter. It is neither better nor worse than other books of the same class, and only here and there does the knowledge we have of its author from other sources enable us to detect some sparkle of his bright wit and quaint humour amid the wearisome monotony of second-rate verse and prose which, though correct and harmonious, is rendered tame by the insipidity of the subject. Introduced into the book, but unconnected with it in subject, is a poetical review, or rather eulogy, of the principal writers of the time, entitled the *Canto de Caliope*. It is hard to judge whether the extravagant praise here expressed is sincere or ironical, or bestowed merely for the purpose of gaining the favour of those to whom it is addressed. Probably the motive that inspired it was a mixed one partaking of each of these elements. Cervantes knew well the defects of the pastoral novel; he has elsewhere ridiculed the unreal shepherds and their sickly sentiment (see p. 87), but the *Galatea* proved successful, and it probably was this success that induced him to adopt literature as a profession, and to become one of the innumerable authors who thronged the approaches to the gate of fame. Literature alone, however, would not suffice to provide the little family with the bare necessities of life, and Cervantes obtained a small post under Government, the duties of which included the purchase of provisions for the forces.

In addition to numerous occasional pieces, Cervantes wrote during middle age thirty dramas. The theatre was still in its infancy, with only slightly more appliances at its disposal than those above described (see p. 66). Judging from the only two plays preserved, Cervantes did something towards its development; but his specific claims of having been the first to reduce the number of acts from five to three (the usual number in the Spanish theatre), and to introduce allegorical personages, must be disallowed. Of these two plays the most remarkable is the *Numancia*, dealing with the siege of that city under Scipio Africanus. It has been praised, perhaps extravagantly, by German critics, but even those who cannot wholly agree with their verdict must admit that the scale on which it is conceived, as well as certain of the scenes, are truly grand. A tragedy of the most harrowing kind, its catastrophe is the fall of a city and the massacre of its inhabitants. It lacks almost every essential of dramatic composition, being merely an assemblage of scenes taken from the life of the doomed city, and worked out with glowing imagination, pathos, and warm patriotic feeling. But there is no unity in its plan, no plot, no true conception of the province, limitations, and methods of the drama. It has, however, a special interest for all admirers of the author of *Don Quixote*, for it is the first work which gives an insight into his genius, and it echoed one of the deepest feelings of the national heart. When Palafox was holding Saragossa against the victorious French armies during the great struggle for Spanish independence, the *Numancia* was played by the defenders of the beleaguered city in order to recall to the minds of the starving inhabitants what Spaniards had dared and done for the same sacred cause in times gone by. Its glowing verse and reckless patriotism, which at other times might have sounded strained and un-natural, found here a ready appreciation and response. The citizens of Saragossa, more fortunate and not less bold than those of Numancia, drove the besiegers from their gates, and outside their shattered walls, sick, half starved, and wounded, they danced throughout the night in a weird frenzy of joy to the strain of the national *jota*.

The interest of the other drama, the *Trato de Argel* (Life in Algiers), is a more narrow one. In it Cervantes attempted to turn to dramatic use his sad experience of a captive's life in the city from which the piece takes its name. Among the characters appears the "Spanish soldier called Saavedra," whose cheerful disposition aided his companions to bear their mis-fortunes, and whose cool daring so often nearly brought about their escape from bondage. Many of the scenes must have been drawn from the author's personal recollections, and the story-teller's talent does something to relieve the heavy verse, part of which is put into the mouth of the frigid allegorical personages whom, as Cervantes proudly imagined, he had first introduced to the stage which they so awkwardly cumbered.

Even to a successful dramatist—and Cervantes tells us that his plays were favourably received—writing for the stage was not a lucrative profession, unless indeed the playwright were endowed with the marvellous fertility of Lope de Vega, whose fame began to spread about the time when Cervantes turned his attention to a department of literature in which he was better fitted to excel. In 1588 Cervantes was living in Seville. *Rinconete y Cortadillo*, a story written in picaresque style, and containing many expressions in *germania* or "thieves' latin," gives the fruit of his observations and a vivid picture of the low and criminal life of the bright city of the Guadalquivir. The descriptions of the organised guild of assassins and pick-pockets, with its president, the famous Monipodio, and the school in which artistic thieving was taught, are still unsurpassed by any one of the numerous imitations to which they have given rise. The *Novelas Ejemplares*, or short stories of which *Rinconete y Cortadillo* is one of the best, were not published until 1613, when the first part of *Don Quixote* had already run through several editions. They were probably written at various periods and laid by until their author could find a publisher for them. In them we see Cervantes in many moods, yet always wearing a bold face, although he must often have been driven nearly to despair by adverse fortune. They are the best of all his works with the exception of *Don Quixote*, and in style, finish, and correctness greatly surpass the masterpiece. Written in an age in which coarseness of expression was scarcely considered a defect, they are, with the exception of one, the authenticity of which has been disputed, almost entirely unobjectionable on this score. Their range of subject is wide, but they are all scenes from contemporary life. *La Gitanilla* (The Gipsy-girl), which forms one of the collection, is the simple story of a dancing girl, told with all the charm of Cervantes' narrative style. In the heroine is found, probably for the first time, a character which has since been made use of in almost every literature. Victor Hugo's Esmeralda represents the same untamed yet womanly spirit preserving much of its innate purity amidst the most degrading surroundings. *La Gitanilla* contains the following praises of gipsy life, probably the finest passage of Cervantes' prose :—

[1] Somos señores de los campos, de los sembrados, de las selvas, de los montes, de las fuentes y de los ríos : los montes nos ofrecen leña de balde, los árboles frutas, las viñas uvas, las huertas hortaliza, las fuentes agua, los ríos peces, y los vedados caza, sombras las peñas, aire fresco las quiebras, y casas las cuevas : para nosotros las inclemencias del cielo son oreos, refrigerio las nieves, baños la lluvia, músicas los truenos, y hachas los relámpagos : para nosotros son los duros terrenos colchones de blandas plumas : el cuero curtido de nuestros cuerpos nos sirve de arnés impenetrable que nos defiende : á nuestra lijereza no la impiden grillos, ni la detienen barrancos, ni la contrastan paredes : á nuestro ánimo no le tuercen cordeles, ni le menoscaban garruchas, ni le ahogan tocas, ni le doman potros : del sí al no, no hacemos diferencia cuando nos conviene ; siempre nos preciamos más de mártires que de confesores : para nosotros se crian las bestias de carga en los campos, y se cortan las faltriqueras en las ciudades : no hay águila, ni ninguna otra ave de rapiña que más presto se abalance á la presa que se le ofrece, que nosotros nos abalanzamos á las

---

[1] " We are lords of the plains, of the fields, of the forests, of the groves, of the springs and of the rivers ; the groves afford us wood gratis, the trees fruit, the vines grapes, the gardens green stuff, the springs water, the rivers fish, and the parks game, the rocks shade, the gorges fresh breezes, and the caves houses : for us the inclemency of the sky is refreshment, the snow coolness, the rain our bath, the thunder music, and the lightning a torch : for us the hard earth is a bed of soft feathers ; the tanned leather of our bodies serves us as an impenetrable armour of defence ; neither fetters nor precipices check our agility nor do walls confine us ; our spirit cannot be bent by bonds nor conquered by the rack, nor stifled by torture, nor vanquished by the block ; we distinguish but little between ' yes ' and ' no ' when it is to our advantage ; our pride is rather to be martyrs than confessors ; for us the beasts of burden are bred on the plain, and purses are cut in the cities ; no eagle or other bird of prey is more swift to pounce upon the quarry than we to seize the opportunity which may result in our gain : many in short are the

ocasiones que algún interés nos señalen : y finalmente, tenemos muchas habilidades que felice fin nos prometen ; porque en la cárcel cantamos, en el potro callamos, de día trabajamos, y de noche hurtamos, y por mejor decir avisamos que nadie viva descuidado de mirar donde pone su hacienda : no nos fatiga el temor de perder la honra, ni nos desvela la ambición del acrecentarla : ni sustentamos bandos, ni madrugamos á dar memoriales, ni á acompanar magnates, ni á solicitar favores : por dorados techos y suntuosos palacios estimamos estas barracas y movibles ranchos : por cuadros y paises de Flándes los que nos da la naturaleza en esos levantados riscos y nevadas peñas, tendidos prados y espesos bosques que á cada paso á los ojos se nos muestran : somos astrólogos rústicos, porque como casi siempre dormimos al cielo descubierto, á todas horas sabemos las que son del día y las que son de la noche : . . . un mismo rostro hacemos al sol que al hielo, á la esterilidad que á la abundancia : en conclusión, somos gente que vivimos por nuestra industria y pico, y sin entremeternos con el antiguo refrán, *iglesia, ó mar, ó casa real*, tenemos lo que queremos, pues nos contentamos con lo que tenemos.

The *Coloquio de los Perros* (Dialogue of the Dogs) recalls by its title and subject Burns's masterpiece, and, like the *Twa Dogs*, contains much of the writer's rough and ready practical philosophy of life. Cervantes saw clearly the weaknesses of his fellow-men, but neither their failings nor the harsh treatment which he received at their hands altered the sweet singleness of his character, or spoiled one of the bravest and most chivalrous natures that the world has ever seen.

Cervantes' dreams of advancement, and of gaining an

arts to which we look for a happy end ; for in prison we sing, on the scaffold we are silent, by day we work, by night we steal or, to speak more correctly, we are a warning to men not to mislay their property : neither does the fear of loss of reputation weigh upon us, nor the desire of increasing it keep us awake : party feeling does not trouble us, nor do we rise early to present petitions, or to attend levées, or beg for favours : precious to us as gilded roofs and sumptuous palaces are these huts and movable tents ; our pictures and Dutch landscapes are those that nature offers in these lofty peaks and snow-covered rocks, broad meadows and deep woods, which we have ever before our eyes ; untaught astronomers we are, for, as we almost always sleep under the sky, we can tell the hour by day or by night, . . . neither heat nor cold, want nor plenty affect our mood : in short we are people that live by our own cunning and resource, and little we reck of the old proverb 'the church or the sea, or the king's household,' * yet we have what we want for we are content with what we have."

* *I.e.* the three professions suitable for a gentleman.

assured position in state employment, were not yet crushed out
of him by continual failure. In 1590 he forwarded to Philip
II., the king whom he had so well served in subordinate
positions, a petition that he might be elected to one of certain
offices of minor importance in America, or "the Indies" as it
was then called. But he was not well fitted to elbow his way
to the throne through the midst of the innumerable place-
hunters by whom it was beset. His petition, though not
absolutely disregarded, was not granted; he became a tax-
gatherer, and shortly afterwards suffered three months' imprisonment on account of his inability to refund certain sums
of trivial amount that had been entrusted by him to a dishonest
person. His fortunes now seemed nearly desperate, but at
this juncture occurred the events that first suggested the work
by which he is best known.

His duties as a collector of rents brought him to the little
town of Argamasilla, situated in the bleak and parched district
of La Mancha. Here, for reasons which will probably remain
for ever unknown, he aroused the enmity of the authorities.
He was for some time imprisoned in the cellar of a house which
stands to this day, and which has recently been used for the
purpose of printing one of the finest editions of the works of
its former tenant. For the wrong thus done him he avenged
himself in *Don Quixote*. The Manchegos are a hardy race,
somewhat rougher in manners and exterior than their neighbours, and endowed with a sharp-wittedness that easily degener-
ates into cunning. They have, however, sterling qualities and
frequent flashes of bright imagination. For all their virtues
Cervantes gives them full credit. The satire upon their failings, interwoven in the *History of the Ingenious Knight*, is far
removed from vituperation; the traces of bitter memories are
few and far between. Unsuccessful attempts have been re-
peatedly made to show that the unamiable characters—they
are not many—in *Don Quixote* are real personages. This

theory contradicts its author's distinct denial of any such hidden meaning, and his reiterated assertion that his purpose was merely to abolish the absurd and mischievous books of chivalry. Cervantes' satire was not directed against individuals. Against innkeepers, duennas, *moriscos*, and a certain class of the clergy, he seems indeed to have cherished a grudge, which probably had its origin in dislike to individual members of these classes.

To analyse a book so well known as the *History of the Ingenious Knight* would be worse than useless, for its merits lie rather in its details than in its general plan. A few general observations must be made, for authorities differ widely about the light in which it is to be regarded, and still the controversy rages as to whether it is gay or sad in tendency, and how far the author was conscious that he was writing what may be taken to be an allegory of human life. As to the former question it would seem certain that Cervantes' intention was to write a book that should provoke mirth; but he wrote as his heart felt. He had not seen a cheerful side of life, and was already on the verge of old age. He declares more than once that his book is destined to have a world-wide reputation, but we must not attach too much importance to these statements, for *Don Quixote* is not the only book for which the author prophesied a brilliant future, and, even when its success was assured, "this withered, wrinkled, capricious child of his genius" does not seem to have been his favourite. It is clear also, both from the carelessness which allowed the first part to remain for years without the corrections of which it stood so much in need, and from the tone in which contemporary writers speak of the book, that it was not supposed to be written with any serious purpose. Some of the great men of the time speak slightingly of it, and Lope de Vega, influenced probably by the jealousy which formed so salient a feature of his character, says in a letter, "nobody is silly enough to praise *Don Quixote*." Even if the allegorical meaning is admitted, it cannot have been this that commended the book to the vulgar and caused its unprecedented success.

At the end of the sixteenth century, literature, with the exception of the drama, had become stereotyped; even the "picaresque" novel was losing its freshness, and as yet no genius had sprung up to create a new form. How popular the romances of chivalry had been is proved by the extraordinarily intimate knowledge of a great number of them possessed by Cervantes himself. But this popularity was on the wane, and while admitting that it was Don Quixote who gave the death-blow to the "innumerable lineage of Ámadis," it is impossible to attribute solely to his influence the fact that after his appearance no single book of this kind was written or reprinted. The real secret of the contemporary success of *Don Quixote* is to be found in the fact that the great body of authors had lost touch with the public; they wrote on certain conventional lines in order to gain mutual commendations and laudatory sonnets. Cervantes' venture brought to the general reader what he wanted, and he refused any longer to be amused according to the goodwill and pleasure of a literary class. Cervantes copied his characters from life, and from types that were common in his own day; they bear strongly the impress of their time and country, but behind lie the motives and passions that have swayed men in all ages. Don Quixote himself was not meant to represent a pure and noble character battling with a world that did not understand it. Its author's experience had taught him that in this world nothing is utterly bad, and nothing is thoroughly good. It seems impossible to ignore the fact that his hero is sometimes grotesque and almost pitiable, and that his creator takes delight in the buffetings he receives. No amount of minute study of its pages can hope to discover the secret of this great book, for it is all things to all men, reflecting continually the mood of the reader, and conveying to him

more or less meaning according to his mental capacity.   Even
so the Spanish peasant sings :—

> [1] En este mundo, señores,
> No hay ni verdad ni mentira,
> Que todo está en el color
> Del cristal con que se mira.

The first part of *Don Quixote* gave to its author fame,
but little, if any, pecuniary profit.   The Duke of Bejar, to
whom it was dedicated, allowed him to languish in poverty.
He followed the court from Madrid to Valladolid under Felipe
III., and an insight is given into his private affairs during his
residence in the latter city by the depositions in a murder case
in which he and other members of his household appeared as
witnesses.   From these we learn that he " wrote and negotiated
affairs," and that his womenfolk contributed with needlework
to the maintenance of the family.   What the nature of the
"affairs " was we do not know ; as for the writing, it seems
likely that his pen employed its bold firm characters in copy-
ing legal documents.   Cervantes had now established his
reputation as a literary man, but the attention he received
took the form rather of malignant attacks prompted by jealousy,
than of acceptance into the ranks of the great authors of the
age.   He had certainly his friends, but with Lope de Vega and
Góngora, the idols of the time, against him, his chance of an
impartial judgment was small indeed.   Those who attacked
him had more interest in undermining his reputation than
friends, such as Quevedo and the Argensolas, had in defending
it.   At any rate he seems now to have had no difficulty in
finding publishers for his works, for it was during the years
1613 to 1615 that the first editions of the *Novelas Ejemplares*,
Viage del Parnaso, and the *Comedias* appeared.   Of the *Novelas*,
for which their author claims, with some show of reason,

---

[1] " In this world, good sirs—there is neither truth nor falsehood,—all lies
in the colour—of the glass through which we look."

the distinction of being the first specimens in Castilian of the novel of adventure, a brief mention has already been made. In the *Voyage to Parnassus* Cervantes once more sought the favour of the poetic muse whom he had so often wooed, and who had so seldom proved kind. In this long poem only here and there does she vouchsafe a smile to her old admirer. Its general plan is, with candid acknowledgments, taken from a book bearing the same title by Caporali, an Italian poet of secondary merit. The author, appealed to by Apollo for help, calls together the good poets for the purpose of driving out the poetasters from the Hill of the Muses. Cervantes had already given proof of his fondness for indulging in mild and generally laudatory criticism in the *Canto de Caliope*, in *Don Quixote*, and elsewhere. His good nature precluded a candid judgment of contemporary merit; moreover serious criticism, if it took an adverse form, would have been considered a breach of good manners in the age in which he lived. He bestows what seems to us extravagant praise with equal lavishness upon good and upon second-rate authors. He redeems his poem from monotony by flashes of quaint rich fancy, and by a sly irony which was the only weapon that the kind heart allowed itself to use even against those who had wounded it most brutally. So much for its literary worth. To all lovers of its writer, to those who know him aright and who seek in his works the brave, generous, and chivalrous nature that inspired them, the *Viage del Parnaso* will always be most precious. With the exception of his last work, it is the one in which we learn most of himself, his ideals, his aspirations, and the long struggle that so seldom wrung from him a bitter word.

The six *comedias* wherewith Cervantes for the second time sought to gain a place among the ever-increasing crowd of playwrights by whom the theatre was beset, are of slight merit; they are never acted and seldom read; even their author did not value them highly. Not so the six farces which appeared together with them. These are written to suit the popular taste, and in more natural tone than the comedies ; their humour is coarser than is general with Cervantes. In their sprightly and rapid movement, and in their artless simplicity of form, they recall the work of Lope de Rueda, whom Cervantes had seen and admired many years before. The scenes, too, of some of them are such as their author knew better than the haunts of the cloaked and sworded gallants after whom the class of dramas that deal with the minor nobility (*hidalgos*) is named. Cervantes had not Quevedo's perverse leaning towards low life, but he was thoroughly intimate with the habits and ways of thinking of the poorer classes, and could treat them with tenderness and delicacy. The creator of Maritornes had indeed wide sympathies.

The profits of the first part of *Don Quixote* had gone into the pockets of the booksellers, both those to whom it belonged and those who, as frequently happened, brought out pirated editions. Whether Cervantes, on concluding it, intended to publish a second part is uncertain, for his final words are ambiguous. Success encouraged him, and he set to work. When his continuation was already partly written, and had been announced in the preface to the novels, there appeared a spurious second part published at Tarragona, bearing on its title-page the probably fictitious name of Avellaneda. Who its author was will probably never be known, but we may infer from passages of his book that he was a churchman, and a friend and admirer of Lope de Vega, between whom and Cervantes there existed a feud of long standing. In this literary quarrel Lope's "universal jealousy," well known to his contemporaries, had caused him occasionally to play a mean and ungenerous part, though at other times he made amends, once even ranking his great rival as equal in wisdom to "Cicero and Juan de Mena."[1] Guided by these slight indications, an

[1] *Premio del bien hablar.*

English Cervantist of the highest merit has started a theory that the book was written by the great dramatist himself, or, at least, with his knowledge and consent, and that its purpose was deliberately to spoil Cervantes' work and bring its author into contempt. Of neither view have we sufficient proof. Mr. Watts' ingenuity and industry, backed by intimate knowledge of the literary history of the time, fail to trace the forgery to Lope, whom he apparently dislikes as much as he loves Cervantes. It may be admitted that the author of the spurious second part utterly failed to grasp the spirit of the story he attempted to continue, and that his book does not in any way bear comparison with that of Cervantes, against whom his animosity continually breaks out in personal attacks in the worst possible taste. But Avellaneda was not the first in Spain to attempt to take an unfair advantage of another's literary success, and it was not to be expected that the same age should produce two geniuses capable of writing *Don Quixote*. The spurious second part is neither better nor worse, nor indeed more indecent, than the generality of "picaresque" stories. If we could be sure that Cervantes had but one enemy, we might safely attribute Avellaneda's book to Lope de Vega.

In 1615 appeared the genuine second part, and in it Cervantes with perfect good temper and dignity retaliates for the great wrong that had been done him, and the brutal personal attack. The real Sancho, overflowing with an increased fund of proverbs, treats his counterfeit with the contempt he deserves, and Avellaneda and his work are pulled to pieces in most masterly style. But the second part has not the freshness of the first; it is more studied, more correct, and more artificial. Its only rival in its own line is the first part; the broad humour, the wit, and the pathos are the same, but the unconscious light-heartedness is gone, and here and there the author, now nearly seventy years of age, seems to grow a little weary; the characters, which have developed since the book began, are here stereotyped, and we cannot help regretting the day when knight and squire first sallied forth discoursing pleasantly, with the whole world before them, and seeking the unknown adventures which were to bring out their strongly-contrasted individuality.

But the second part of *Don Quixote* was thoroughly successful, and Cervantes was now held in great esteem. He was still very poor, but to that he was accustomed. After fifty years of effort his genius was at last appreciated, and his head was full of literary projects, including a second part of the *Galatea*, which still held a high place in his affections. This book was never written, but Cervantes lived to finish his *Pérsiles y Sigismunda*, struggling to beat back fast-approaching death until it should be completed. It had been in hand for some time, and he said that it would be "either the best or the worst book of entertainment in Spanish." It is neither. Persiles and Segismunda are lovers to whom the fates are adverse, and who roam about the world somewhat aimlessly until at last they are happily united. The chronology and geography of the book are intentionally hazy; the changes of scene are so rapid, the characters and their adventures so numerous, and the plot so complicated, that it reads rather like the argument of a book than a complete story. This wealth of imagination in a man so old, worn, and broken, is indeed astonishing. For Cervantes was now near his end; his disease, as he well knew, was dropsy, but he worked on till the last, brave and unrepining. Three weeks before his death he penned the touching dedication of his last work to the Count of Lemos, the same to whom he had addressed the second part of *Don Quixote*. In the Prologue, one of the most characteristic passages of his whole works, he had already bid good-bye to life with cheerful resignation in the simple words: "Good-bye to quips; good-bye to cranks; good-bye to light-hearted friends; for I am a-dying, and longing to meet you soon in the happiness of another life." [1]   On the 19th of April he passed away, within ten days of the date of the death of Shakespeare.

That all his life he had been a faithful son of the Church is made abundantly certain in his writings, in spite of the inferences that bigotry has attempted to draw from his slighting words about ecclesiastics of a certain kind, and from the fact that the Inquisition at its worst period found excuse for defacing some of his works.   Before the end he assumed the habit of St. Francis according to the custom of his age and country. He was buried by his own request according to the simple rite of his order, in the Trinitarian convent in which his daughter had taken the veil.   When the nuns changed their quarters, his bones were removed, along with others, so that they are no longer distinguishable.

Looking back on his great work we try to explain the charm which it possesses for high and low, rich and poor, learned and simple.   In it we find no model of literature, no splendour of style; nay, the writing is often careless and slipshod.   Surely the truth is that Cervantes and his work interest humanity because he and, consequently, it are so intensely human; because he neither railed at nor eulogised his fellow-men, but wrote of them as one who felt in himself the germ of all their failings, and all their virtues; and thus the love he bore his kind is returned to him in full.   The interest of *Don Quixote* is the same as that afforded by the study of human nature and the conditions under which we live; in both are found the same inexplicable contrasts and contradictions between higher aspirations and uncompromisingly brutal realities; in both but a hair's-breadth separates the sublime from the ridiculous.   Sad it is to think how those of his own time failed to appreciate the supreme courage of this war-worn and broken soldier, with

---

[1] "Adios, gracias; adios, donaires; adios, regocijados amigos, que yo me voy muriendo y deseando veros presto contentos en la otra vida."

"aquiline profile, chestnut hair, smooth and unwrinkled brow, bright eyes, and silvery beard,"[1] who with uncomplaining cheerfulness bore poverty, neglect, and the harsh treatment of his fellows, and as a token of great-hearted forgiveness left behind him one of the world's treasures, a book that will laugh with the gay and light-hearted, will weep with the despondent, afford pleasure to the most foolish, and food for thought even to the wisest.[2]

[1] See the Prologue to the *Novelas Ejemplares*.
[2] See the Prologue to *Don Quixote*.

CHAPTER XIV

LOPE DE VEGA

AFTER the somewhat crude though powerful efforts of Cervantes the drama passed at once into the hands of a remarkable man, who not only gave it its final form and excelled in all its departments, but by the amount rather than by the merits of his work eclipsed all other Spanish dramatists.

Lope Felix de Vega Carpio, the most voluminous writer of ancient or modern times, was born in Madrid in 1562, and received his early education in the newly founded Imperial College. We have it on his own authority that he gave proof in early infancy of his faculty for versification. His first plays were written before he was twelve years old. The roving and adventurous spirit characteristic of the men of his age and country was strong within him. At thirteen he ran away from school with one of his companions, but fell into the hands of the police at Astorga and was sent back to Madrid by a kindly magistrate. At fifteen he enlisted and served under the Marqués de Santa Cruz during the Portuguese and African campaigns in the same regiment with Cervantes. He did not remain long in the army, but returned to Madrid, where he entered the household of Don Jerónimo Manrique, the bishop of Ávila, who wisely sent the stripling poet to Alcalá to continue his studies. Of his first patron he always speaks in terms of respectful affection, but so grave a centre was ill-suited to the gay young soldier-poet, and he became secretary to the Duke of Alva, grandson of the great nobleman of that name. His first important work is the *Arcadia*, a pastoral novel in no wise remarkable except for the facility of its verse, and the fact that it contains many episodes of its author's life under the name of Belardo, which he habitually adopts when he figures in his own writings; the unusual sprightliness of its "shepherds" amidst their unnatural surroundings constitutes it a favourable specimen of a grotesque and almost worthless class.

Love adventures succeeded one another rapidly in Lope's life, and at one moment we find him preparing to take orders. But a new affection threw all his grave thoughts to the winds, and he married Doña Isabel de Urbina. Shortly afterwards he fought a duel with a gentleman whom he had ridiculed in public and, having wounded him seriously, was obliged to leave Madrid. He took refuge in Valencia, then the centre of a brilliant circle of dramatists and poets including in their number Guillén de Castro. While at Valencia he heard of his wife's illness in Madrid, and hurried back in time to spend some months in her company before her death. He mourned for her in an " Eclogue," so full of mannerisms and so artificial that it utterly fails to express the grief that he probably really felt. His home being broken up he again took military service and joined the Invincible Armada, which was then being fitted out. During this disastrous expedition his brother was killed, but neither this private bereavement nor the public misfortunes checked the flow of his verses. Encouraged probably by the partial success that had been attained by Luís Barahona de Soto in his *Lágrimas de Angélica*, Lope conceived a plan of continuing Ariosto's great poem, and whiled away the dreary hours of his voyage by the composition of *La Hermosura de Angélica*, a work possessing such merit as is consistent with the circumstances of its being a continuation of the work of a great poet and hastily written by a very young author.[1]

On his return to Spain with the shattered remnant of the great fleet, Lope again married, and for some time appears to have lived quietly and happily, working hard for the stage. A son was born to him, but died at the age of seven years, and shortly afterwards Lope found himself again a widower. His little son, Carlillos as he affectionately calls him, had been very dear to him, and he felt the blow most deeply. Fame and even riches had come to him after years of hard work, but he was alone in the world, for his natural daughter, Marcela, whom he fondly loved, entered a Trinitarian convent, and her brother became a soldier. Lope now joined the order of St. Francis, a congregation of which his great rival Cervantes was a member, and afterwards became a priest and a familiar of the Inquisition. In the fulfilment of the duties of these grave offices he was punctiliously exact, but they did not prevent him from continuing to write for the stage which he had now, as Cervantes says, "nearly monopolised." Year by year the immense mass of his works continued to grow, while their author lived alone in his little house in Madrid, occupied in works of charity and in tending the little garden which we know so well from his own descriptions and those of his contemporaries. It is sad to relate that certain documents, lately brought to light, go to show that age had not stamped out his passions, and that, though a priest, Lope's life was, for a time at least, not altogether blameless. Great personages sought the friendship of the idol of the populace, the "prodigy of nature" (*monstruo de la naturaleza*), as he was called, and brought with them into his retirement the passions and struggles of the outer world. Certain it is that Lope repented bitterly before the end. Misfortunes, the precise nature of which we do not know, overtook

---

[1] For Lope's other epic and mock epic poems, see the chapter on Epic Poetry, pp. 223-228.

his old age and he relapsed into a settled melancholy. He had always been an agreeable companion, simple and unassuming in manner, and to the end he continued to receive his friends and converse with them, chiefly on religious matters. He died in 1635, worn out as much by the harsh discipline to which he had latterly submitted himself as by the weight of years.

During his lifetime his popularity had been extraordinary; kings and popes had done him honour, and his funeral was made an occasion for an elaborate display, befitting the esteem in which he was held. The magnificent procession of friends, noblemen, men of letters, and ecclesiastics, that accompanied him to the grave, turned aside in order that Marcela, the nun, might look forth on it from the lattice windows of her convent. The mourning of Spain was shared by other countries whither the Spanish language had followed her victorious arms; Paris, Milan, and Naples contributed to the laudatory poems dedicated to his memory. These fill two large volumes; for his contemporaries rated him higher than any poet of ancient or modern times.

Turning to the works on which this exaggerated estimate is founded, one is struck, at first view, merely by their bulk. The exact number of Lope's dramatic works cannot be known, for, as he himself complains, even during his lifetime, many inferior works were brought out in his name by unscrupulous authors and actors desirous at any price of gaining the public ear. Many of the plays also to which he lays claim in the list which he drew up at the request of his friends have disappeared. A reasonable estimate brings up the number of his plays to fifteen hundred, exclusive of seven hundred *autos*, short farces, and interludes. Besides these Lope wrote innumerable sonnets, occasional verses, and a whole series of excellent ballads, as well as novels and epic and mock poems. His dramas have been classified as tragedies; legendary plays, heroic, historical, and sacred; comedies of intrigue, of manners, and picaresque; and *autos sacramentales*. But this is obviously a cross-classification and is of little use in dealing with the immense mass of his plays, only about a third of which have been published. The difference between his comedies and tragedies consists often merely in the nature of their ending. Change but the names of some of his so-called legendary or religious plays, alter an expression here and there, and they at once become comedies of the ordinary Spanish type.

In every branch of the dramatic art Lope attained such eminence that his works were treated as models by all later Spanish writers, and so long as the national drama existed his influence is everywhere apparent. The play of the "cloak and sword" (*comedia de capa y espada*) may almost be said to be his own invention, and it was he who introduced its peculiar features into every department of Spanish fiction. The cloak and sword play is essentially the play of manners; its characters offer little or no variety; the scene is always some Spanish town, and the plot invariably centres round the love intrigue of persons in the middle or upper classes of life, regulated by a conventional code of honour so strict that it replaces the abstract "Necessity" of the allegorical drama. A host of minor characters are introduced generally as servants, and among these a secondary plot is developed, running parallel to the main one. Careful delineation of character is not attempted; the whole interest lies in the ingenious intricacy of the plot and the vivid representation of a brilliant and picturesque but somewhat shallow and uniform state of society. In reading these pieces, the greatest attention is required in order to follow the main thread throughout the maze of complications (*enredos*) so dear to a Spanish audience. A simplified outline of "Fair Words Rewarded" (*El Premio del bien hablar*), a favourite and not exaggerated specimen of the class, will illustrate and confirm the above assertions.

Don Diego, a Sevillian gentleman, speaks disrespectfully in public of Leonarda, the lady to whom his brother Don Pedro is about to be married. He is reproved by Don Juan, a stranger from the north, who is staying in Seville accompanied by his sister Ángela. A fight ensues and Don Diego is seriously wounded. Don Juan accidentally seeks refuge in the house of Don Antonio, the father of Leonarda; his defence of her honour is rewarded by Leonarda's love and he remains concealed in the house. Meanwhile, Don Pedro is seeking his brother's assailant, accompanied by Feliciano, the brother of Leonarda. The latter on seeing Ángela at once falls in love with her and persuades his sister to offer her hospitality, little thinking that Don Juan is already concealed in the house. Leonarda now becomes suspicious of the relationship existing between Don Juan and Ángela, while Don Juan is jealous of Don Pedro; the situation is still further complicated by Don Antonio's attempt to marry Leonarda to Don Pedro. An elaborate game of cross purposes is played in Don Antonio's house, and the ingenious lying, wherewith the parties extricate themselves from delicate situations, renders confusion worse confounded. Feliciano endeavours to prevent the match between his sister and Don Pedro, which would extinguish his own hopes of obtaining the hand of Ángela ; for it would of course be impossible for him to ally himself with the enemy of his brother-in-law. At last Feliciano and Leonarda come to an understanding, and the way out of the difficulty becomes obvious. Don Pedro arrives in bridal attire only to find Leonarda betrothed to Don Juan, and Feliciano betrothed to Ángela. His brother is now out of danger, so like a sensible man he resigns himself to the inevitable and accepts an invitation to the forthcoming double wedding.

The foregoing exceedingly condensed analysis wholly leaves

out the secondary intrigue formed by the love-affairs of Rufina, the mulatto slave-girl of Leonarda, and Martín, the unusually comic lackey of Don Juan.

La Moza de Cántaro (The Water-Carrier) is a typical instance of Lope's manner, and still commands an enthusiastic audience at its periodical revivals on the Madrid stage. It differs from the foregoing in its simpler structure and greater unity of interest. Ticknor places it in a special class because some of its characters belong to the lower orders, but it is really a *comedia de capa y espada*, as may be seen from the following abstract of its main argument.

The scene opens in Mérida, where Doña María de Guzmán, a lady of great beauty, is wooed by a host of admirers, all of whom she rejects somewhat disdainfully. One of these suitors, enraged at the treatment he has received, inflicts a blow upon her father. This outrage, according to all the rules of the Spanish stage, demands a bloody reprisal, and Doña María herself undertakes the part of avenger of her father's honour. She murders her father's brutal assailant in prison, and in order to escape the consequences of her act, sets out in humble disguise for Madrid. On her way thither she meets with an *indiano* or Spanish American, in whose household she takes service. Her simple dress does not conceal her attractions. While carrying her pitcher to the fountain she is seen by Don Juan, the stereotyped *galán* or lover, who, becoming enamoured of her, rejects for her sake the overtures of Doña Ana, a lady of great attractions. This lady has another suitor, a nobleman ; but she loves Don Juan in spite of his coolness, and her jealousy makes her desirous of seeing her successful rival, the water-carrier. In order to gratify her wish, she contrives to bring Doña María to her house. Here Doña María takes advantage of the opportunity afforded by the marriage of a fellow-servant to dress herself in the costume which befits her real station and best shows off her charms. Thus attired she is irresistible; Don Juan proposes marriage to her and is accepted, in spite of the protests of Doña Ana. The reason for disguise is now at an end; Doña María declares her rank and parentage, and is at last happily married.

Recklessness of human life is characteristic of the Spanish stage: here the unfortunate hot-tempered suitor is murdered, not that his death may form the catastrophe of the piece, but incidentally that it may give his murderess an opportunity of obtaining the disguise on which the necessary dramatic situations depend. Doña María's crime provokes no moral reprobation, nor is it meant to do so; a lady so careful of the family honour is likely to make the best of wives, and her conduct is considered natural, if not praiseworthy.

Lope de Vega is a master of easy and natural dialogue written in even and flowing verse. Calderón's characters, if not more natural, are better studied, but their stilted speeches, modelled on the language of the court, give them an air of un-reality. Calderón's verse, too, often rises to heights that Lope never attained or even aimed at, but Lope's is more even in quality. Though never attaining first-rate rank, it is seldom mere commonplace, as is too often the case with his great successor.

Calderón undoubtedly proposed to himself serious aims in his drama; Lope had none except the amusement of his hearers. This he admits candidly, and almost cynically, in his *Arte nuevo de hacer Comedias* (New Method of Play-writing), a brief treatise in verse, of great importance to those who would understand his conception of the art. In it he states that his predecessors, by their barbarous attempts at the imitation of classical models, destroyed the public taste for the drama in its highest forms. He too had tried to write correctly and had emptied the theatres. Finding that playgoers pre-ferred even the most extravagant pieces, written to suit the national taste, to the most correct of those written according to rule, he followed their humour. "And when I have to write a comedy," he says, "I fasten up the rules of the art with six keys. I turn out Terence and Plautus from my study so that they may not cry aloud against me ;—for truth is wont to make its voice heard even in dumb books. I write according to the method which was invented by those who became candidates for popular favour, for as it is the mob that pays for the play, it is but right to gratify it by speaking in the uncultured language which it understands." Speaking of the object of the drama, he says it is "to imitate the actions of men, and paint the manners of the age"; of moral purpose there is no mention at all in this place. He recommends that the tragic and comic element should be mingled in the same play, for although the result, judged according to the Aristotelian rules, will be "a second Minotaur," it will combine the grave and the laughable and produce the variety which is essential to pleasure, a variety warranted by the analogy of nature which the drama should strive to imitate. With regard to form he lays down precise rules for the employment of the recognised metres : *décimas* (combinations of octosyllabic lines) are fitted for complaints ; the sonnet is suited to moments of suspense ; descriptions require *romance* (octosyllabic assonant), though *ottava rima* is very effective ; *tercets* are suitable to serious matters, and *redondillas* (octosyllabic, A.B.B.A.) to love-scenes. He concludes his precepts by declaring that of the four hundred and eighty-three plays he had then written all but six sinned grievously against the classical rules.

Acting on this simple and elastic code, and discarding from his mind all the work of previous dramatists, Lope de Vega perfected the Spanish drama, truly national in character and more popular in form than that of any other country. Its defects are, as has been already stated, feeble delineation of character and an utter lack of moral purpose ; but in richness of plots, in variety of incident, in intrigue and powerful dramatic situations, it stands unrivalled. The great authors of other countries drew upon its inexhaustible treasures, sometimes imitating whole pieces, sometimes adapting single incidents or situations to their own requirements, generally without acknowledgment. Animated and picturesque, gay and reckless, narrow in ideas but outspoken and chivalrous like the men for whom it was intended, it affords a picture of a restricted and more or less imaginary society, so lifelike and so minute as to be unrivalled.

It was undoubtedly to his dramatic works that Lope owed his great fame, but to consider him as a dramatist only would be to study but one side of his remarkably versatile genius. His miscellaneous works fill more than twenty large volumes. One or two of the eleven epics that show his industry and skill in versification rather than his talent for this kind of composition will be considered elsewhere : for the present, space allows only a brief notice of his occasional poems and novels. In the latter class the *Dorotea* demands special mention, for Lope held it dearest of all his works. It is written in prose dialogue divided into five acts and, like other pastoral novels, contains a large amount of verse. The *Dorotea* is one of Lope's earliest books, but he published it for the first time only three years before his death. Its plan is ill-studied and poorly carried out ; it has, properly speaking, no plot ; the slight thread of story that connects the various scenes is seemingly taken from its author's life, and Lope himself may be recognised in the principal shepherd, Fernando. Numerous wearisome digressions and the unnecessary length to which it is dragged out combine to make the *Dorotea* very heavy reading, relieved only here and there by the occasional interest of the episodical matter and the quality of the verses, some of which are indeed charming. It was probably for the sake of introducing these that the *Dorotea* was composed, and their natural and passionate tone contrasts strongly with their formal and frigid setting. As Lope connected his scattered love-verses by means of the *Dorotea*, so he connected his carols and rustic songs by means of the *Pastores de Belén* (Shepherds of Bethlehem), another pastoral novel, superior to most of its class in that it treats a time and country of which its readers knew little or nothing, and thus gives more legitimate scope for the free play of imagination. Its story is roughly the gospel accounts of the birth of Christ; its shepherds are those who glorified Him and proclaimed the message of the angels. Lope was familiar with, and made good use of, many of the beautiful traditional legends that have gathered round the childhood of Jesus, as for instance that of the meeting of the Holy Family, during the flight into Egypt, with gipsies who enigmatically foretell the Saviour's fate from the lines on His baby-hand; and that of the kindness shown to the Virgin and Child by a poor woman whose son is a leper, but is healed by the water in which Jesus has been bathed, and afterwards appears in Scripture as the thief who repented on the cross. The pastoral and rustic tone of the book is spoiled in parts by exaggerations on either side : sometimes the shepherds are so uncouth and grotesque as to be altogether unpleasing; at others they amuse themselves by poetical competitions such as those in which Lope himself had so often won the prize. Many of their carols (*villancicos*) admirably combine grace and simplicity, and afford some of the best specimens of a very ancient traditional form. The most beautiful of all is probably that cited by Ticknor, but the following one serves equally well to illustrate their general characteristics :—

> [1] " ¿ Quién llama ?   ¿ Quién está ahí ? "
> " ¿ Dónde está, sabéislo vos,
>   Un niño que es hombre y Dios ? "
> " Quedito, que duerme aquí."

---

[1] " 'Who knocks?   Who is there ? '—' Do you know where is—a child who is man and God ? '—' Softly, he's sleeping here.'—' Asleep on the ground ? '

" ¿ En el suelo duerme ? "   " Sí."
" Pues decidle que despierte :
    Que viene tras él la muerte,
    Despues que es hombre, por mí."
" Llamad con voces más bajas
    Si le venís á buscar ;
    Que cansado de llorar,
    Se ha dormido en unas pajas."
" Bien podeís abrirme á mí
    Que puesto que busco á Dios,
    Ya somos hombres los dos."
" Quedito, que duerme aquí.
    Á fe que es mucha malicia
    Que acabado de llegar,
    Le vengáis a ejecutar
    Y con vara de justicia "
" Él mismo lo quiere así
    Por satisfacer á Dios."
" Entrad, decidselo vos."
" Quedito, que duerme aquí."
" ¿ Qué prendas queréis sacar,
    Si no tiene más hacienda
    Su madre que aquesta prenda
    Para que pueda pagar ? "
" Si tiene tantas en sí,
    Que es igual al mismo Dios,
    ¿ Qué más prendas queréis vos ?
" Quedito, que duerme aquí."

Besides the above-mentioned pastoral novels Lope published *El Peregrino en su Patria*, which stands half-way

' Yes.'—' Then bid him awake,—for death comes after him,—when he reaches man's age, for me.' — ' Call in a gentler voice,—if him you come to seek ;—for worn out with weeping—he has fallen asleep on the straw '—' Well may you open to me,—for though it is God that I seek,—now we are both but men.'—' Softly, he's sleeping here,—and, certes, it is hard indeed—that scarce has he arrived,—when you come to slay him thus—with an officer's wand in hand.'—' It is he who wills it so—to make amends to God.'—' Enter and tell him yourself.'—' Gently, he's sleeping here.'—' What pledge would you have of him ?—His mother has no other treasure *—than him she loves so well—wherewith to satisfy you'—' Such riches has he in himself—that he is even as God ;—what other pledge would you have ? '—' Gently, he's sleeping here.' "

---

* It is impossible to translate the play on ·the word *prenda*, used here in its three significations—a pledge or surety, a treasure, a good quality.

between the romance of chivalry and the modern novel, and three short stories of adventure in the less conventional form which Cervantes claimed to have originated. They were, as he tells us, written to amuse a lady, but are by no means favourable specimens of their class.

Among the bewildering number of Lope's sonnets it is scarcely possible to find one of first-rate merit, but very few are utterly worthless. They were thrown off without effort from his fertile brain, and probably never retouched. This form is eminently ill-adapted for a poet whose facility almost amounted to improvisation, and whose immediate inspiration was impatient of all restraint. Of Lope's poems on sacred subjects (*poemas á lo divino*) the best are the five meditations (*Soliloquios amorosos de un Alma á Dios*) which mark the outburst of religious fervour that accompanied his ordination. They are instinct with the passionate, personal, and intensely realistic feelings produced in the plastic southern nature by reflections on the great tragedy which was the beginning of Christianity. It is hard to recognise in the enraptured and mystical devotee the inventor of the duels and intrigues of the cloak and sword plays.

Of a very different character are the poems written in honour of Isidro, the rustic saint, who in Lope's lifetime became the recognised patron of "the very noble and loyal city of Madrid." Isidro was a peasant of the neighbourhood of what is now the Spanish capital; during the twelfth century he gained such a reputation for sanctity that it was reported that angels visited him, and carried on the field-work which he neglected in order the better to perform his religious duties. Until the year 1598 his reputation was a merely local one, but it was vastly increased when Felipe III. was cured of a dangerous fever by means of his relics which had been carefully preserved. It was on this occasion that Lope wrote his long poem, *San Isidro Labrador*, in which he relates the life and miracles of the holy man in a style that often approaches burlesque.   Twenty years afterwards, at the instance of the king whom he had healed, San Isidro was beatified, and two years later he was canonised.   Each of these events was made an occasion for rejoicing and display of every kind, and not the least important part of the ceremony was the *justa poética* (poetical tournament) over which Lope presided, and in which Guillén de Castro, Calderón, and other famous poets took part.   Lope entered thoroughly into the spirit of the proceedings ; his "universal jealousy" did not trouble him here, for he was placed by general consent far above all competition.   From a lofty tribunal he read out the successful compositions, and introduced a kind of buffoon who pronounced a running commentary on the events of the day in burlesque style that greatly delighted the populace.   The name, Tomé de Burguillos, assumed by this comic character was meant to veil, without obliterating, the personality of Lope himself, whose dignified position rendered it impossible for him to speak in person in so light a strain on so solemn an occasion.   The whole collection of poems delivered during the festivities was subsequently published, and those of Tomé de Burguillos were found to contain some of the best lighter verse of Lope de Vega.

A curious and unamiable feature in Lope's literary career is his fondness for "capping" Cervantes' work.   Cervantes published his *Novelas Ejemplares ;* Lope published short stories in the same style ; Cervantes' *Galatea* was followed by Lope's *Dorotea ;* Cervantes' *Viage del Parnaso* was imitated in Lope's *Laurel de Apolo*.   Of the two former works by Lope mention has already been made ; of the latter it is enough to say that its fulsome praise, shallow and pedantic criticism, and feeble plot, are unrelieved by the touches of humour that redeem from commonplace his rival's poetical review of contemporary authors.

The estimate of Lope's position as a poet involves the

whole question of the nature and function of poetry. Lope was a great poet according to the notions of his time, and within the limitations of his own peculiar views. He so exactly represented the highest poetical ideal of his century and of his country that all his works have a peculiarly "local" flavour which is absent from the great books that appeal to humanity at all times. He lived in an artificial age, and his genius was not sufficiently strong to rid itself of its influence. His position is possibly best expressed by saying that he was not absolutely a great poet, but "a great Spanish poet of the seventeenth century."

CHAPTER XV

DON FRANCISCO DE QUEVEDO Y VILLEGAS, who played with equal facility and success the parts of court wit and moralist, statesman and novelist, erotic poet and writer of religious treatises, is one of the most distinctive and extraordinary figures in the history of Spanish literature.

Like many of the most celebrated Spaniards, Quevedo was descended from an old Asturian family. His father was secretary to María de Austria, the daughter of the Emperor Charles V., and his mother was lady of honour in the household of the Infanta Isabel. Born in 1580, he was sent early to the University of Alcalá, where he gained a high reputation as a scholar, graduating in civil and canon law and in theology, besides reading deeply in Latin, Greek, Hebrew, French, and Italian ; he is also supposed to have studied medicine. His studies at Alcalá formed, however, only one side of his university life ; he mixed freely in the loose Bohemian society of the place ; for though in later life he became a strict moralist, in youth and even in middle age he was by no means severe towards himself, and his erotic poems are remarkable for their shameless indecency, even in an age not too nice in such matters. A ringleader among the turbulent students in their coarse sports and still coarser pleasures, he was early noted for personal valour, and in spite of his somewhat uncouth figure and short sight was a most skilful fencer, as more than one of his antagonists found out to their cost. The description he gives of his personal appearance tallies very closely with the portraits of him still extant. " My hair," he says, "is black, my head large, my forehead broad and white with some old scars that bear witness to my courage, the brows arched and reddish in colour, eyes well opened, bold glance, large and strongly marked nose, well grown beard, full lips, strong teeth and firm ever ready to bite, long neck, broad and sloping shoulders, thin but well-formed arms, hands broad enough to please a courtier, deep chest, slim waist, one leg lame and deformed." Elsewhere he thus whimsically admits the correctness of an enemy's brutally plain statement of his physical defects—" He says that I am lame and cannot see : I should lie from head to foot if I denied it : my eyes and gait would contradict me." By reason of his short-sightedness he habitually wore eye-glasses, called after him " *quevedos.*"

On leaving Alcalá, Quevedo betook himself to the court at Valladolid, where he at once distinguished himself among the wits and poetasters of the day by a number of coarse but brilliant short poems. He also wrote at this period of his life a " picaresque" story remarkable for its freedom from the moral-ising tendency by which such works are generally rendered unreadable. *El gran Tacaño* (The great Rogue), as it is called, consists of a series of roughly drawn but animated scenes from that low student and Bohemian life which he knew so well and which always fascinated him. But Quevedo had not abandoned graver studies, though it is with some surprise that we find him at the age of twenty-four in correspondence with Justus Lipsius, one of the most celebrated scholars of the day, on the subject of his book *de Vestâ*. This correspondence is in Latin and gives a high idea of Quevedo's attainments. Lipsius addresses him in the most flattering terms, and Quevedo com-municates to his friend his intention of publishing a defence of

Homer against the injurious treatment to which he had been subjected by Scaliger.

In 1606 the court returned from Valladolid to Madrid, and with it Quevedo, overjoyed like the rest of the courtiers at the change, and bidding adieu to the former city in the couplet—

> [1] Para salirse de tí
> Tienes agradables puertas.

The next seven years passed at Madrid firmly established Quevedo's reputation. Besides a translation of Anacreon, dedicated to his future patron Don Pedro Girón, Duke of Osuna, he published verse translations of Epictetus and Phocylides, and commenced the series of *Visions* (*Sueños*) which have always been among the most popular of his writings. These *Visions*, seven in number, are short satires on the vices and follies of the age, and on certain professions; they probably contain caricatures of real personages. Though many of the allusions are either obscure or have lost their point, the *Sueños* are still amusing. They illustrate their author's mordant wit and grasp of human character, and proclaim his withering contempt for the hypocritical and artificial life of the capital. Always honest and blunt, often intentionally brutal, Quevedo wields the lash with no sparing hand. His satires are simple in plan, and roughly executed. Before their publication Quevedo had created an amusing character in his *Knight of the Grapple* (the man to whom any excuse or any humiliation is acceptable, provided he be not obliged to loosen his purse-strings), but this time it is classes of society and particular professions rather than individual vices that he sets up for the butt of his keenly-pointed shafts. The fiction of the dream makes it easy to bring forward types, but this method, long popular in Spain, had seldom been put to such good use.[2] We choose for short analysis one of the best known,

---

[1] "Thy gates are a joy to those—who pass through them as they quit thee."

[2] The most famous specimen of this class of satire is *Le Diable Boiteux* by Le Sage, who took the idea from Luís Velez de Guevara's *Diablo Cojuelo*, published in 1641.

the *Alguacil endemoniado* (The Bailiff Possessed). The author, speaking in the first person, relates how he happened to go into the church of St. Peter to seek the Licenciado Calabrés, a priest of questionable character. He finds his friend engaged in an attempt to drive out a devil from an *alguacil* or bailiff. On being called upon to justify his conduct with regard to the unfortunate demoniac, the devil replies that his victim is not a man but a bailiff (a very different creature), and complains that he is there against his will, for it is not he who has taken possession of the bailiff, but rather the bailiff who, after the manner of his kind, has taken possession of him. The evil spirit moreover shows that he is not so utterly bad as the bailiff, in that it was through attempting to gain the dominion of Heaven that he fell, whereas his victim owes his present condition to the lowest of motives. The licentiate proceeds to sprinkle holy water, and the demoniac forthwith attempts to escape ; whereupon the devil protests that it is not he who fears the water because it is holy, but the bailiff who fears it because it is water, and begs the exorcist to release him from his distasteful quarters. The author now explains to the devil that he is an old friend, and asks for information as to the organisation and administration of the lower regions. This the evil one gives freely, treating of the various orders of the lost, and beginning by the poets, who, as he explains, abound to such a degree that their accommodation has had to be increased, and their influence in hell has become almost as important as that of the notaries. Some are tormented by hearing the verses of their rivals read, others are obliged to correct them : some wander disconsolate round hell in search of a rhyme. The dramatists, however, are in the worst case on account of the many crimes which they have caused to be committed, and the many noble characters that they have spoiled. Between blind men and lovers, madmen and astrologers, murderers and doctors, no distinction is drawn by the devils into whose hands they all eventually fall. The author inquires anxiously after lovers, for he has a personal interest in their fate. The spirit replies that the term lovers includes the whole of the lost, for all love themselves, some love their money, and some their works. Lovers, in the general acceptation of the word, are rare below, for the treatment they receive at the hands of their mistresses is such as generally to produce repentance before the end. The devils, it appears, are much offended at the horned and hoofed representations of themselves that pass current in the upper world, and also at the way in which the generic name is lightly used as a term of abuse for low personages, and in the phrase "the devil take it." Kings form a rich prey down below, for they often bring with them their favourites and the whole of their court. Merchants are there by thousands, and are so bold as to attempt to create a monopoly for keeping up the fires, and to offer to undertake the torturing at a fixed rate. Judges are the devil's pheasants and afford a most profitable crop, for each brings with him a host of notaries, bailiffs, and scribes. Women come down in such numbers that their enforced entertainers are weary of them, and hell would be a pleasanter place had it no female inhabitant. The ugly ones are the most numerous, for the pretty ones repent. When asked if the poor are to be found in hell, the devil does not even recognise the name. After having it explained to him, he states that men are damned for their part in the world, and as the poor have no part in the world and are neither flattered nor envied during life, they never come to the lower regions after death. The demon brings his revelations to a close by stating that, if he has told secrets that might produce contrition in the heart of a stone, it is only in order that his hearers may not be able to say that they have had no warning. He is thereupon silenced by the exorcist.

Quevedo's burlesque treatment of this and other serious subjects incurred, as was to be expected, the displeasure of the Inquisition. In later life he struck out or altered all such passages of the *Sueños* as could be considered objectionable in their manner of treating subjects appertaining to religion; simple indecency he did not consider it necessary to alter.

On Holy Thursday, 1611, Quevedo saw a lady grievously insulted in the church of San Martín at Madrid. He reproved her aggressor, and a duel took place. Quevedo slew his adversary, and was obliged to seek safety in Sicily, where his patron, the Duke of Osuna, was now viceroy. Shortly afterwards he returned to Spain, and resided at the village of La Torre de Juan Abad, a manor which he had inherited from his mother. In his writings at this time he praises a country life, and indulges in much severe moralising. We need not doubt his sincerity, but the serious mood was due merely to his surroundings, and did not last long. In 1613 he joined Osuna in Sicily, and without occupying any definite official position became the viceroy's confidant and agent in his public administration, and also, it is whispered, in the love intrigues for which he was celebrated. Quevedo was subsequently entrusted with the important charge of furthering Osuna's interests at court by means of bribes. This sort of duty, which gave him an insight into the weak side of human nature, he thoroughly enjoyed, and it was probably thanks to Quevedo that his patron was promoted in 1615 to the viceroyalty of Naples. How far Quevedo was cognisant of Osuna's bold schemes of personal ambition we shall never know; it is, however, certain that he nearly lost his life in the rash attempt to seize Venice in 1618, and that shortly afterwards Osuna dismissed him from his service on account of the many enmities he had provoked by his somewhat brutal treatment of a matter so delicate as bribery. Quevedo now again withdrew to his estate, and employed his leisure in writing a *Life of Saint Thomas of Villanueva*, as well as some of the most free-spoken of his satirical verses.

When, in 1620, Osuna returned to Spain in disgrace, he became reconciled to his former ally. This reconciliation provoked the suspicions of the reigning favourite, and Quevedo was exiled from the court. In his retirement he finished his ambitious work on statecraft and morals, *The Politics of God and the Government of Christ*, wherein, with much pedantic learning, he developed a scheme of government founded on the precepts of the Bible. So good an opportunity for gratifying a grudge was not to be lost, and Quevedo filled his pages with what might reasonably be considered as reflections of the severest kind on the existing administration. Only a complete change in the position of affairs could now restore his shattered fortunes. The death of Felipe III. and the accession of Felipe IV. brought this change, and on hearing the welcome news Quevedo remained in the country only long enough to write an extravagant dedication to the new favourite, the Count-Duke of Olivares. He then hurried to Madrid like the rest to worship the rising sun. The large body of writings in which he refers to the events of this time show the greatest diplomatic skill in their evident attempt to propitiate the powers without utter loss of self-respect and betrayal of former obligations. But the writer was known as a dangerous man, and after a few months he was again exiled from Madrid. Quevedo did not lose heart; the *Sueño de la Muerte*, composed as a peace-offering, is a witty and powerful panegyric, in the form of a fiction, on the new order of things. It is quite possible that in his actions and in the expressions of his opinions at this time, Quevedo may have been more than half sincere; he was not the only one to be deceived by the promises of the brilliant young Count-Duke. The flattery of such a man was irresistible; in 1623 Quevedo was again in favour, and employed his poetical talents in relating the festivities that celebrated the visit paid to the Spanish court by the Prince of Wales (afterwards Charles I.), between whom and a sister of Felipe IV. a marriage had been negotiated. The versatile nature of Quevedo had found its proper element in the court, and he discusses with equal facility grave questions such as the disadvantages of public executions, or light ones, such as the amusements of the society of which he was the most noted wit.

Quevedo played an important part in a curious controversy that agitated the whole of Spain about the year 1627. From time immemorial Santiago (St. James) had been patron of the country. In 1627 the Pope, urged by certain zealots, chiefly of the Carmelite order, put forth a bull promoting the lately canonised Santa Teresa to be joint patron with Santiago of Spain. The amount of discussion and angry feeling produced by the change appears almost incredible at the present day. Quevedo became the champion of St. James, and published several pamphlets. Thanks, in part at least, to his efforts, the obnoxious bull was cancelled in 1630, and the ancient patron was restored to his full honours. The king and Olivares had espoused the cause of Santa Teresa, and Quevedo's second banishment, which took place about this time, is attributed by contemporaries to the energetic part he took in the heated controversy. His return to favour was the signal for a combined attack on the part of his enemies, among the most virulent of whom was Luís Narvaez, a fencing-master, and author of a treatise on the art of fencing. This man is said to have conceived a grudge against Quevedo through having once been worsted by him in an assault-at-arms. It is characteristic of the manners of the time that he took vengeance by delating his enemy and his works to the Inquisition, but Quevedo saved himself by bringing out in 1629 the corrected edition of his early works. In the same year he rendered an important service to the literature of his country by publishing the works of Luís de León. · In the controversy between the modern euphuists and the writers of the old Spanish school, Quevedo sided strongly with the latter, though his own works are by no means specimens of classic simplicity. In 1631 he published a collection of poems in very pure and simple style by the Bachiller de la Torre (see p. 122).

Quevedo was now growing old, and his thoughts turned to religious subjects. He set to work to reform his life, and he, the scoffer at marriage and the dread of husbands, took to himself a wife, chosen by the Countess of Olivares. He gives a very uninviting description of himself at the age at which he became a bridegroom, but he is very particular in the instructions which he gave to his lady adviser as to the kind of wife he would prefer. Finally their choice fell upon a lady of good family and some wealth. The marriage was apparently not happy, for the couple soon separated. Age had not sweetened Quevedo's temper, and again his enemies closed in upon him. But the old man defended himself vigorously ; his position as secretary to the king gave him a certain advantage over them, and for a time he beat them back. Even amid the bustle of the court he found time for serious studies. Disappointed in the *régime* to which he had looked for so many good results, he prepared a second part of his work, entitled *The Politics of God*, speaking out boldly what he well knew to be the truth. He seems to have been aware that he stood on the brink of a precipice, and with the courage of despair he openly rebuked the king and his favourite in language the more offensive because of its unwonted sobriety and the keen wit which clenched its arguments. The year 1639 saw his final fall. The reason of it is shrouded in a considerable amount of mystery. The king on seating himself one day at table found on his plate a memorial setting forth in the strongest terms the miserable condition of the country, and urging him to amend his ways, rouse himself, and be no longer a puppet in the hands of his favourite. Quevedo was suspected, rightly or wrongly, of being the author of the memorial ; he was dragged half-naked from his house, and was imprisoned for nearly four years at León. At first he bore up and wrote boldly in his defence, but at length his spirit was broken, and he addressed humble petitions for mercy to the favourite. His prayers and protestations were disregarded. The treatment he received during his captivity seems to have been brutal in the extreme. Convinced at length that he had nothing to hope for, he betook himself for consolation to religion and the philosophy of the Stoics, of which he had always been an earnest student. He was not, however, fated to end his days in prison, but was finally set free in 1643, probably because, broken in health and spirit, he was rightly considered harmless. He retired at once into the country, where he set in order his papers, and nursed his feeble body until 1645, when he died as a good Catholic.

Of the huge mass of writings left by Quevedo the greater part has lost its interest. Even his moral and political writings are so deeply tinged by the controversies of his day that they are not of great permanent value. His works throughout are defaced by a perverse leaning to all that is disgusting and obscene. In this, as in other respects, he may be aptly compared to Dean Swift. His sudden transitions from a semi-ascetic to a loose life, and back again, ought not to throw doubt upon the sincerity with which he handles grave questions. His conduct was generally brave and disinterested, but he possessed a very versatile character, and was deeply influenced by his surroundings. He served his patrons faithfully, and had at heart the good of his country. If he sometimes abandoned lost causes and fallen individuals, he did so less rapidly and less shamelessly than most of the men of his day. In the mastery of his native language he is probably unrivalled, but this, like other of his talents, he did not turn to the best possible use. He showed his appreciation of pure style and of the best models by publishing the works of Luís de León and of the Bachiller de la Torre, but his own writings are deeply tinged with a kind of bad taste widely different from that of the *culto* school, which he heartily despised. His fondness for double meanings, for strong antitheses, for playing upon words, and for condensing a whole train of thought into an epigram, paradox, or conceit, make him the best Spanish example of the school called *conceptistas*. These peculiarities, together with the extraordinary richness of a vocabulary to which he admitted many of the slang words and expressions of the low life of his time, render a great part of his writings unintelligible to those who have not made them a special study. For the proper understanding of many of them a special vocabulary and commentary would be required, the composition of which would tax the powers even of those best versed in the literature and inner history of his time. This is the more remarkable because he always abhorred classical pedantry, and in one of his early burlesque compositions (*Origen y Definiciones de la Necedad*) he pronounces himself thus: "We declare and at once admit as fools of four quarterings all who by their speech and example attempt to introduce new fashions of talking and to change the vocabulary of their age . . . and if any such . . . make use of Latin words or meanings . . . he shall take rank above his brethren in folly."

Half scholar, half adventurer in style as in life, Quevedo attempted almost every branch of literature, and in almost all he attained some degree of success; but his wide interests and restless character, together with the fatal facility of writing so common in his time, combined to prevent him from attaining to quite the first rank in any one department. He is, in his faults and in his virtues, characteristically Spanish, and no one who wishes to understand the Spaniards of his time can afford to neglect Quevedo.

CHAPTER XVI

CALDERÓN

CERVANTES was a world-wide genius; Lope de Vega was a strictly local one, with all the limitations of his time and country; Calderón stands midway between them. He is the Christian poet of an age that has begun to reason and inquire, and, conscious of its own decadence, looks back for its models to the virtues of a glorious past, defending old causes with modern arguments.

Pedro Calderón de la Barca was born in Madrid in the year 1600. His family, like that of Lope, belonged to the old Castilian nobility, and sprang from the valley of Carriedo, where stood its ancestral home. From the first fortune seemed to smile on Calderón. His father held a position of importance as secretary to the finance department. He himself had the advantage of the best education that his age could afford at the University of Salamanca. Here he shone in the different branches of the scholastic and formal learning which he somewhat ostentatiously parades in many of his plays. He grew up handsome in person, grave and majestic in deportment; his life was pure and blameless, and his sweet and noble character endeared him to those around him. When thirty-five years old, his reputation as a dramatist was already so well established that he was made court poet, succeeding Lope in the office. The king conferred on him the mantle of the noble order of Santiago, a dignity singularly well adapted to his Christian, chivalrous, and courtly disposition.   During the preceding ten years he had served as a soldier in Flanders, and again at the time of the rebellion in Catalonia he abandoned the court and took part in its suppression.   Immediately afterwards he abandoned the profession of arms and gave himself up entirely to the dramatic art.   At the age of fifty-one he took orders, and afterwards became chaplain of honour to the king and familiar of the Inquisition.   Outliving his patron, Felipe IV., he died in 1681 with faculties and reputation unimpaired.   For forty years he had been the darling of the court and of the populace.   His remains were borne by the Congregation of Priests, natives of Madrid, to be buried in the city which had been the scene of his triumphs.   Only a few months before his death he had written a play (*Hado y Divisa*) which shows no sign of failing powers, and he left unfinished an *auto sacramental* intended for representation at the feast of Corpus Christi.

The published works of Calderón consist of about one hundred and twenty plays and eighty *autos*, besides some light interludes, one-act farces, and occasional verses.   Of all his writings the *autos* are those that he most highly valued.   He it was who improved and stereotyped this form and became its greatest exponent.   A description and analysis of one of these pieces is necessary in order to understand this important and characteristic department of the drama, which remained popular until its suppression in 1765.

From very early times the stage was pressed into the service of the Church.   The great religious festivals, Easter and Corpus Christi, were marked by theatrical representations of the events which the day recalled.   Traces of the old nativity plays are to be found in the *nacimientos* or Christmas puppet-shows still made in almost every old-fashioned Spanish family for the delight of the children, and occupying much the same traditional position as the Teutonic Christmas-tree. A *nacimiento* is a kind of model of the scene at Bethlehem, more or less exact according to the education and means of those for whom it is intended. The grouping of the puppets, the cardboard mountains, and the trees, generally represented by sprigs of evergreen, often produce a very pretty effect, to which the conventional shepherds and Magi contribute.[1] The name *auto* was applied by the earliest Spanish dramatists to all classes of dramatic composition. In Calderón's time its use had become restricted to sacred plays, the subjects of which had gradually been reduced to one—the mystery of the Sacrament, dramatically represented on the day of Corpus Christi. The order of proceeding on such occasions was as follows :—In the morning the Host was paraded round the principal streets of the town in much the same manner as is still customary in Roman Catholic countries, but with a grotesque accompaniment of *gigantones* and *tarascas*, huge pasteboard monsters of hideous aspect whose origin and signification is lost in obscurity. The accompanying procession included all the principal personages of the place, and the religious brotherhoods (*confradías*) which play so large a part in Spanish life, with their banners and bands of music. The streets through which the procession passed were thronged with the kneeling populace. At the head of the column gambolled the selected dancers, who in no irreverent spirit took a prominent part in the solemnity. In the afternoon the procession set forth again, but this time without the Sacrament, which had in the meantime been carried back with all ceremony into the church from which it started. Huge cars bore the actors, who at this time of the year were forbidden to represent secular plays. The cars were drawn up before some public building or the house of some great personage, generally in the principal square or

---

[1] A pretty description of a *nacimiento* is to be found in Fernán Caballero's *Noche de Navidad*.

plaza of the town. Placed side by side under the open sky they formed a rough stage, and the *auto* began. The spectators either stood in the open space around the cars, or if fortunately placed, looked on from the windows or balconies of the neighbouring houses. Of the turmoil and fatigue of such a day a good description is put by Calderón into the mouth of one of his *graciosos* or buffoons,[1] who, by the way, is supposed to be an inhabitant of Antioch during the early years of Christianity !

The *autos* must be distinguished from the *comedias de santos*, religious plays bearing on the lives of saints or Biblical characters, but without special reference to the Sacrament. In the *autos* proper the personages are principally allegorical. A list made by a Spanish author includes, besides many others, the synagogue, paganism, the Church, grace, sin, pleasure, grief, beauty, love, the law, religious rite, the vices and virtues, the senses and faculties, trees and flowers, air, fire, and water, the seasons and months of the year, flattery and discretion, the sciences and professions. All these were pressed into the service, and all played their parts in honour of the sacred mystery.

The plots of the *autos* are simple in the extreme. An idea of their construction may be formed from the following analysis of *The Cure and the Disease*, chosen at random among Calderón's *autos*. Lucifer appears invoking Sin and Shade to come forth from the abyss and admire the marvels of the Creation. Shade stops short on the borders of Light and beholds the four spheres—that of Fire, the abode of the stars ; that of Air, where the birds fly ; that of Water, the haunt of the fishes ; and, finally, the Earth. All these sing hymns in praise of Humanity, inviting one another to do it service and honour. Humanity comes forth with much pomp and receives gifts from the Elements. Pride causes the downfall of Humanity, and thinking to become equal to God, it eats the

---

[1] *Mágico Prodigioso.* Jor. i.

fruit in which Sin has hidden its poison. The Elements, formerly so friendly to Humanity, become its enemies, until at last it is healed of its morbid sickness by the Pilgrim who reveals to it the secret of the sacramental food, the antidote against the poison of Sin.

In many of the *autos* heathen mythology is oddly mixed up with Christian doctrine ; good taste is often entirely lost sight of, and the result is grotesque and unpleasing in the extreme. But there can be no doubt of the truly religious spirit in which the performances were carried out and received, and many of the plays themselves, and the *loas* or commendatory introduc tions which preceded them, contain magnificent passages of verse.

In Calderón's opinion these dramatised theological discus-sions were the only part of his work worth preserving, but it was not owing to them that his reputation was destined to live. During the last century certain German critics called the atten-tion of the world to his so-called philosophical dramas, and notably to *La Vida es Sueño* (Life is a Dream) and *El Mágico Prodigioso* (The Marvellous Magician). These two plays are intended severally to illustrate a central idea or theory. The former inculcates the unreality of outward impressions, and dis-cusses the question whether these, as received in our waking state, are in any way nearer to " things in themselves " than are the fantastic imaginations of dreams. The latter upholds the doctrine of freedom of the will, and maintains the logical necessity of God as a First Cause. Philosophy and meta-physics require for their appreciation on the stage audiences brought up on *autos sacramentales*. Many passages of sublime and harmonious verse which are to be found both in these and in other dramas by Calderón must have lost half their effect when spoken in the course of a play, the action of which they gener-ally in no degree furthered. The long scholastic arguments carried on by the characters must have been intolerably wearisome even in Salamanca, their proper home. The faults of Calderón are the faults of his time and of the Spanish stage generally, namely, *culteranismo*, exaggerated sentiment, deficient study of character, and artificial complication of detail combined with an ill-considered general scheme. The greater part of his work, it must be remembered, was not meant for publication. Had he been able thoroughly to carry out his great conceptions, he would have been unequalled in one department of his art. His ideas are profound but vague, and all his work lacks a clear-cut outline to show off its minute carving ; he cannot profitably be-compared with Shakespeare or Goethe, or with the great Greek tragedians, on account of the radical differences which separate his conception of subject and treatment from that of the great masters. In his philosophical dramas he avoids the complication of plot (*enredos*) which forms so marked a feature of the Spanish theatre. The plan of *La Vida es Sueño* is, in fact, extremely simple. Basilio, king of Poland, by shutting up his son Segismundo in a solitary tower, and bringing him up like a wild animal, attempts to evade the evil which, as his astrological studies have taught him, he is destined to suffer at his hands. Relenting in his purpose when Segismundo is already grown up, he determines to allow him an opportunity of giving proof of his disposition. For this purpose Segismundo is rendered unconscious by means of drugs and is conveyed to the palace. On waking up and finding himself the central point of the pomp and splendour of a court, he immediately, by his haughtiness and unbridled passion, gives proof of the brutality which, owing to an entire lack of moral training or restraint, easily defeats the fine instincts of his truly noble nature. Basilio now considers that he has done all that justice demands. By his orders Segismundo is again rendered unconscious and conveyed back to his prison. On his second awakening amid the familiar surroundings, his guardian tries to persuade him that the experiences of the previous day were merely the hallucinations of a dream. Segismundo, comparing the vividness of his present impressions with those that remain stamped on his memory, concludes that the whole of life is but a dream, and that the impressions of our waking state are not more real than those of sleep. His situation gives rise to the following soliloquy :—

> [1] *Clotaldo.* . . . aun en sueños
> No se pierde el hacer bien.
> *Segismundo.* Es verdad ; pues reprimamos
> Esta fiera condición,
> Esta furia, esta ambición,
> Por si alguna vez soñamos :
> Y sí haremos, pues estamos
> En mundo tan singular,
> Que el vivir sólo es soñar ;
> Y la experiencia me enseña
> Que el hombre que vive sueña
> Lo que es, hasta dispertar.
> Sueña el rey que es rey, y vive
> Con este engaño mandando,
> Disponiendo y gobernando ;
> Y este aplauso que recibe
> Prestado, en el viento escribe,
> Y en cenizas le convierte
> La muerte (¡ desdicha fuerte !) :
> ¿ Qué hay quien intente reinar,
> Viendo que ha de dispertar
> En el sueño de la muerte ?
> Sueña el rico en su riqueza
> Que más cuidados le ofrece ;

---

[1] " *Clotaldo.* Even in dreams—good deeds are not in vain.
Segismundo. It is true ; so then let me restrain—this fierce temper of mine —and this unbridled arrogance—lest at any time I dream :—and dream I shall, for we dwell—in a world so strange—that living is but dreaming :—my own fate teaches me—that all men living dream—their lot, until they awake.—The king dreams of his royalty, and lives—thus deceived, commanding,—ordaining and governing :—the adulation he receives—is his only for a time ; he writes it on the wind,—and straightway is reduced to ashes—by death, the king of ills :—'Tis strange that men should long to reign,—seeing that awakening will come—in the dream of death ?—The rich man dreams of riches—which but

Sueña el pobre que padece
Su miseria y su pobreza ;
Sueña el que á medrar empieza,
Sueña el que afana y pretende.
Sueña el que agravia y ofende,
Y en el mundo, en conclusión
Todos sueñan lo que son
Aunque ninguno lo entiende.
Yo sueño que estoy aquí
Destas prisiones cargado.
Y soñé que en otro estado
Mas lisonjero me vi.
¿ Qué es la vida ?   Una frenesí ;
¿ Qué es la vida ?   Una illusión,
Una sombra, una ficción,
Y el mayor bien es pequeño ;
Que toda la vida es sueño.
Y los sueños sueño son.

Yet his belief in the eternal laws of right and wrong is not shaken, for even in dreams, he says, the distinction between good and bad exists.   He determines for the future to restrain his passionate outbursts.   In this mood he is found by the leaders of a revolution, who, having discovered that a legitimate heir exists, are come to deliver him from prison, and to place him on the throne.   Ambitious longings are at once awakened in Segismundo's breast, but he is now conscious that they, like the rest, are but dreams.   He leads his party to battle against his father, and by his victory fulfils the gloomy prognostications of the astrologer.   No obstacle now stands in the way of his passion for revenge, but his moral consciousness is aroused, and he acts with moderation and even generosity.

In the development of Segismundo's character, so suddenly

---

increase his cares;—the poor man dreams of suffering,—of misery and poverty;—one dreams that fortune smiles on him ;—another, that he fights and struggles,—or that his malice wins success :—the world, in short, is all made up—of dreamers dreaming each his lot,—but no man knows that it is so.—I dream that I am here—and loaded with these chains :—I dreamed once that a different fortune—and more flattering was mine.—What is life? Delirium.—What is life? An illusion,—a shadow and a fiction,—and the greatest good is but small,—for all life is a dream,—and dreams are but a dream."

brought about, many links are missing, but Calderón, as we have said, is a poet of fine passages rather than of consistent merit. For the success of his plays he depends on interesting situations or opposing motives, and not on a subtle analysis of character. The dialogue of his plays is of the stiff and artificial type prevalent at the Spanish court, and the poet realises his genius only when he can shake off the dramatist, launching out into inspired monologues or tirades which fortunately lose nothing of their beauty by separation from their commonplace context.

In *La Vida es Sueño* the sublime and grotesque are brought very close together, according to the author's wont, by the continual interference of the *gracioso* or buffoon. This character is not Calderón's own creation. In the drama *de capa y espada* of other authors his poor witticisms abound, but Calderón makes a peculiar use of him, and in his hands the type becomes invariable. The *gracioso* is the foil to the principal character, and is almost always his servant. After the fashion of the Greek Chorus, he furnishes a running commentary on his master's actions, and when, as often happens, the exaggerated sentiment of the love intrigue is taking too lofty a flight, his uncouth pleasantries bring it somewhat suddenly to earth again. The love affairs of the *gracioso* and ladies'-maid form a parody on the main plot, a caricature so harsh, and placed in such close juxtaposition to that which it is meant to relieve, that the effect is often painful in the extreme.

Beside the *gracioso*, Calderón has made peculiarly his own the passion of jealousy (*celos*) of a peculiar kind. This jealousy is connected rather with the point of honour than with love. The slightest shade of offence against the husband's honour calls for the most sanguinary vengeance, not in order to satisfy the natural instinct of reprisal, but in order that the husband's character for nicety as to the point of honour may not be degraded in his own eyes, or in those of the world. This

characteristic undoubtedly corresponds to a strongly marked
feature in the national character.   Spaniards are peculiarly
inclined to forgive any crime that can plead jealousy as its
motive, but Calderón asks too much of us when he tries to
enlist our sympathies in favour of husbands who, for the sake
of appearances, deliberately, and in cold blood, murder the
wives of whose innocence they are assured.[1]

In this, as in other respects, it is to be noticed that many of
Calderón's characters, though they bear familiar-sounding names,
are really allegories.   The habit of writing *autos* has reacted upon
the author's method in other departments.   Of the complexity
of the motives that generally determine action he has but little
notion ; he adopts and exaggerates the ideas of religion, morality,
honour, and loyalty as they existed in his time, or had existed
during the earlier period which Spaniards were already learning
to regard as their Golden Age, and places them unmixed upon
the stage.   It follows, therefore, that in his characters there is
singularly little variety, his heroes are generally passionate and
brave, carrying out to the full the narrow code of honour which,
in courtly circles, had supplanted the moral law.   Even when
committing crimes of a very deep dye they remain gentlemen
at heart, that is to say, Spanish gentlemen of the sixteenth or
seventeenth centuries ; and as such they act and speak, in
spite of the incongruous environment of age and country to
which the caprice of their creator occasionally transplants
them.   His women are weak and passionate, mere puppets,
so colourless that scarcely a feature distinguishes the Rosauras
and Estrellas from the Isabels and Leonors.   Yet they are
seldom bad, and never abject ; they, like the men, probably
represent the types among which Calderón moved during
his residence at the court.

Calderón created one fine and simple character in his
Alcalde de Zalamea.   The play and the hero from which it

[1] Cf. the plot of *El Médico de su Honrd.*

takes its name have ever remained popular in Spain, for in it the poet ceased to appeal to a select circle, and held up before his countrymen at large what he and they conceived to be the national virtues personified—sturdy independence, unflinching bravery, recklessness of consequences when the affections are involved, a high sense of personal and family honour, hospitality, and loyalty.

Judged by modern standards, most of Calderón's secular plays will be found either wanting in moral purposes, or, more frequently, decidedly immoral. It is hard to find a villain among his characters; even the devil generally acts with the utmost propriety, and enlists our sympathies by his artless nature, which frequently allows him to be defrauded of his just dues. But hideous crimes, murders, betrayals of trust, and breaches of hospitality abound, nor do they seem to produce much regret in their perpetrators, or to incur the reprobation of the other characters. This is undoubtedly, in part at least, an inherent defect of Calderón's method; he depended upon situations for effect, and the situations had to be strong ones in order to arouse the interest of his hearers.

Behind the code of honour, and supplementing it as a rule of life, stands the teaching of the Church, the doctrines of which Calderón sometimes pushes to such extremes as to wellnigh reduce them to absurdity. An example of this is the *Devoción de la Cruz*, in which the hero, after leading an utterly depraved life and committing a series of most hideous crimes, is finally found worthy of resuscitation and salvation, simply because throughout his career he has always preserved a superstitious reverence for the sacred symbol. It is easy to imagine the effect of such teaching as this among a people which, though not bloodthirsty, has always been somewhat more reckless of life than its neighbours. In spite of these obvious blemishes, Calderón will ever remain a great Christian, or rather, a great Catholic poet; he has a wide sense of the beauty and harmony of the universe, and a perfect belief in the wisdom and justice of God and of His representative on earth, the Church. He must not be blamed if his love for nature is somewhat artificial, if he occasionally speaks as though flowers and birds had been created for the purpose of providing him with the rich imagery in which he excels, nor for the hollow sentiment and hair-splitting sophistry which he puts into the mouths of his characters even at the most thrilling moments. He did not create the Spanish drama, he merely followed the lines that had been already laid down. He attempted by exaggerating the type to give freshness to stock characters, and these he places in situations that are unparalleled in the experience of everyday life. By so doing he created a world such as never existed in any time or country, and, departing from truth and nature, he hastened a decadence the signs of which were everywhere apparent. Calderón is the greatest Spanish dramatist because he is the greatest poet who adopted the dramatic form, but he does not, like Shakespeare, stand alone among his contemporaries. Lope de Vega, Tirso de Molina, and Guillén de Castro knew better than he the requirements of the stage, but none of them possessed his versatility, imagination, and poetic sense of harmony.

In spite of the great number of his works, and the short-lived purpose for which they were intended, Calderón seldom wrote carelessly, and never slovenly. In order to save himself trouble, he frequently introduces passages of which he has before made use in a slightly different form. But it is hard to believe that some of his plays, with their beautiful lyrics, sonnets, and highly complicated metaphors, were meant to be heard but few times, and even then amid the hurry and bustle of the stage. To us they seem adapted rather for reading than for acting. The elaboration and perfection of many passages will repay the closest attention, and in fact require it for their proper understanding. A noticeable feature of most of Calderón's finest passages is their defiance of all attempts at translation. To this peculiarity two causes contribute. Many words, expressions, and metaphors, that in Spanish sound quite natural, become inflated, bombastic, and absurd when rendered literally into other languages. Calderón frequently plays on the various shades of meaning of words and expressions, so that the translator is obliged either to give a grotesque literal rendering, or to alter the passage and substitute expressions of his own. Calderón was a perfect master of one of the richest languages in the world, and he frequently makes use of this power in working out long passages of double meaning, the exact bearing of which, on account of the delicacy of their structure, it is almost impossible to render satisfactorily. Certain English translators who have attempted the task have produced exquisite verse, but the fruit of their labours must be regarded rather as poetry inspired by the reading of the Spanish original, than as a translation.

In humour Calderón is distinctly lacking. None of his plays are essentially comic, but in almost all the *gracioso* is introduced. The *gracioso* is, as has been stated above, a stock character, exhibiting even less variety than the more dignified personages to whom he acts as a foil. He is invariably a conceited, talkative, meddlesome coward; his witticisms are generally of the feeblest kind, and if he occasionally succeeds in raising a smile, it is generally because of the strange situations into which his many failings bring him.

CHAPTER XVII

OTHER DRAMATISTS OF THE GOLDEN AGE

Observations on the Spanish Theatre and the Causes of its Decay

LOPE DE VEGA and Calderón are deservedly the two most widely - known, as well as the two most representative and typical dramatists of their country, but several others are entitled to rank very near to them. If authors are to be judged by single works, neither Lope nor even Calderón is the greatest Spanish playwright. No other country and no other age has produced so large a quantity of plays as Spain in the latter half of the sixteenth and the early half of the seventeenth century. Their very numbers and their uniform standard of excellence have obscured the fame of individual pieces ; the national taste too has changed and been corrupted, and when one of the great classical dramas is revived, the limited degree of enthusiasm that it arouses is generally half factitious. During the last hundred and fifty years the Spanish stage has been occupied chiefly by translations, or adaptations, of the lighter kind of French plays : the national tradition is dead, and modern Spanish dramatists look beyond the Pyrenees for their models ; even among scholars few can boast an adequate knowledge of the huge mass of obsolete literature that constitutes the Spanish drama. Space will not allow more than a brief mention of the most famous works of some few of the play-writers of the Golden Age who are distinguished from the general body by special qualities or notable individual works.

Guillén de Castro, a Valencian of noble family, was a contemporary and friend of Lope de Vega. Born in 1567, he gave early proof of his literary talents, and became a member of the local academy or poetasters' club, known as the *Nocturnos*, in which were enrolled some of the best writers of his time. The young De Castro did not at first look to literature for a living; he joined the army, and became a captain of cavalry. His literary fame, unusual in one of so high a position, soon brought him into notice; he left the army, and, for a time, enjoyed the protection of some of the great men of the age. The Conde de Benavente, viceroy of Naples, conferred upon him an important appointment in the government of that kingdom, and when he returned to Spain he received a pension, first from the Duke of Osuna, and afterwards from the Count-Duke of Olivares. His literary reputation stood very high; Cervantes mentions the great popularity of his dramas, and Lope made use of Guillén de Castro's help in organising the festivities that celebrated the canonisation of San Isidro in 1620. In spite of the many advantages which birth and position put within his grasp, he died miserably in dire poverty at the age of sixty-six, after gaining for some years a scanty living with his pen. His harsh and stubborn character had alienated all his friends; that which had been forgiven to the brilliant young soldier and man of letters was sufficient to wreck the fortunes of the worn-out literary hack of the Madrid theatres.

As a dramatist, Guillén de Castro followed closely in the steps of Lope de Vega. It is not necessary to suppose that he always consciously kept his great master in view, but Lope was the acknowledged law-giver in almost every branch of the drama, and on each had left the impress of his individual genius, thereby rendering the drawing of parallels between himself and his successors an easy task. The Spanish play-writers had long been aware of the inexhaustible treasure that lay ready to their hands in the national traditions embodied in the ballads. Patriotic feeling of a jealous and exclusive kind was strong, and anything that could for a moment blind an audience to the national decay which was becoming every day more and more apparent was sure to be received with rapturous applause. The virtues of an earlier and hardier age were not the less appreciated because they had ceased to be practised, and those who helplessly beheld the dismemberment of the Spanish power paid ready homage to the heroes who, in days long past, had helped to lay its foundation. Of this bent of the popular mind, and of the readiest means of satisfying its cravings to forget the present in the past, nobody was more keenly aware than Guillén de Castro, and nobody has made better use on the stage of the ballads which at his time still lingered on the lips of the people. It is easy to imagine the thrill of enthusiasm that must have run through a Spanish audience of the seventeenth century when well-known verses such as *El conde Alarcos* or *El conde d'Irlos*[1] were thundered from the stage, with their effect heightened by all the glamour of dramatic action, or, better still, when the Cid, the great champion of the re-conquest, and representative of the national ideal, appeared before them, surrounded by the heroes well known to popular tradition, and speaking the well-known words in the familiar but ever stately and impressive ballad-measure. But Guillén de Castro's two plays on the youthful exploits of the Cid (*Las Mocedades del Cid*) owe their fame less to the enthusiasm which they aroused at the time of their production, than to the fact that they furnished the groundwork for the *Cid* of Corneille,

[1] These two ballads occur in the plays of Guillén de Castro that bear their names.

and through it exercised a wide and lasting influence on the drama of Europe.

In these plays, as elsewhere in their author's writings, not only is the story of the ballads (see p. 49) closely followed, but the ballads themselves are frequently introduced into the dialogue. The first of the two opens with the scene in which the young Rodrigo is dubbed a knight. The insult suffered by Diego Lainez at the hands of the Conde Lozano, the vengeance exacted by Rodrigo, the son's high spirit and the father's stern confidence in his valour, coupled with anxiety on account of his youth and inexperience, are well set forth. The meeting of the two after the father's honour has been avenged, gave an opportunity for fine writing and manly sentiment, which Guillén de Castro used to the best advantage. It is, however, for his treatment of the character of Jimena, the daughter of the haughty Count, that most credit is due to him. In this particular he departs from, or rather develops and justifies, the tradition of the *romancero*. According to the old legend, the marriage arranged by the king between the Cid and the daughter of the enemy whom he has slain is merely a matter of policy, the means of staying a dangerous feud and appeasing the offended honour of a great lady. The heroine of Guillén de Castro's play, on the contrary, is placed in one of the most thrilling dramatic situations that can be imagined. She has long and deeply loved the young Rodrigo, and cannot but admire the haughty spirit that has cost the life of her father. Against these feelings are ranged her filial affection, the strict code of honour under which she has been brought up, together with all the fierce instincts of her family, age, and country. But she crushes her heart within her, and passionately begs the king to do justice on the slayer of her father. It is only by the report of Rodrigo's death that the confession of her love is at last wrung from her. The great Corneille saw clearly the power and beauty of this almost unique situation, but bound by the rigid rules of " unity " to which the French drama was submitted, he was forced to compress the action of his play into the space of twenty-four hours, thus making the revulsion of Jimena's feeling too violent to be natural, and too sudden to carry with it the sympathy of the onlooker.

The latter part of the traditional story of the Cid offered no such situation, and is adapted rather for epic than for dramatic treatment. The unhappy love of Doña Urraca, the treachery of Bellido Dolfos, the gallant conduct of Count Ordoñez and his sons, would each furnish material for a play ; the apparition of St. Lazarus would probably be rejected altogether by an experienced playwright of the present day ; but Guillén de Castro combined them all in a single drama, and gained applause by the intrinsic merits of his subject rather than by his treatment of it. His second play on the *Mocedades del Cid* is crowded with personages and episodes which do nothing to further its action ; it has no plot properly so called.

The other plays of Guillén de Castro are less well known. Two of them derive their subjects from *Don Quixote.* Of these, one bears the name of the Manchegan knight, the second is a dramatised version of *El Curioso Impertinente* (Misplaced Suspicions), an episodical story of no great value introduced by Cervantes into his book. Don Quixote on the stage speaks and acts in exact conformity with that which is related of him in his *History*, but the dramatist was forced to have recourse to minor characters, such as Cardenio and Dorotea, for his plot, and the result is worthless, save for the sprightly dialogue and correct versification that distinguished all the works of its author.

Like most of his contemporaries, Guillén de Castro drew upon the Bible and the Lives of the Saints for subjects for his plays. His most successful effort in this direction is his *Santa Bárbara*, in which he introduces the devil in person, tempting the saint whose unshaken constancy when suffering martyrdom secured the conversion of her lover and her friends, together with a signal triumph for the faith. In this play, as elsewhere, human love is treated as symbolical of divine, in a manner that even ingenuity and delicate handling cannot make pleasing to modern taste.

With the exception of the *Mocedades del Cid*, there is little in Guillén de Castro's work to distinguish him from the general body of the dramatists of Lope de Vega's school. His "cloak and sword plays" are so similar in character to those of Lope that it would be almost impossible to distinguish by internal evidence between the work of the disciple and that of the master, who was his contemporary.

Another dramatist who, like Guillén de Castro, owes his reputation outside his own country chiefly to the creation of a character which has become the literary property of the world, is Gabriel Tellez, who published a number of plays under the pseudonym of Tirso de Molina. Of his life little is known, save that he was a native of Madrid, and studied in his youth at Alcalá. He took orders somewhat late in life, and it was probably out of regard to his position as an ecclesiastic that he concealed his real name when publishing the collection of his plays, many of which are of a much looser character than is usual on the Spanish stage. He died about the middle of the seventeenth century.

The legend of Don Juan is probably founded on real events that happened at Seville. The all-embracing genius of Lope de Vega introduced parts of the story into the play entitled *El Dinero es quien hace Hombre* (Money maketh Man), but Lope failed to catch the gloomy horror of the subject, and had it not been for Tirso de Molina it would probably have been speedily forgotten. Quite apart from the distinction of having inspired artists so widely different in character as Molière and Corneille in the past, and Byron, Mozart, and Zorilla (see p. 259) in the present century, Tirso de Molina's play *El Burlador de Sevilla*

(The Mocker of Seville) is of the highest order of merit, both as regards general plan and execution.   Nowhere has the strange character of Don Juan been better portrayed.   Its interest lies in the powerful appeal that it makes to some of the most complex feelings of human nature, and the shrinking and unwilling admiration which its very boldness in vice compels even from those in whom its atrocious villainy has aroused the strongest reprobation and repugnance ; one virtue alone, and that not of the highest order, contributes the human element in a character which, without it, would be inconceivable. Courage is usually represented as springing from reliance on a good cause and the promptings of a good conscience, but here we have the unparalleled spectacle of cool daring in the face of superhuman terrors, supported by nothing stronger than the ordinary passions of mankind, to the gratification of which it ruthlessly wins its way.   It is strange to reflect that so monstrous and powerful a creation sprang from the brain of Gabriel Tellez, the prior of the convent of Soria.

The following brief outline of the play will show to what extent those who afterwards made use of the story are indebted to Tellez for its form.   The scene opens in Naples, where Don Juan abuses the confidence of Isabel, who in the dark mistakes him for her lover, the Duke Octavio.   An alarm is raised and Don Juan is captured ; he is, however, allowed to escape by his uncle, the Spanish ambassador, to whom he has surrendered himself.   The next scene introduces a further piece of treachery. Don Juan, on his return to Spain, is shipwrecked on the coast, and is entertained by a fisherman's daughter named Tisbea, who in turn becomes his victim.   He abandons her, and, on arriving at Seville, finds that the king has arranged a marriage for him with Ana, the daughter of the Comendador Don Gonzalo de Ulloa.   But Don Juan's father has in the meantime heard of his son's conduct with regard to the unhappy Isabel, and demands that he shall be compelled to marry the lady whom he has so deeply wronged, and that Doña Ana shall be given to the Duke Octavio. Doña Ana, however, has already an accepted admirer in her cousin, the Marqués de la Mota, with whom she arranges a nightly interview. The letter containing the assignation falls into the hands of Don Juan, who again personifies another man. This time the trick is discovered and Doña Ana raises an alarm ; her father, the Comendador, hurries up and is killed by Don Juan. One more infamous act is needed to make the measure full. The scene suddenly changes to a village wedding. The bride attracts the baneful attentions of Don Juan and falls a prey to him. The consequences of the villain's crimes now begin to overtake him. Isabel comes to Spain seeking justice, and falls in with Tisbea. Don Juan is obliged to seek sanctuary in the church where stands the statue of the Comendador whom he has slain. The sight of it provokes no remorse ; he mocks at it and jestingly invites it to sup with him. The appearance of the statue at the appointed time produces no terror in Don Juan, nay it does not even check his mocking humour. He glibly accepts an invitation from his supernatural guest for the following evening. The last scene is laid in the chapel where lie the bones of the Comendador ; the man and the statue sit down together, the former more provoking in attitude and more bitter in language than ever. Suddenly the statue seizes and slays him, the earth opens, and this type of superhuman wickedness is swallowed up. The scene in which the statue of the Comendador appears at supper is unsurpassed in grisly impressiveness :—

> [1] *Don Juan.*   ¿ Quién va?
> *Don Gonzalo.*   Yo soy.
> *Catalinón.*   ¡ Muerto estoy !

---

[1] "*D. J.* Who is there?
D. G. 'Tis I.
C. I am dying of fright !

Don Gonzalo.	El muerto soy, no te espantes.
	No entendí que me cumplieras
	La palabra, según haces
	De todos burla.
Don Juan.	¿ Me tienes
	En opinión de cobarde ?
Don Gonzalo.	Sí que aquella noche huiste
	De mí, cuando me mataste.
Don Juan.	Huí de ser conocido ;
	Mas ya me tienes delante ;
	Dí presto lo que me quieres.
Don Gonzalo.	Quiero á cenar convidarte
Don Juan.	Cenemos . . .
Don Gonzalo.	Valiente estás.
Don Juan.	Tengo brío
	Y corazón en las carnes.
Don Gonzalo.	Siéntate.
Don Juan.	¿ Dónde ?
Catalinón.	Con sillas
	Vienen ya dos negros pages . . .
Don Gonzalo.	¿ No comes tú ?
Don Juan.	Comeré,
	Si me dieres áspid, áspides
	Cuantos el infierno tiene.
Don Gonzalo.	Tambien quiero que te canten.
Catalinón.	¿ Qué vino beben aquí ?
Don Gonzalo.	Pruébalo.

D. G. I am the dead man, be not afraid.—I did not think thou wouldst fulfil thy promise, so lightly dost thou hold promises.

D. J. Dost thou take me for a coward ?

D. G. Yea ; for on the night when thou didst slay me thou didst flee.

D. J. I fled for fear of being known ; but now we are met, say quickly what thou wouldst with me.

D. G. I would have thee to sup with me.

D. J. Let us sup then.

D. G. Thou art a bold man.

D. J. I have courage and a good heart within me.

D. G. Be seated.

D. J. Where ?

C. Two sable pages approach with chairs.

D. G. Dost thou not eat ?

D. J. If thou wilt give me adders I will eat as many as hell doth hold.

D. G. I would have music.

C. What wine do they drink here ?

D. G. Taste it.

Catalinón.	Hiel y vinagre
	Es este vino.
Don Gonzalo.	Este vino
	Exprimen nuestros lagares.
Cantan dentro.	Adviertan los que de Dios
	Juzgan los castigos grandes
	Que no hay plazo que no llegue
	Ni deuda que no se pague.

. . . . .

Don Juan.	Ya he cenado : haz que levanten
	La mesa.
Don Gonzalo.	Dame esa mano
	No temas la mano darme.
Don Juan.	¿Eso dices? ¿Yo temor?
	(*le da la mano*)
	¡ Que me abraso ! No me abrases
	Con tu fuego.
Don Gonzalo.	Esto es poco
	Para el fuego que buscaste.

. . . .

	Esta es justicia de Dios
	Quien tal hizo que tal pague.
Don Juan.	¡ Que me abraso ! No me aprietes.
	Con la daga he de matarte.
	Mas ¡ ay, que me canso en vano
	De tirar golpes al aire !
	—Á tu hija no ofendí ;
	Que vió mis engaños antes
Don Gonzalo.	No importa, que ya pusiste
	Tu intento.

C. This wine is gall and vinegar.

D. G. 'Tis such as our presses give.

Voices singing. Take warning all who — reflect on God's great chastisements — that the future is near at hand — and all debts must be paid.

D. J. I have supped. Let the table be cleared.

D. G. Give here thy hand. Fear not to give me thy hand.

D. J. What sayest thou? I, afraid? (*Gives him his hand.*) I am burning ! Burn me not with thy fire.

D. G. It is nothing in comparison of the fire that thou hast incurred. Such is God's justice, as a man sins, so is he punished.

D. J. I am burning ! Stifle me not. With my dagger I will slay thee. Alas, I struggle in vain, showering thrusts on the air ! I did thy daughter no wrong ; she was not deceived by my wiles.

D. G. It matters not, for thy purpose was clear.

Don Juan.	Deja que llame
	Quien me confiese y absuelva.
Don Gonzalo.	No hay lugar, ya acuerdas tarde.
Don Juan.	¡ Que me quemo ! ¡ Que me abraso !
Don Gonzalo.	Esta es justicia de Dios
	Quien tal hizo que tal pague.

(húndense.)

The consideration that Tirso de Molina built up his play merely on the bare tradition that a libertine member of the noble family of Tenorio was found dead hard by the statue of the Comendador de Ulloa, whose daughter he had wronged, justifies a lofty estimate of his imaginative and dramatic power. The successive introduction of so many of Don Juan's victims undoubtedly somewhat draws off the attention from the main interest, but it gives a more distinct idea than could otherwise be produced of the utter iniquity of the man, and brings the audience into thorough sympathy with the hideous punishment that finally overtakes him.

Such a play from the hands of Tirso de Molina is the more surprising, as his taste led him to adopt light and even comic subjects for most of his dramas. In this latter style he wrote *Don Gil de las Calzas Verdes* (Don Gil of the Green Breeches), one of the most thoroughly popular plays in Spain, and a type of the play of intrigue as conceived in its author's age. So intricate is the plot, and so many are the characters and the transformations they undergo, that it is extremely difficult to follow the thread of the action throughout.

Molina's lighter plays are, as has been said, defaced by a licentiousness fortunately rare on the Spanish stage. His ideal of love, the main theme of the *comedia de capa y espada*, is a low one; his female characters are rather loose than passionate;

D. J. Let me call a confessor to shrive me.
D. G. It cannot be, thy purpose comes too late.
D. J. I am burning ! I am scorching !
D. G. Such is God's justice, as a man sins, so is he punished.

(They sink into the earth.)"

the strict rules of the Spanish code of honour have but little weight with his libertine heroes. His characters, however, are really life-like ; his dialogue is bright and natural ; his knowledge of his native language is remarkable, and his versification correct and flowing. A play that illustrates his merits, while free to a great extent from his defects, is the *Vergonzoso en Palacio* (Shameface at Court).

The grave and deeply religious side of the Spanish character is represented in Molina's works by *El condenado por desconfiado* (The Doubter Damned), a play that will bear comparison with Calderón's philosophical dramas. A holy hermit, named Paulo, has doubts as to his ultimate salvation, and prays that his end may be revealed to him. A devil makes known to him in a dream that his end will be the same as that of Enrico, a well-known libertine and criminal. Paulo, in despair, abandons his holy life and becomes a bandit. Enrico dies on the scaffold, but is saved by his final repentance and his dutiful conduct towards his father. Paulo, trusting to the promise made by the devil, makes light of repentance when his end draws nigh. He dies and is damned, but reappears to bear witness that the devil's promise is false, Enrico being already in glory. Truly dramatic is the scene in which Paulo, disguised as a hermit, visits Enrico, whom he has condemned to death, in order to discover if he will finally repent. After a striking interview in the prison, finding that Enrico's heart is still hardened, Paulo releases him for fear that, by putting him to death while still impenitent, he may be condemning himself.

Besides his dramatic works, Tirso de Molina published two celebrated collections of short stories after the Italian fashion, both of which won great celebrity. The first, the *Cigarrales de Toledo*, describes the festivities that are supposed to take place, on the occasion of a wedding, at certain country houses (*cigarrales*) in the neighbourhood of Toledo. The stories and verses which go to make up the book are told by the guests who attend the wedding and own the houses which, on successive days, are the scene of the rejoicings. This method of connecting various detached stories shows the influence of Boccaccio, and the stories themselves are marked by the artificial taste and language of the time in which they were produced; but the verses, like all those by the same hand, are good, and the book is by no means a dull one. The same cannot be said for the second attempt of the author in the same direction. In his *Deleitar Aprovechando* (Pleasure with Profit) Molina adopts a severe and moral tone well suited to the ecclesiastic, but sounding somewhat strangely in the mouth of the author of certain of his plays.

Juán Ruiz de Alarcón y Mendoza, a native of Mexico, was born about the end of the sixteenth century. Coming over to Europe early in life to finish his legal education, he studied at Salamanca, and, after an attempt to find suitable employment in his native country, entered the household of a nobleman of the Spanish court and began to cultivate literature. His plays brought him speedily into notice; he was named Commissioner for the Indies, an office which he enjoyed until the time of his death, which took place in 1639. In spite of the excellence of his work, Alarcón seems never to have enjoyed any wide popularity. He was attacked with great bitterness by several of his rivals, some of whom were probably prompted by jealousy; even his physical deformities were held up to ridicule; the harsh and scurrilous lines which Quevedo wrote on the unfortunate hunchback are well known. Alarcón's work has special features that distinguish it from that of the other dramatists of his time. He attempted a more perfect study of character, and did something to vary the stock *dramatis personae*, whereas the Spanish theatre generally relied for its interest solely on complications of plot; most of his plays, too, contain a direct moral lesson; he is justly styled by A. Morel-Fatio the most serious and observant of Spanish poets. His most successful play is *La Verdad Sospechosa* (The Truth Distrusted), to which Corneille owned himself indebted for the plot and principal characters of his *Menteur*, and which thus exercised an influence on French comedy at its best period, similar to that which the *Cid* of Guillén de Castro exercised on tragedy. The main idea running through the piece is embodied in the Spanish proverb—*en boca del mentiroso lo cierto se hace dudoso* (on the lips of the liar the truth is held as falsehood). Don García, a student of Salamanca, is cursed by an inveterate habit of lying. Falling in love with Jacinta, he tells her a series of untruths about himself and his position. In the meanwhile his father has, without his knowledge, arranged to marry him to the lady of his affections. Ignorant of the fact that the lady whom his father has selected for him is really his beloved Jacinta, and anxious to avoid a marriage which he thinks would be distasteful to him, Don García pretends that he is already a married man. The confusion thus created is sustained and made worse by a mistake that Don García has made, attributing to Jacinta the name of Lucrecia, one of her friends. This mistake not only prevents father and son from coming to an understanding, but entangles García in an engagement with Lucrecia, who receives and answers his letters, imagining them to be addressed to herself. Finally the liar is obliged to marry Lucrecia, whom he does not love, while Jacinta becomes the wife of his rival. This somewhat intricate plot gives occasion to a quantity of amusing incidents and a good deal of careful character-drawing. The attempts of Don García to extricate himself from his entanglements are most ingenious; the scenes in which, driven to confess the truth, he is disbelieved and treated as a liar, are among the best of their kind in the Spanish theatre.

Of Alarcón's other plays, more than twenty in number, the most famous is *El Tejedor de Segovia* (The Weaver of Segovia), which turns on the popular Spanish theme of unswerving loyalty tried by the greatest injustice. Like the rest of its author's work, it displays true dramatic instinct, careful and sober versification, and considerably more finish than was usual at his time.

One of the most deservedly popular plays of the Spanish stage is *El Desdén con el Desdén* (Pride conquers Pride), turning on the same central idea, as *Milagros del Desprecio* (Contempt works Wonders) by Lope de Vega, but vastly better worked out. The author, Augustín Moreto, was a native of Madrid. Born at the period when the Spanish drama had reached its most brilliant development, and when even the king[1] himself was a playwright, Moreto studied at the University of Alcalá, and wrote all his plays, more than a hundred in number, before he reached middle age. The strong and somewhat gloomy religious feeling that forms so marked a feature of the Spanish character became all-powerful in his declining years; he became a member of a charitable brotherhood, and passed the latter part of his life in the service of the poor. To them he left his fortune, and he shared their burying-place after death.

Diana, the heroine of *El Desdén con el Desdén*, is the daughter of the Count of Barcelona. Gifted with great beauty and talent, she shows a rooted dislike to marriage. Her father, thinking to overcome her prejudice, summons to his court the neighbouring princes who are suitors for her hand. Among them comes the Count of Urgel who, determined to win the lady, conceals his passion under an affected indifference, and makes profession of views similar to her own on the subject of marriage. Piqued in her womanly pride by his coolness, Diana determines to conquer it, and marshals all her charms in order to bring him to her feet. In this dangerous game she soon begins to lose her heart to him, and he is not

---

[1] Two plays are attributed to Felipe IV., and others, by the same hand, are supposed to be contained among the large number of those by anonymous writers.

slow to perceive it. Urged by his own impatience the Count declares his love before matters are ripe. Diana seeing him, as she supposes, in her power, treats him as she had treated former suitors. The lover's presence of mind, however, does not desert him ; he craftily passes off the matter as a joke that could not possibly have any evil consequences when passing between parties whose opinions with regard to marriage are so notorious. Finally, Diana's jealousy is roused; she declares her passion, and a thoroughly agreeable and healthy play ends with a wedding. The secondary characters are carefully and consistently drawn ; the *gracioso* forms an exception to his class by being really witty and amusing. On Moreto's play Molière founded his *Princesse d'Elide*, closely following the original in many scenes.

Moreto, like Alarcón, is distinguished by unusual care in the drawing of character, and also by light and graceful fancy and suitable and natural dialogue. His sense of humour is more keen than that of most of the Spanish dramatists, as may be seen by reading his *Tia y Sobrina* (Aunt and Niece) or his *Lindo Don Diego* (Don Diego the Fop). In the latter play the hero, carried away by his own vanity, falls at last a prey to a designing waiting-maid, who trades upon his folly and represents herself to be a person of high position. But Moreto did not always devote himself to light subjects ; his *Caer para Levantar* (a Fall precedes a Rise) and *San Franco de Sena* have a gloomy side, and show the powerful working of the deeper passions. Moreto was the first to make good use of *figurones* or comic types of character such as had been first introduced by the universal genius, Lope de Vega. His handling of these is particularly skilful ; the caricature under his hands never becomes repulsive, nor do the *figurones* themselves lose their freshness. His work was much admired by his contemporaries ; the great Calderón himself collaborated with him in the production of certain plays.

A considerable figure in the literary world of his own time, though he has left little that an after age cares to treasure, is Juan Perez de Montalván, the intimate friend and biographer of Lope de Vega. Montalván was the son of the royal librarian ; his education was the best that his age could furnish, and he early attained a considerable reputation as a scholar. Like many other Spanish men of letters, Montalván entered the Church ; but his literary activity was not checked by his ecclesiastical duties ; when he died in 1638, at the age of thirty-six, he had already produced nearly fifty plays, besides writing novels and taking a conspicuous part in the literary tournaments common at the time. The esteem in which he was held was very great ; his reputation, even during his short lifetime, had crossed the seas ; a Peruvian, to whom he was personally unknown, assigned him a considerable pension to which certain obligations of a religious nature were attached. He had, however, enemies, chief among whom was Quevedo. These were never weary of ridiculing the author and his work, and even went so far as to say that all that was worth preserving of the books published in his name had been written by Lope, who is known to have helped him in his literary undertakings. Montalván's *Para todos* (Everybody's Book) is a collection of bright stories, spoilt in many instances by pedantry and affectation. The stories are loosely connected, after the same fashion as the *Cigarrales de Toledo* by Tirso de Molina, which Montalván evidently had in view when writing them. The book was so successful that it produced imitators, who took no trouble to conceal their plagiarism ; they adopted even the title with but slight modification. Matías de los Reyes called his collection of stories *Para algunos* (Some People's Book) ; Peralta called his *Para sí* (One's Own Book). Montalván was encouraged to try again, and afterwards published eight more stories which are, in some degree, free from the faults of the former ones.

As a dramatist Montalván does not rise above second-rate merit, but his *Amantes de Teruel* deserves notice on account of its graceful treatment of a story which has for several centuries formed an important part of the stock-in-trade of Spanish authors. In the town of Teruel in Aragón is shown a sepulchre which is said to hold the bones of two lovers whose fate created a deep impression on the popular mind. The legend told of them is undoubtedly of early date. It is as follows. Both were natives of the town, and their passion was of the deepest and most tender description; but the suitor was refused by the lady's family on account of his scanty means. Relying on the constancy of his lady, and the promises made to him that she shall not be compelled to marry before the lapse of a certain number of years, the lover sets out to seek his fortune. After many adventures he at last attains his object, and gleefully starts for home. But during his long absence he has been unable to send any news of himself to the lady who pines for him in his absence, and she has been worked upon to believe that he is dead. He arrives just at the moment when her wedding with a rival is being celebrated. Making his way to her room he falls dead at her feet. The lady, who throughout has been faithful to him, expires before the day of his funeral, and the two are buried together. The first to make use of the story was an inferior dramatist named Artieda, who wrote his *Amantes de Teruel* in 1581. In 1616, a long poem on the same subject, but also embracing many others, was published at Valencia by Yagüe de Salas. This was followed, in 1635, by a play, bearing the same name, from the pen of Tirso de Molina. Montalván made use of Molina's play in his own, improving upon his predecessor's work, and endeavouring to add interest to the story by bringing it several centuries nearer to his time and connecting it with well-known events that occurred in the reign of Charles V. During the present century this legend—for legend it must be called, in spite of the evidence manufactured in order to give it an historical character—has been made to furnish a plot for a novel and also for another play, the latter from the hand of Hartzenbusch the Academician.

A witty and original Spanish playwright, whose merits French authors were more ready to perceive than to acknowledge, was Francisco de Rojas, a contemporary and also imitator of Calderón. Of his life very little is known. He was a native of Toledo; was at one period of his life a soldier; and received in 1644 the mantle of the order of Santiago, which may be interpreted as a sign of court favour. Of his literary abilities we are enabled to judge by a collection of about fifty plays—in the composition of some of which Rojas collaborated with other dramatists—and a dozen *autos* of but slight merit. These numbers are merely approximate, for Rojas himself published only two volumes of his works comprising twenty-four plays. Many others, published separately, are undoubtedly written by him, but such was the carelessness of dramatic authors as to literary property in what they considered merely ephemeral productions, and such the unscrupulousness of booksellers and the indifference of the public, that to Rojas, as to many others of his contemporaries, works are ascribed which are certainly not his own, whilst the credit of some authentic ones has gone to swell the account of his rivals.

The two most celebrated plays of Rojas are a comedy and a melodrama. The former is entitled *Entre Bobos anda el Juego* (The Simpletons' Sport). The argument is as follows. Doña Isabel is affianced against her will to Don Lucas del Cigarral. She does not, however, confine her attentions to her somewhat commonplace betrothed, but encourages another admirer, Don Luís, and really loves Don Pedro, the poor and attractive cousin of the uncouth Don Lucas, thus carrying out fully the precept of the popular *copla*—

¹ La niña que quiere á dos
No es tonta sino advertida,
Si una vela se le apaga
Otra le queda encendida.

Don Pedro has also won the affections of Alfonsa, the sister of his cousin and rival, Don Lucas. The whole party is assembled at an inn. A nightly interview is arranged by Don Pedro with Isabel. Don Luís, searching for Isabel in the dark, meets Alfonsa and enjoys the favours which are meant for Don Pedro, for whom the lady mistakes him. Don Pedro, in order to allay the suspicions of Don Lucas, is now obliged to pay marked attentions to Alfonsa. The jealousy of Isabel is aroused, and an explanation between the parties ensues. Meantime Don Luís has been pushing his suit, and, thinking that he has gained Isabel's affections, he demands of Don Lucas that he should abandon his claim upon her. This Don Lucas very wisely does, but not in favour of Don Luís ; for, having learned the truth from Alfonsa, he marries Isabel to his cousin Don Pedro, and leaves to time and poverty the charge of avenging his injured feelings.

The above-mentioned melodrama is the celebrated *Del Rey abajo Ninguno* (None but the King alone). In spite of many dramatic faults, this play deserves its wide popularity. The argument brings into play in the strongest manner the two ruling passions of the Spanish theatre—the sense of personal honour and the obligation of unswerving and exaggerated loyalty to the king. In the present instance these two feelings strive for the mastery of a typically Spanish mind, and the result could not fail to be acceptable to those for whom the play was intended. To those who have not been brought up in the traditions of the Spanish stage, both sentiments must seem somewhat strained and unnatural. The hero of the piece, García del Castañar, lives retired from the court by

¹ "The lady who has two lovers is wise rather than foolish : if one flame goes out another is still alight."

reason of an unjust suspicion under which his father has fallen. By the munificence of his contribution to the expenses of a forthcoming expedition against the Moors, the attention of Alfonso XI. is called to him. Failing to recognise the nobleman under his assumed name, the king determines to disguise himself and to visit his wealthy and generous subject. Don García is informed of his intention, and receives him hospitably, but mistakes one of the suit, Don Mendo, for the king. Don Mendo falls in love with his host's wife, and is surprised by Don García while attempting to enter her apartment. For such an outrage the penalty is death ; but the king's person is sacred, and Don García, though persuaded of his wife's innocence, determines on her murder as the sacrifice demanded by his injured honour. His design is frustrated by her escape to the court. Thither Don García follows her and immediately learns his mistake. His course is now clear, and he faithfully carries out the precept of the stage code of honour by slaying his enemy in the royal ante-chamber. He is, of course, pardoned by the king, who very naturally concurs in the opinion that *None but the King alone* has any right to look for forgiveness in such a case.

The above notice of Spanish dramatists might be indefinitely extended were mention made of all those who supplied the stage during the best period with plays of a high order of merit. Even the most successful were only represented a few times, so that the demand was continual; moreover an audience, educated by Calderón and Lope, could not be expected to tolerate inferior work. The fertility and inventiveness of the Spanish dramatic authors during a period of one hundred years is unparalleled. In spite of the somewhat narrow and conventional limits which they had fixed for their art, there is scarcely any department of the drama in which Spaniards did not attain a success that owed nothing to imitation of foreign masterpieces. Many of the stock characters and most ingenious plots of the French and English stage, which now, through the wearing-down process of time, seem to bear no mark of their Spanish origin, can be historically traced to the great body of writers of whom, by reason of the limits of space, so few are here named.

From the time of Lope de Vega onward, little change or development in the form of the drama is perceptible. Later playwrights followed the lines which he had laid down, not so much from a slavish wish to copy the master, as because in every branch of the art he had tried his hand, and had everywhere won such success that, to those of his own time, it seemed as if no further development or improvement were possible. And, in one respect, they were right. With the plays of Goethe and of Shakespeare, plays that probe deep into the human heart and discuss the great problems of human life, the Spanish drama has nothing to compare, unless it be some few grandly conceived but hastily executed dramas of Calderón, and of one or two others. In the delineation of character the Spanish stage is still more markedly inferior. For the great geniuses of other countries it provided certain materials of which much could be made, and for this it must be given due credit, but the provider of the rough materials must not claim the finished work as his own. When Corneille, Molière, Le Sage, and Scarron steal from the Spanish stage, they almost in every instance justify their theft by marked improvements on the adopted theme. The one form of the drama which Spain not only created, but in which she stands unrivalled, is the play depending for interest entirely on its plot, the play in which certain stock characters, whose actions under any given circumstances can be infallibly foretold, are always on the stage, and are made to afford amusement by the inexhaustible combinations of which they are susceptible, and the ready wit of the creators of their picturesque adventures and surroundings. This may not be the highest form of the art, but it is no small glory for Spanish authors to have evolved unaided almost every form of the modern drama and to have excelled in one.

So attached were the Spanish audiences to the stock characters, the *galán* and *dama*, the *gracioso* and *barba* of their "sword and cloak" plays, that they introduce them with but slight disguises into religious plays. The Church, during the Golden Age of Spanish literature, looked on the drama with varying degrees of disfavour; on one or two occasions plays were prohibited altogether and the theatres were closed, but generally the slightest veil of religious purpose in the selection of the plot and naming of the characters was sufficient to disarm suspicion; the *galán* sighed and quarrelled, and the *gracioso* cracked his jokes none the less glibly because he found himself suddenly transported to Babylon or to Antioch, or to the period of the persecution of the early Christians.

The universal passion for play-going was condemned by some of the most thoughtful Spaniards, and Mariana,[1] among others, raised his voice against it when as yet the evil had not reached its height. Yet, setting aside the matter of bloodshed arising frequently from causes too slight to be credible, the national drama as a whole can scarcely have been considered immoral by writers of the seventeenth century unless their views were far in advance of the age. Indecency is very rare, and when it appears, as it does in Tirso de Molina's plays, it is generally confined to coarseness of expression. From villains and abject characters the Spanish stage is almost entirely free. The sentiments and motives represented are either those of Spain's heroic period, exaggerated for the purpose of greater effect, or those of a purely imaginary age.

For the sudden decay and final extinction of so strong a growth, several reasons may be given. The drama in its

---

[1] See his violent attack on the theatre, *Contra los Juegos Públicos*, caps. 1-12.

origin was entirely popular, and it remained so until the time
of Lope de Vega; afterwards it became more and more
artificial, and the successful playwright was the darling of the
court, writing to please the taste of munificent patrons such as
the later kings of the house of Austria. The people deserted the
theatres which had ceased to cater for their tastes, and betook
themselves to lower forms of amusement, more especially to
stage-dancing of a more or less licentious character, which
often drew down repressive measures from the Government.
The dramatists who wrote to secure court favour produced
some of the best of Spanish plays, but with the accession of
Felipe V., French taste was introduced in high places, and the
Spanish authors found themselves unable to vie with their
neighbours to whom, during the foregoing century, they had
provided models. But those who would seek the real cause
of this decay must go much deeper and study the influence
of the national fortunes upon national character. The most
brilliant period of Spanish literary glory, according to a rule
that seems well-nigh universal, coincided with the most brilliant
period of military glory and national activity. As the Spanish
empire widened, so did the national character develop, and
the joyous and free side of it so gained the upper hand as
to cause the gloomy and harsh side to be almost forgotten.
But reverses came; the Spaniards had adopted an attitude
that cut them off from the rest of Europe at a time when
increased facilities for the communication of ideas should have
made their genius more cosmopolitan. Buoyancy, such as the
French possess, has been denied to the Spanish nation, and,
finding themselves no longer masters of the world, they withdrew into a haughty and gloomy retirement; unable any
longer to hold the foremost position, they proudly gave up the
struggle altogether. The harsh fanaticism that produced the
Inquisition took the place of the strong religious feeling that
had upheld them during their struggle of seven centuries with

the Moors. The spirit of enterprise died out, and Spain remained at a standstill during the period in which the rest of Europe was advancing most rapidly. Something of the immutability of the East seemed to have remained with her ; she clung fondly to her ideals ; but her ideals were those of an age that had departed never to return.

CHAPTER XVIII

EPIC AND NARRATIVE POETRY IN THE SIXTEENTH AND SEVENTEENTH CENTURIES

A FEELING of weariness and depression at once overtakes the reader on opening the two volumes which Rivadeneyra, in his series of *Autores Españoles*, devotes to Epic Poetry. They contain nearly two hundred thousand lines of verse, none of which rises above second-rate merit, while by far the larger proportion is utterly worthless and prosaic; yet they entirely omit Lope de Vega, whose heroic compositions would fill another volume of the same size without materially altering the general standard.

In the chapter specially devoted to Lope's writings, mention has been made of his *Hermosura de Angélica*, but four more long poems must be noticed in order to give some idea of his success in this kind of composition. Two of these draw the little inspiration they possess from a rooted hatred towards the English race, natural enough in a soldier of the Invincible Armada. The subject of the *Dragontea* is Sir Francis Drake, *El Draque* as he is called by the Spaniards, who regarded the bold freebooter as an embodiment of the wickedness of Protestantism, and as a scourge of the devil sent to chastise their country for its sins. The *Dragontea* is crowded with allegorical personages; its style is hollow and bombastic; it neither increases our sympathy for the nation it was meant to glorify, nor does it succeed in vilifying those against whom it was written.   A celestial and a terrestrial argument are carried on without a hero, properly so called, unless it be the feeble allegorical "Spain," or "Providence," who freed her from her hated foe by his death at Puerto Bello in 1596.

Once again Lope used his pen in a bitter invective against the champions of Protestantism.   The execution of Mary Queen of Scots has been the theme of many poems, but none is so extravagant as the *Corona Trágica*.   Mary is extolled as a martyr, and Elizabeth treated with a violence that amounts to brutality and coarse abuse.   On such a subject all Lope's grace forsook him, and he filled his pages with frigid and feeble religious controversy.

Lope's longest and most characteristic epic is his *Jerusalén Conquistada*, a curious misnomer, for it treats of the unsuccessful expedition under Philip Augustus and Richard Cœur-de-Lion.   It is indeed strange that a Christian poet should have chosen such a subject, but stranger still is his rambling and diffuse treatment of it.   Regardless of historical truth, Lope drags Alfonso VIII. of Castile into the miserably wasteful and badly planned campaign round which so much legend centres. But the Alfonso of the poem is a very different person from the historical king of the same name ; he is, in fact, no other than our old acquaintance the *galán* of the "cloak and sword" play in a new dress.   The action—or rather actions of the poem, for they are many—drags wearily from Europe to Asia and back again, seldom relieved by a fine scene or really stately verse.   The only person who comes well out of the indiscriminate slaughter is Saladin, but the character is so inconsistent that it fails to retain the interest that it arouses.

In his mock epic, the *Gatomaquia* (Battle of the Cats), Lope avoids the monotony of the eleven-syllable octaves (*octavas reales*) cultivated by almost all Spanish narrative poets, and writing in lines of irregular length (*silvas*) is now and then really amusing and brilliant.   The *Gatomaquia* is undoubtedly imitated from the old Greek *Battle of the Frogs and the Mice*, but the best parts of the struggle between the rival pretenders to the hand of the tabby Zapaquilda are parodied from Ariosto and other Italian poets. Lope's caricature of the works of these authors is far more successful than his serious imitation (*Hermosura de Angélica*), but, like it, errs on the side of inordinate length.

Another and equally successful comic poem is the *Mosquea*, by José de Villaviciosa, a canon of Cuenca. Twelve long cantos are devoted to the heroic exploits of flies and ants, whose pompous speeches and spirited single combats are described in the style of the *Æneid*. One of the most powerful passages describes the dashing assault made by the flies on the skull of an ass in which the ants have taken up a strong position.

The poems contained in Rivadeneyra's volumes may be roughly divided, according to subject, into three classes—those that treat of religious matters, those that sing the glories of the earlier members of the Austrian dynasty, and those that celebrate the conquest of the New World.

Under the first of these headings comes the *Monserrate* of Cristóbal de Virnés, published in 1588. This long poem, written in verse, the tame correctness of which at length becomes wearisome, tells of the foundation of the monastery of Cataluña, from which it takes its name. Juan Garín, a holy hermit, dwelling amidst the eastern spurs of the Pyrenees, is tempted by the devil in person to violate and murder the daughter of the Count of Barcelona, who has been brought to him to receive healing at his hands. Stricken by remorse, he makes his way to Rome seeking absolution. By way of penance he is bidden to return to his country on hands and knees like a brute. Finally, assured of his pardon from God by the words of a child of tender years, forgiven also by the father of his victim, he repairs to the spot where the body is buried. Our Lady appears and brings to life the long-buried girl, and the monastery is founded to celebrate the miracle.

A more truly religious spirit inspired the *Cristiada* of Fray Diego de Hojeda. Its twelve cantos relate the Passion of our Lord, beginning with the Last Supper and ending with the descent into Hell. Hojeda versifies with some spirit, and he feels deeply the events which he relates; but for effective treatment his subject demanded much higher talents than he possessed, and the best parts of his poem are little better than a rhymed sermon.

The *Carolea* by Jerónimo Sempere, and the *Carlo famoso* by Luís de Zapata, which profess to be epic poems, are really rhymed chronicles, written, as Nicolás Antonio says, " *neque pura neque poetica dictione.*" The weary story of the wars of their hero is told in prosaic style and chronological order. Where the authors give play to their imagination, it generally takes a mythological form, and the result is cold and artificial in the extreme. The *Carlo famoso* contains a few interesting details, which are, however, but slightly connected with its subject, and would be much better told in prose.

The exploits of Don Juan de Austria and the battle of Lepanto are feebly sung by Juan Rufo. His *Austriada*, published in 1584, has, however, the honour of being classed by Cervantes along with the *Araucana* and *Monserrate* as the best Spanish epic, a compliment which, even if true, does not amount to much.

Don Alonso Ercilla y Zúñiga began life at the court of Felipe II., whom he accompanied to England on the occasion of his marriage with Queen Mary. As a young man he went to America, and took part in an expedition against the brave Indian inhabitants of the valley of Arauco in Chile. He was condemned to death for mutinous conduct by the leader of the expedition, but the sentence was commuted to banishment. Finally he found his way back to Spain, bringing with him the first part of the poem that celebrates the campaign. He died in poverty during the last years of the sixteenth century.

Ercilla himself tells how his *Araucana* was composed, "at times with sword in hand, at times with pen" (*tomando, ora la espada, ora la pluma*), and that parts of it were written in circumstances of difficulty and danger, but its greatest fault is its inordinate length. The whole poem is made up of no less than thirty-seven cantos in *ottava rima*. In the first part (fifteen cantos) the author restricts himself to the events of the campaign in Chile. The doings of each day are recorded in the form of a rhymed journal, but occasionally the poem takes a loftier flight. It is remarkable that such sympathy as it calls forth is entirely in favour of the Indians, the more or less imaginary characters of some of whom are truly heroic. The Spaniards are represented as brave, but their cruelty and bad faith are evident, and cannot be excused by their avowed object of converting the heathen. The second and third parts of the poem deal in visions and mythology. By this means the battles of Lepanto and of St. Quentin are introduced. The story of Dido is told with much detail in order to solace the soldiers in their march through the Andes. The language of the *Araucana* is dignified and simple, and its versification correct; but little that is worthy of the name of poetry is to be found in it, though it is admittedly the best attempt at formal epic in the Spanish tongue.

Ercilla found an imitator in Pedro de Oña, who in his *Arauco domado* (Arauco Conquered) celebrates the exploits of García Hurtado de Mendoza, the leader of the expedition, whom Ercilla, probably from personal motives, had neglected to mention. Oña lacks the chivalrous character that cast a halo over the tedious poem which Ercilla, as Morel-Fatio well puts it, "wrote with a pike."

The heroic deeds of Cortés are told at great length in indifferent verse by Gabriel Lasso de la Vega in *El Cortés valeroso*, and by Antonio de Saavedra in *El Peregrino Indiano*.

Juan de Castellanos, after serving as a soldier, settled as a priest at Tunja in Mexico, and wrote the *Elegías de varones ilustres de Indias*. Many curious facts about the early discoverers and conquerors of America, as well as interesting details as to the manners and customs of the inhabitants, are recorded in this gigantic work, but, like the foregoing, it is almost entirely devoid of poetry.

Ariosto found two Spanish imitators. Luís Barahona de Soto continued the Italian poem with but slight success in his *Lagrimas de Angélica* (Tears of Angelica). Bernardo de Balbuena, imitating a foreigner, took for his hero his namesake and fellow-countryman *Bernardo del Carpio*. In spite of a warm imagination and great inventive faculty the twenty-four crowded cantos of slipshod verse did little towards increasing the reputation of the hero or founding one for the author. The *Bernardo* is in fact a rhymed romance of chivalry, just as the *Carolea* is a rhymed chronicle.

CHAPTER XIX

FROM THE BEGINNING OF THE EIGHTEENTH CENTURY TO THE WAR OF INDEPENDENCE

WHEN at the beginning of the eighteenth century the last feeble representative of the great House of Austria died, and the succession fell to the Bourbons, it was inevitable that French influences should become paramount in Spain. The country had lost its national traditions, and the glorious past was as yet too little removed for the descendants of its heroes to be conscious of its importance. It was not in Spain only that the influence of the great French writers of the age of Louis XIV. made itself felt; all Europe bowed before it, but in Spain it found a free field, and its artificial expansion was furthered by the well-known sympathies of the court. Its effects were, on the whole, salutary; nothing could be built on the ruins of the old literature, and French influences cleared the ground for a fresh development. The literature which has been briefly examined in the foregoing pages is, in the main, essentially popular in character, and a natural outgrowth of the national life. The makers of the ballads, the founders of the drama, and the inventors of the picaresque novel, were not hampered by literary canons or prejudices; they had no models in view; they wrote to please the multitude, and their works went straight to the popular heart. This tendency is directly opposed to the classicism of the French school. To blend the two systems was impossible, and thus it is that the precepts of the classical school killed the little that remained of the old Spanish genius without taking root themselves. The whole of Spain was suffering from the exhaustion that follows on a mighty effort. In arms, in arts, and in letters she had produced her best, and the rude shock of finding her very national independence gone was needed in order to rouse her from the state of lethargy into which she had sunk. When at last she awoke the aspect of the world was changed : the eighteenth century was dead and buried ; the old literature was gone ; the struggle between it and the French influences had ended fatally for both, and the vacant field was about to be occupied by the romantic school and the modern novelist. But before this came about a dreary period had to be gone through.

During the period of its hardy youth, Spanish literature had received but scanty protection at court. Monarchs like Carlos V. and Felipe II. had other matters to occupy them. With the approaching decadence matters changed ; Felipe IV. was not only a patron of men of letters, he went down into the lists and competed with the poets of his time. The first Bourbon king was an intelligent lover of letters, and, in spite of his strictly French education in literary matters, he showed a tolerant and even indulgent spirit to what he could not but regard as a barbarous branch of art. He could not revive the old creative spirit, but he could encourage the Spaniards to work upon the inheritance that had come to them from the past, and this he did. Already in the seventeenth century one man of untiring devotion had spent a studious life on the bibliography of his country. This was Nicolás Antonio. His great work is divided into two parts, of which the former, the *Bibliotheca Vetus*, comprises notices of all the Spanish writers from the earliest times till the end of the fifteenth century. The *Bibliotheca Nova* brings up the work to the author's own time. To the student of Spanish literature Antonio's work is invaluable ; in careful accuracy and solid learning it stands as a model for compositions of a similar character, whilst the fact that it is written in Latin makes it accessible to those who are unacquainted with the author's native language.

At the beginning of the eighteenth century, in imitation of French institutions of a like nature, were founded the two Academies—of the Language, and of History—which have justified their existence by rendering signal service in the departments to which they are severally devoted. In 1732 the Academy of the Language produced its great dictionary, the *Diccionario de Autoridades*, as it is called—a work which has done much to preserve the purity of the Spanish tongue, but which is unfortunately miserably incomplete even for the period which it affects to embrace.

Little had hitherto been done in the way of antiquarian research ; modern authors had thrust the ancient ones into the background, and, if any turned over the musty records of the past, it was, unfortunately, often with the sinister design of falsifying some document. In 1575 Argote de Molina, the first Spaniard who deserves the name of antiquary, had published at Seville a part of the works of Don Juan Manuel, but the study of the older literature languished until, in the last century, Sanchez published his *Poetas Anteriores al Siglo XV.*, and Mayans y Siscar his learned and valuable *Orígenes de la Lengua Castellana.* Both Sanchez and Mayans y Siscar were royal librarians ; their works are not only the earliest instances of the critical treatment of old Spanish documents, but are of permanent importance to all students of the subjects of which they severally treat.

During the first half of the eighteenth century discussion raged hotly over the *Poética* of Don Ignacio Luzán, a book written with the avowed object of supporting the doctrines of the French classical school, and explaining the mysteries of the unities to a nation sunk in darkness. Luzán was a clever man of narrow views, which caused him to exaggerate the importance of his precepts. A staunch disciple of Boileau and his school, he supports his views by pouring contempt on the great but "incorrect" authors of his country. His contemporaries could not find answers to his arguments, but they were wise enough to see that there must be something faulty in a system which would exclude Cervantes and Calderón from Parnassus. Thus it was that Luzán's polemic had the effect of strengthening the cause it was meant to weaken.

Among the multitudinous names of second and third-rate Spanish poets of the last century, it is scarcely possible to select one that is worthy of mention. Those who attempt to follow the old tradition lack the inspiration that atoned for its artistic faults, while most of their opponents, supporters of the French school, produced compositions which can scarcely be rivalled for frigid insipidity. Of them Quintana (see p. 241) well says, " The presses groaned and the newspapers overflowed with pamphlets, satires, and epigrams, hurled at each other by Spanish wits to no other purpose than the causing of well-deserved contempt for art so degraded and time so wasted." Even those who did not sink to this level were "careful rather to avoid defects than bold and ambitious to secure beauty," and thus even the best of their work has no place in a History of Literature. Only very rarely do we catch something of the sparkle of the old poetic fire in compositions such as the *Fiesta de Toros en Madrid*, by Nicolás Fernandez Moratín, or in the *Fables* of Samaniego and of Iriarte, whose obvious imitation of the great Lafontaine does not entirely preclude all literary merit. A proof of the poverty of the age is the reputation that these poems enjoyed, and still enjoy, to such a degree that it is difficult to find a Spaniard who does not know some part of the *Fiesta de Toros* and some of the *Fables* by heart. The falling off from the best poets of the seventeenth century to Iglesias, Cienfuegos, and Menendez Valdés in the eighteenth is almost incredible. All that can be said for the latter is that they are tolerable versifiers, and did something to preserve the purity of their native language.[1]

The condition of the theatre in the century that succeeded Lope and Calderón was truly pitiable. The old dramas were neglected for bad translations, adaptations, or imitations from the French; those who affected to follow the national models followed them in their faults alone. In this department, however, two notable exceptions occur, and two names stand out strongly from the surrounding littleness. The first is that of Leandro Fernandez de Moratín, a son of the author of the *Fiesta de Toros en Madrid* and of other short and sprightly compositions in verse. Moratín the younger began life as apprentice to a jeweller, but literary instincts were strong within him. He wrote verses, and first brought himself into notice as a successful competitor for prizes offered by the Academy for compositions on set subjects. By dint of powerful protection he obtained advancement both in civil and ecclesiastical life, and travelled in various European countries. During the French domination Moratín swam with the current, and was named royal librarian by Joseph Buonaparte. He left Spain with the French invaders, and spent most of his later life at Paris and at Bordeaux in the company of other exiled members of his party. Moratín, in spite of his foreign sympathies and his want of patriotism at one of the most critical periods of his country's history, was one of the first to study the Spanish drama anterior to Lope de Vega, and his notices of a large body of old plays are both curious and valuable. His own works consist of satires, mostly on the feeble literature of his time and its producers and admirers; of epigrams, written with a spirit and grace that call to mind

---

[1] For the works of these and the other poets of the eighteenth century see *Poetas líricos del Siglo XVIII.*, 3 vols. (Bib. Autores Españoles), together with the admirable preface by L. A. de Cueto.

Góngora and Quevedo; and of plays. In the latter department he deserves to rank as the most successful among
Spanish imitators of the French. Molière is his model and, if
he cannot bear comparison with his master in brilliant wit, he
comes near him in careful delineation of character, and in
elegance and correctness of language. The most celebrated of
his plays is *El sí de las Niñas* (The Ladies' Consent) written
in prose. Its main argument is simple. The heroine is
betrothed by her ambitious mother to an old man, who does
his best by kindness to atone for his years. But the lady's
affections have already been secured by a young officer, who
has contrived to make his passion known to her while she was
still being educated in a convent. The young lover, hearing
of her distasteful engagement, sets out hurriedly in order to
prevent the marriage, and overtakes the betrothed couple,
accompanied by the lady's mother, at an inn. His perplexity
is increased by the discovery that the elderly lover is his own
uncle, to whom he is deeply indebted for favours received.
After many amusing and well-studied scenes the truth dawns
upon the old man and, with simple generosity, he abandons
his pretensions in favour of his nephew. The best characters
in the piece are the uncle himself and the mother of the
lady, the hypocritical and intriguing nature of the latter
contrasting strongly with the old man's frankness and high
spirit.

The other dramatic author above alluded to is Don Ramón
de la Cruz, a gentleman of good family, who was born in 1731
and lived nearly to the end of the century. Don Ramón
occupied an official position, but its duties can scarcely have
weighed heavily upon him, for he produced about three
hundred dramatic pieces, and for thirty years was the favourite
of the Madrid stage. This popularity was thoroughly deserved.
In his own department Ramón de la Cruz is unrivalled. He
made peculiarly his own the *sainetes*, or short dramatised

scenes from everyday life, without plot or regular dramatic structure, and relying for their interest on the accurate representation of popular types and manners.   This kind of composition is closely paralleled by the *entremés*, *paso*, or *baile*, that used to be introduced between the acts (*jornadas*) in order to relieve the heavier dramas of the older theatre; but it was Ramón de la Cruz who perfected it and gave it its peculiar character.   His *sainetes* present an incomparably vivid and animated picture of one side of the life of Madrid as it was before the French invasion, with its picturesque colouring, its squalor and corruption, its light-hearted gaiety and thoughtlessness in the midst of national calamities.   Love of pleasure and the recklessness of despair seemed for a time to have overshadowed the strong elements of the national character, which, however, were shortly to make their power felt in the heroic rising against the French, known from its date as the *dos de Mayo*.   The characters of the *sainetes* are all taken from the low life of the city or from the middle-class citizens; their dialogue is animated and characteristic, freely sprinkled with the *sales* or witticisms for which the Madrileños are celebrated, and with the national songs which they love so well and sing with so much expression.   Any incident sufficient to bring a certain number of popular types into play serves to form the foundation of a *sainete*—a street row for example, or a picnic-party (*merienda*), or the quarrels of the inmates of a lodging-house.   These short farces can neither be described nor translated; either process utterly destroys the wit and animation in which they abound; away from the place of their origin they are almost meaningless; they must be read or seen on the stage in Madrid, where such pieces as *La Casa de Tóqueme Roque* or *Las Castañeras Picadas* will provoke as much enthusiasm among the Spaniards of to-day as they did a hundred years ago.   The types that they represent must be studied in real life in order thoroughly to appreciate the *sainetes:* plenty such still exist, though they have lost some-thing of their picturesqueness and brilliant colouring.

One more name will bring the scanty list of important writers of the eighteenth century to an end. José Francisco Isla was a Jesuit priest of considerable celebrity on account of the learning which had obtained for him chairs at more than one of the Spanish universities. He was already an old man when, in 1765, he was driven out of Spain, together with the other members of his order, by the still unexplained decree of Carlos III. He retired to Bologna, where he won the esteem of all who came into communication with him, and died in 1781 at the age of seventy-eight. Isla possessed an intelligent love of his country and a strong sense of humour. Himself a preacher, he saw clearly the abject state into which pulpit oratory had fallen in his country, and set himself to cure the mischief by ridicule. His *History of the famous Preacher Fray Gerúndio* relates the adventures of a poor boy who is brought up for the Church, and who, by concealing poverty of thought under ridiculously bombastic and pedantic language, gains both the reputation of a great preacher and the admiration and respect of his hearers. This subject, including as it does the decay of learning in all departments, and offering an opportunity for sketches of various classes of society, might have made a splendid book had it been treated at reason-able length. But Padre Isla, like Fray Gerúndio himself, is long-winded and prosy, though here and there in his book passages are to be found that are worthy of the pen of a Cervantes or a Quevedo. The following one, which describes the bringing up of Fray Gerúndio and the school of oratory to which he owed his fame, may be reckoned among the best :—

---

[1] " Punto en boca, señores," exclamó Antón Zotes de repente, "ahora me incurre un estupendísimo nombre que jamás se empuso á ningun

---

[1] " 'Hold your tongues,' exclaimed Antón Zotes suddenly, 'a stupendous name has just occurred to me, which has never been borne by any man and shall

nacido, y se ha de impuner á mi chicote. Gerúndio se ha de llamar, y no se ha de llamar de otra manera, aunque me lo pidiera de rodillas el Padre Santo de Roma." . . . Hízose así ni más ni menos, y desde luego dió el niño grandes señales de lo que havía de ser en adelante, porque antes de dos años ya llamaba *pueca* á su madre con mucha gracia, y decía *no chero*, *querno*, tan claramente como si fuera persona : de manera que era la diversión del lugar, y todos decían que havía de ser la honra de Campazas. Passando por allí un Frayle Lego, que estaba en opinión de Santo porque á todos trataba de *tú*, llamaba *bichos* á las mugeres, y á la Virgen *la Borrega*, dixo que aquel niño havía de ser Frayle, gran Letrado, y estupendo Predicador ; el suceso acreditó la verdad de la profecía ; porque en quanto á Frayle lo fué tanto como el que más ; lo de gran Letrado, si no lo verificó en esto de tener muchas letras, á lo menos en quanto á ser gordas y abultadas las que tenía ; y en lo de ser estupendo Predicador, no huvo más que desear, porque éste fué el talento más sobresaliente de nuestro Gerúndico, como se verá en el discurso de la Historia. Aun no sabía leer y ya sabía predicar. . . . En cierta ocasión estuvo en su casa á la questa del mes de Agosto un Padrecito de estos atusados, con su poco de copete en el frontispicio, cuellierguido, barbirubio, de hábito limpio y plegado, zapato chusco, calzón de ante, y gran cantador de jácaras á la guitarrilla. . . . Pues como supieron que predicaba en Cabrerizos el sermón de Ánimas, concurrieron con efecto todos á oírle . . . y el buen Religioso quedó tan pagado de su sermón que repitía muchas

be given to my brat ; Gerúndio he shall be named and not otherwise even though the Holy Father of Rome were to beg it on bended knees.' . . . And so it was, exactly, and from the very first the child gave remarkable proofs of what he was destined to become, for before he was two years old he had the wit to call his mother 'piggy' and used to say 'I shan't, so there,' as distinctly as if he were a reasonable being : so that he was the delight of the village and everybody said that he would be a credit to Campazas. There chanced to come that way a lay friar who was looked upon as a saint because he thee'd and thou'd everybody, called the women 'dear creatures' and the Virgin 'the Ewe' : he declared that the boy would make a friar, a great man of letters and surprising preacher : events proved the truth of his prophecy for, as regards being a friar, he was so as much as the best of them ; as for letters, if he did not fulfil it by becoming very learned he did so at any rate by the pompousness and weightiness of such as he possessed : as a preacher he left nothing to be desired, for this was the greatest of all the talents of our Gerúndio as will be seen in the course of the story. Even before he could read, he could preach. . . . On a certain occasion there happened to be stopping in the house for the August offertory one of those smart little Fathers with a little curl on his forehead, head erect, fair beard, clean and pleated cassock, neat shoes and leather breeches, a famous singer of lively ditties to the guitar. . . . So when they heard that he was going to preach at Cabrerizos the sermon for the souls in Purgatory, all were eager of course to hear him. . . . and the good monk was so delighted with his sermon that he used to declaim paragraphs of it. 'Listen to the exordium,'

cláusulas de él. . . . "Oigan ustedes como comenzaba" dixo la primera noche, "¡Fuego, fuego, fuego! que se quema la casa : *Domus mea domus orationis vocabitur.* Ea Sacristán tocá esas retumbantes campanas : *In cymbalis bene sonantibus.* Assí lo hace ; porque tocar á muerto y tocar á fuego es una misma cosa. . . . Pero qué veo ? ¡ Ay Christianos que se abrasan las Ánimas de los Fieles ! *Fidelium animae:* y sirve de yesca á las voraces llamas derretida pez : *Requiescant in pace, id est in pice,* como expone Vatablo ; ¡ Fuego de Dios, como quema ! *Ignis a Deo illatus.* Pero albricias, ya baxa la Virgen del Carmen a librar á los que traxeron su devoto excapulario : *Scapulis suis.* Dice Christo 'Favor á la justicia' : dice la Virgen 'Válgame la gracia. Ave María.' . . ." Á todo esto estaba muy atento el niño Gerúndio y no le quitaba ojo al Religioso. . . . Acostóle su madre . . . y á la mañana, luego que dispertó, se puso de pies y en camisa sobre la cama, y comenzó á predicar con mucha gracia el Sermón pero sin atar ni desatar, y repitiendo no más que aquellas palabras mas fáciles que podía pronunciar su tiernecita lengua. . . . Antón Zotes y su muger quedaron aturdidos : diéronle mil besos. . . .

There is no doubt that Isla's satire was keenly felt by those to whom it was addressed. A warm polemic followed, and the bogey of the Inquisition, shorn by this time of most of its terrors, was brought in to scare the witty Jesuit. Besides *Fray Gerúndio*, Isla wrote several other satires of less note, some works of devotion, and an admirable translation of the *Gil Blas* of Le Sage which, as he says, he wished to restore to its native language.

Two other churchmen, one a Jesuit and the other a

said he the first night, ' Fire ! fire ! fire ! the house is on fire ! *Domus mea domus orationis vocabitur.* Ho, sexton ring those echoing bells : *In cymbalis bene sonantibus.* That's the way, for the knell for the dying and the tocsin for fire are all one. . . . But what is this ? ah Christians, the souls of the faithful are burning, *fidelium animae :* and melted pitch feeds the voracious flame : *requiescant in pace, id est in pice,* as Vatablus interprets : God's fire, how it burns ! *ignis a Deo illatus :* Good news, good news ! the Virgin of Carmel is coming down to deliver those who have worn her scapulary with devotion : *scapulis suis :* Christ says " Help in the king's name "; the Virgin says "Heaven protect me ; Ave María " . . .' All this little Gerúndio listened to with much attention not taking his eyes off the preacher. . . . His mother put him to bed . . . and next morning, on awaking he rose up in his shirt upon his bed and began to preach the sermon very prettily, but without stops, or breaks, and repeating only such easy words as his childish tongue could pronounce. . . . Antón Zotes and his wife were amazed : they kissed him a thousand times. . . ."

Benedictine, both of them natives of Galicia, attained considerable reputation during the eighteenth century, but rather as scholars than as men of letters. In an age more productive of first-rate writers their names would probably have been passed over, but Spain undoubtedly owes a good deal to Father Sarmiento, whose *Essays on the History of Poetry* and on *Spanish Poets* did much to bring the older literature again into fashion; also to his master, Benito Feyjoo, whose lifelong efforts were devoted to an attempt to bring up the level of knowledge in his own country to something like that which was general throughout the rest of Europe. The vast amount of subjects treated of by Feyjoo in his *Teatro crítico* and *Cartas eruditas* made it impossible for him to be an original worker in any one department, but he had a keen critical faculty, and though his work is defaced by an abominable style and is of little value at the present day, to him may be traced the origin of a sort of revival of learning in Spain which is still going on.

Bare and scanty as is the foregoing notice of the eighteenth century, it probably errs on the side of excessive length if the relative merit of writers is to be taken as the standard of the space they should occupy in a History of Literature. Not only are the majority of the works themselves worthless, but they form, as it were, a useless continuation of a departed period without serving to bridge over the gulf that separates the old Spanish school from the new.

CHAPTER XX

THE nineteenth century dawned darkly for Spain : to those who could look back two hundred years and compare the Spain of their own day with the Spain of Philip the Second, the prospect must have been dismal indeed. The foreigners held the land in an iron grip, and the men who ought to have been the leaders of the people in the gallant struggle for liberty that was shortly to break out, were, for the most part, the first to accept the bondage that had been laid upon their country, and to decry their national institutions and deride their national history in a real or affected admiration for its oppressors. The influence of the French Revolution was everywhere felt, and it combined with selfishness to drown the voice of patriotism among the upper classes in Spain. But the heart of the people remained true, and never for an instant lost sight of the national independence which it held so dear.

A great war and mighty revolution passed over the country, and when the air cleared again Spain found herself dragged from the middle age in which she had lingered into the full blaze of nineteenth century life. The gallant struggle against the French in which every province joined did much to increase the feeling of Spanish unity, and old feuds and jealousies were forgotten. The renewed national life bore fruit in fresh activity in every direction, and in literature, as well as in politics, Spain began slowly but surely to win back her position among the nations.

The struggle between the Classical and Romantic schools which was fought out in Europe at the beginning of the present century has left its traces in Spain. The strongest growths of Spanish literature had had a popular origin; the modern classical spirit penetrated the country only with the French influence, and was never accepted by the general body. Its productions are many, but are of little note, for classicism in Spain was but the imitation of an imitation. It is a curious fact that some of the most stirring verses addressed to the people at the time of their struggle for independence are written in this essentially unnational and artificial style. It cannot be denied that those who roused the Spaniards to throw off the yoke were those who had imbibed the ideas of their oppressors rather than those who clung to the old Catholic and monarchical traditions.

Among such must be noted Manuel José Quintana, a friend and pupil of the patriot Jovellanos, himself a poet and an orator of no mean order. Quintana drew his inspiration from the events of his own day, or from such recollections of the past as would make his countrymen less tolerant of their dependent condition. His odes *To the Sea, To the Invention of Printing, To the Rising of the Spanish Provinces against the French*, and *To Guzmán the Good*, are full of spirit, and in spite of their widely different subject, may be compared in tone to the finest poems of Herrera. The liberal ideas of his day never for a moment weakened the strong national feeling in the heart of this truly patriotic Spaniard. Quintana wrote, moreover, in the classic style two tragedies on national subjects which never attained any popularity, as well as a collection of graphic and well-told *Lives of Celebrated Spaniards* and *Selections from the Spanish Poets*, with admirable short critical prefaces.

The list of the classical poets of the earlier part of the present century includes several other names of second-rate importance. These men departed from the literary traditions of their country, and, possessing but little individuality, their works lost even the small interest which they for a time possessed, when the reaction began in favour of the school which had produced all the great works of which Spain can boast.

Martinez de la Rosa is the author of a frigid satire *el Cementerio de Momo ;* of a most artistically composed but hollow-sounding *endecha*, or lament, addressed to the Duke of Frias on the death of his wife ; and of several plays of some merit. Alberto Lista, a weaver of Seville, who became Professor of Mathematics, wrote a fine poem on the *Death of Jesus*, which has something of the inspiration and delicacy of Luís de León. Juan Nicasio Gallego, a priest and a chauvinist, drew genuine inspiration for his verses from the rising against the French in Madrid, known as the *dos de Mayo*, and from the defeat of the English at Buenos Ayres in 1807.

The Romantic school produced two poets of vastly greater importance than those above mentioned. These are the Duke of Rivas and Espronceda. The former was a nobleman of enlightened views and cultivated tastes. His early writings bear traces of the classical traditions amidst which he had been brought up. Carried away, however, by the current which was setting strongly towards Romanticism throughout Europe, he produced a long and rambling poem with epic pretensions, to which he gave the name of *Moro expósito ó Córdoba y Burgos en el Siglo X*. A few fine passages were not enough to save it from speedy oblivion, and the author's best title to fame lies in his ballads, which are really successful imitations of old models, and in his *Don Álvaro*, a tragedy of the most harrowing kind, full of the bloodshed and gloomy passion which excited the admiration of a past generation, but which would now be laughed off a French or English stage.

Don José de Espronceda is undoubtedly the greatest Spanish poet of the present century: thus much can be gathered from the fragments which form the larger part of his works—fragments which would probably have remained incomplete even had their author not been carried off by an early death. Espronceda was the son of a Spanish colonel, and was born in Extremadura. On going to Madrid to complete his studies he threw himself with all the eagerness of an impassioned nature into the revolutionary schemes which were then to the fore. His violent and open opposition to the existing order brought upon him a decree of banishment, and he left his country to seek his fortunes abroad. A characteristic anecdote is told of his journey into exile. On approaching Lisbon he threw away the last coin he possessed, "so as not to enter so great a city with so little money." He found his way to London, where for some time he lived a miserable and precarious life, keeping up his communications with the revolutionaries in his own country and elsewhere. The revolution of 1830 in Paris found him fighting on the barricades and taking a prominent part in what he believed to be the cause of liberty. The general amnesty brought him back to Spain, where his genius was now recognised; he obtained important preferment under Government, and contributed stirring articles to the newspapers. He died in 1842, aged only thirty-two, but worn out by his feverish temperament, strong passions, and the hardships he had endured.

Very early in life his sensitive and passionate temperament found its natural expression in poetry, and he commenced an epic, taking for its subject Pelayo, the earliest hero of the reconquest. The fragments that are preserved are very uneven in merit, but give ample proof of great talent and real inspiration, the defects being those of youth and inexperience. During his residence in England it was inevitable that he should come under the influence of Byron, which was at that time supreme. The two poets possessed many qualities in common, especially a morbid selfishness and a restlessness not unconnected with ambition. The younger henceforth affected, even when he did not feel, the defects as well as the merits of his master. Espronceda's verse is an accurate reflection of his life and character, full of gloomy fire, of passions too great to be satisfied with vulgar debauchery, and of impossible ideals. As a sceptic and revolutionary he has little that is characteristically Spanish, but he turned the sonorous grandeur of his native language to good account in portraying the sombre self-consciousness and superhuman adventures of men of the Byronic world. His *Estudiante de Salamanca*, Don Felix de Montemar, is a Don Juan in slightly altered circumstances ; a man with passions unchecked by religious belief or scruples of honour, and with the same undaunted courage in face of the supernatural world. The first part of the poem is powerfully written, and, in spite of the villainous character, we cannot help feeling some sympathy for the very recklessness of the hero whose superhuman wickedness must inevitably bring him to a hideous end. But, when Don Felix falls in with the ghostly being who, disguised as a lady, draws him on to his fate, the horror is too long drawn out ; the warnings are too many for a human being to resist ; the poet's imagination runs riot ; what is meant to be awful becomes merely fantastic ; and the catastrophe, when it does come, brings with it a sense of relief, and is not to be compared for simplicity and power with that of its prototype, *The Mocker of Seville*.

The second of Espronceda's longer pieces is incomplete. In the *Diablo Mundo* the poet, as he himself tells us, set himself the task of resolving the problem of human life from the sceptic's point of view. It is scarcely to be wondered at that the undertaking appalled him, and that he abandoned it after writing a few cantos, some of which have apparently no connection with the subject. The plan of this remarkable poem, so far as we can judge of it by the fragment, seems to have been taken from *Faust*. The principal personage is restored from old age to youth, and enters on his new life with some of the feelings and tendencies peculiar to either age. The execution is very uneven, and most of the fine passages seem to be introduced at haphazard, and to be inspired by the authors whom Espronceda may have been reading at the time. Some of the reflections on human life are sublime, as are also the *Song of Life* and the *Song of Death*, which seem to have caught something of the inspiration of Calderón's *autos sacramentales*.

Among the shorter pieces notable specimens of Espronceda's power of description and expression may be found in *The Beggar* (El Mendigo) and *The Executioner* (El Verdugo), subjects chosen for the sake of their grotesque and repulsive character, which undoubtedly attracted Espronceda's morbid temperament. Their treatment would satisfy a "naturalist" of the modern French school. The *Serenade to Elisa* is tender, dignified, and harmonious, even beyond the wont of Spanish verse. The ode *To Jarifa* expresses finely the disgust produced in a really noble mind by the orgy into which it has allowed itself to be drawn, but it is not without a tinge of the loathing produced by satiety. Those entitled *To my Country* (*A la Patria*) and *To the 2nd of May* (*Al dos de Mayo*) breathe the fiery patriotism of their author. From the former are extracted the following verses :—

> [1] ¡ Cuán solitaria la nación que un día
> Poblara inmensa gente !
> ¡ La nación cuyo imperio se extendía
> Del ocaso al oriente !
> Lagrimas viertes, infeliz ahora,
> Soberana del mundo ;

---

[1] "How forlorn is now the nation that was once—thronged with innumerable folk !—The nation whose empire spread—from the setting to the rising sun ! —Thy tears flow fast, unhappy now,—once sovereign of the world ;—will no

¡ Y nadie de tu faz encantadora
Borra el dolor profundo !

.   .   .   .   .

Tendió sus brazos la agitada España
Sus hijos implorando ;
Sus hijos fueron, más traidora saña
Desbarató su bando.
¿ Qué se hicieron tus muros torreados ?
¡ Oh mi patria querida !
¿ Donde fueron tus héroes esforzados,
Tu espada no vencida ?
Un tiempo España fué ; cien héroes fueron
En tiempos de ventura,
Y las naciones tímidas la vieron
Vistosa en hermosura.

.   .   .   .   .

Mas ora, como piedra en el desierto,
Yaces desamparada,
Y el justo desgraciado vaga incierto
Allá en tierra apartada.

.   .   .   .   .

Desterrados ¡ oh Dios ! de nuestros lares
Lloremos duelo tanto :
¿ Quién calmará ¡ oh España ! tus pesares ?
¿ Quién secará tu llanto ?

The Spaniards have contributed but little to modern philosophy. Their theologians have always enjoyed a deservedly high reputation, but in other departments of thought their development has certainly been checked both by the tradition of rigid and unquestioning orthodoxy, which is so dear to "the most Catholic nation," and by the objective character of their minds. This latter peculiarity is noticeable throughout their

one from thy beauteous face—blot out the woe profound ?—Distracted Spain stretched out her arms—calling upon her sons for help :—her sons they were, but traitor's hate—dispersed the band,—Where are thy battlemented walls,— sweet fatherland ?—Whither are gone thy valiant sons,—and thy unconquered sword ?—Once Spain was Spain : a hundred heroes had she—in happy days, —and nations with affright beheld her—glorious and beautiful—Now like a rock in the wilderness—thou liest all forlorn,—thy patriots wander full of gloom—in foreign lands afar.—Exiled, oh God ! from our own hearths—our grief and tears must flow :—who shall assuage, oh Spain, thy woes,—and who shall dry thine eyes ?"

literature, and leads them to express all profound thought in the concrete form of metaphors.

Two Spaniards have, during the present century, entered the lists of religious controversy as champions of orthodoxy, and have thereby won a high reputation in their native country. The first of these is the famous Don Jaime Balmés, whose *Cartas á un Escéptico* (Letters to a Sceptic), according to the verdict of a recent Spanish writer, "bring within the grasp of the most limited intelligence the loftiest truths of religion." His *Protestantism compared with Catholicism* is supposed by his countrymen to have set the question of which it treats at rest for ever.

Contemporary with Balmés was Don Juan Donoso Cortés, whose important political service in troubled times raised him from the chair of literature in the University of Cáceres to the post of ambassador in Paris, with the title of Marques de Valdegamas. His most celebrated work, *An Essay upon Catholicism, Liberalism, and Socialism,* is dogmatic rather than controversial; it is, in fact, a statement of the author's own ideas in somewhat pompous terms, with a haughty disregard for all other opinions.

The revival that took place after the War of Independence has produced good results, and Spain in spite of her comparatively small reading public can challenge comparison in one or two departments of literature with other European nations. Only a generation ago the most cultivated of the Spaniards looked to foreigners to supply them with books, while the multitude was satisfied with bad translations of the worst class of French works. South America now lies open as a great field to Spanish authors, and every day the demand for good literature increases at home. The old bad feeling of Spanish exclusiveness and the detestation of things foreign, which took the name of patriotism, are wearing off; the regret of a past that can never be repeated no longer prevents a hopeful looking forward to the future.

The novel in Spain, as elsewhere, is the most vigorous of modern literary growths. The *pícaro* of the sixteenth and seventeenth centuries became at last a prosy moralist of third-rate order, and then disappeared to make room for the sickly sentimental gallants and ladies of the last century. These too died of inanition and left the field free for something more adapted to modern times, and something more natural than the shepherds and shepherdesses of a former age.

The first who made the modern novel popular, and gave the impulse which was destined to result in works worthy to be compared with those of the great days of Spain, was Cecilia Boehl de Faber, a lady of German descent, born at the end of the last century and widely known under the assumed name of Fernán Caballero. She was married successively to three Spanish husbands, and thoroughly identified herself with the country of her adoption. In her literary work she made use of the improved methods with which she had become familiar in the course of a German education. At court she enjoyed favour as the champion of the Neo-Catholic movement. Her works consist mainly of short stories and sketches from Spanish life, drawn with great accuracy and true appreciation of the picturesque, and told in idiomatic and unaffected language. Her moral aim is high, and she was bold enough to openly attack some of the most cherished national institutions, not excepting the bull-fights. But her love of Spain, its traditions and scenery, its strongly marked characteristics and robust beliefs, is so evident that her foreign parentage has been forgotten, and the Spaniards proudly count her as one of themselves. Forty years have changed the form and character of the novel, and Fernán Caballero's work now appears somewhat old-fashioned and tame to those who are steeped in the modern French fiction. But it will ever remain popular with those whose tastes have not been corrupted by a stronger food, and who consider that delicacy of thought and language and a high moral tone are appreciable merits in a story.

Somewhat similar to Fernán Caballero in method and in aim is Don Telesforo Trueba y Cossío, an Asturian who emigrated to England in 1823 and there wrote the greater part of his works, in which the influence of Sir Walter Scott is everywhere apparent. Trueba's vivid imagination enabled him in his *Spanish Tales* to bring up before his eyes the typical representatives of the country which in his exile he loved so well. He is not in any sense a great writer, but, aided by abundance of material of an attractive kind, and a true appreciation of the way in which it should be utilised, he has left behind him a collection of stories which well deserve the popularity which it enjoys. From Fernán Caballero the Spaniards learned that a simple well-executed sketch from nature is more valuable than an elaborate copy : from her and from Trueba they learned that it was not necessary to go outside their own country for interesting material.

Among writers of short stories and magazine articles on the national manners and customs, or on events of the day, three names deserve special mention. The first of these is that of Don Mariano Larra, who committed suicide in 1837 at the age of twenty-eight. His articles on political and literary subjects give proof of profound observation and keen wit ; they are, however, in some degree spoiled by a bitter and cynical tone which, coupled with the author's idiomatic and somewhat harsh style, reminds us of Quevedo, whom he probably took for his model. He wrote under the names of *Fígaro* and *Un pobrecito Hablador*.

A writer of somewhat similar character to the foregoing, though otherwise marked by strong idiosyncrasies, is Don Serafín Estebañez Calderón, an Andalusian gentleman who played a considerable part in the politics of the troubled times in which he lived. He was a great admirer of the old-fashioned

Spain, which in his time was rapidly passing away, and a vigorous opponent of foreign influences and what he considered to be new-fangled ideas. His *Escenas Andaluzas* have been often quoted as models of pure Spanish prose, free from the bastard words and expressions which bad translations from the French had brought into the language. Undoubtedly he is deserving of credit for having headed the reaction in favour of pure Spanish, but his works can scarcely be considered as models of the kind. In the attempt to be idiomatic his style becomes strained and unnatural, and he abuses the extensive vocabulary of his native tongue, making use by choice of archaic, provincial, or little-used words. The memory of Estebañez Calderón owes much to his distinguished kinsman Don Antonio Cánovas del Castillo, the present Prime Minister of Spain, who wrote his biography under the title of *El Solitario y su Tiempo*, making it the vehicle for the expression of his own straightforward and manly views on many subjects both political and literary.

More truly popular and more elegant than either of the two above-mentioned writers is Mesonero Romanos (*El Curioso Parlante*). He was a native of Madrid ; his birthplace inspired in him the same affection as it did in Ramón de la Cruz, and he turned to equally good use an extensive and sympathetic acquaintance with his fellow-townsmen. His *Escenas Matritenses* are charming sketches of manners and of popular types, some of which were rapidly losing their strongly marked characteristics even when the book was written. His language, pure, idiomatic, and graceful, is unspoiled by the mannerisms and affectation of Calderón. His name is still held in affectionate esteem in the city he loved and described so well in *El antiguo Madrid*. Both in form and matter he is one of the most thoroughly agreeable of modern Spanish authors.

Together with Mesonero Romanos, though belonging by his date to the next chapter, must be mentioned Gustavo Becquer, who, at his early death, left behind him a collection of *Legends* of uneven merit, some of them founded on popular stories, others derived entirely from the author's passionate and romantic imagination. When he treats of Spanish subjects as in *la Rosa de la Pasión, Maese Perez el Organista*, and *el Cristo de la Vega*, Becquer is almost always successful; but he is less so in stories such as *Ojos Verdes*, in which he attempts to reproduce the weirdness and melancholy peculiar to Scandinavian or Celtic stories. Becquer at his best is extremely good, but the necessities of a continual struggle with poverty compelled him to publish much that his reason and taste must have condemned. Some of his verses are beautiful and full of pathos; the following recalls certain passages of Alfred de Musset's impassioned lines, or Espronceda's longings after the ideal :—

> [1] Yo soy ardiente, yo soy morena,
> Yo soy el símbolo de la pasión,
> De ansia de goces mi alma está llena
> —¿Á mí me buscas?—No es á tí : no.

> —Mi frente es pálida : mis trenzas de oro :
> Puedo brindarte dichas sin fin ;
> Yo de ternura guardo un tesoro.
> —¿Á mí me llamas?—No : no es á tí.

> —Yo soy un sueño, un imposible,
> Vano fantasma de niebla y luz :
> Soy incorpórea, soy intangible :
> No puedo amarte.—¡ Oh, ven ; ven tú !

---

[1] "'Fervid and dark-haired am I,—the very type of passion,—my soul is overflowing with longing for delights.—Is it me thou seekest?'—'No, not thee.'—'My forehead is pale : my tresses of gold :—I can offer thee unending bliss ;—my heart is a well of tenderness.—Is it me thou callest?'—'No, it is not thee'—'I am a dream, impossible,—a phantom vain of mist and light : —bodiless, intangible,—I cannot love thee,'—'Oh come, come thou.'"

CHAPTER XXI

THE following notices of contemporary authors, most of whom are still alive, will for obvious reasons be very brief, intended rather to direct a course of reading than to criticise. The series opens with a really great writer, Juan Valera, poet, critic, and novelist. It is more especially in the latter direction that Valera has developed his great talents. His *Pepita Jimenez* is worthy of a place among the best novels of the century. Whether regarded as a study of character, or as a study of manners, or from the point of view of style, it is equally admirable. It combines all the passion of the South with the most delicate and refined taste, and might serve as a text from which to prove that, in the hands of really great writers, nothing is coarse or unclean. It has been well rendered into English, but must lose greatly by translation, for, since the time of the mystic writers of the sixteenth and seventeenth centuries who served as his models, nobody has handled the most beautiful of living languages with the same unaffected grace as Valera. The reputation established by *Pepita Jimenez* is well sustained by *Doña Luz*, *El Comendador Mendoza*, and other stories. Of Valera's poems the chief merit is grace and correctness. His essays show wide sympathies and an eclectic taste which, combined with what Morel-Fatio so happily calls his " fine scepticism," have more than once brought their author into difficulties with the champions of narrower national and religious sentiments.

Perez Galdos enjoys a wide reputation earned by his *Episodios Nacionales*, careful and doubtless accurate studies of the feelings and views that have prevailed at different epochs of Spain's stormy history during the last hundred years. From them his countrymen may derive much political teaching that may be useful for the future ; but the stories themselves lack dramatic interest ; a certain sameness pervades the whole series, making them dull reading to such as are not thoroughly familiar with the country and the intricate party organisation of the periods of which they treat. Galdos' style is pure without pretensions to brilliancy ; but he would probably find more readers if he would descend to the level of those who consider that a plot is an essential part of the novel.

Pedro Alarcón followed the Spanish expeditionary forces in their brilliant campaign in Morocco, and wrote a good description of the expedition and of the country through which it passed. He is also a poet and critic of no small merit, but his reputation would not stand so high as it does were it not for his novels. Of these the most remarkable is the *Sombrero de Tres Picos*, a charmingly quaint and graceful sketch of old-fashioned village life which in subject as well as in treatment forms a marked contrast with his sensational stories such as *El Escándalo* or *La Pródiga*. In his longer works Alarcón loses most of the charm that pervades his *Historietas Nacionales*, *Narraciones Inverosímiles*, and *Viages por España*.

Pereda is a native of Santander ; he has a deep love and appreciation of the character and peculiarities of his fellow-countrymen whom he so successfully portrays in his works. *Sotilezas*, his most famous book, is a powerful picture of life amongst the fisher-folk of the northern town before it became a great industrial centre. The characters are sharply defined and well drawn, but the plot, like others by the same hand, is somewhat melodramatic. In *Sotilezas*, as elsewhere, Pereda writes a great deal of his dialogue in dialect. A less pretentious and more successful story, though not possessing the same perfection of detail, is *Don Gonzalo Gonzalez ;* in it, however, the principal person comes dangerously near caricature.

Emilia Pardo Bazán enjoys the distinction of being one of the very few distinguished authoresses of her country, and of possessing an education and breadth of view that are rare among Spaniards even of the other sex. She is a native of Galicia and, like its other celebrated children, she is enthusiastic in her affection for her native province. Its men and manners, its scenery and life, are the themes of her works, and all who read the *Pazos de Ulloa* and the *Madre Naturalza* will feel himself brought into sympathy with their authoress's point of view. Her articles on the social and intellectual condition of her country are valuable both as authorities for the existing condition of things, and as guides for the direction in which the desired improvements may be carried out. Patriotic feeling, which she possesses in a marked degree, does not blind this gifted authoress to the faults of her countrymen and to the backward state of her country. She belongs to the liberal party whose head is the great orator Castelar, himself a novelist, and author of a pretty Italian story in the style of George Eliot's *Romola* entitled *La Hermana de la Caridad*.

The position of Armando Palacio Valdés with regard to the contemporary literature of his country is as yet undecided. His *Hermana San Sulpicio*, published four years ago, is a work of great merit, thoroughly Spanish in tone, well executed, and containing some very clever character-drawing. It was greatly admired both in Spain and abroad, and much was expected from its author. A great disappointment, however, awaited his many friends. In *La Espuma* (Foam), published in 1890, he shows a decided leaning to the French "naturalistic" school, and wilfully introduces repulsive or indecent scenes and incidents which, though powerfully drawn, add nothing to the merit of his story, and sometimes have no bearing whatever on its main action. If in this respect he will take his country-man Valera for a model, he will secure the admiration and respect of a larger class of readers without finding himself restricted as to subject or treatment.

In 1890 appeared *Pequeñeces* by the Padre Luís Coloma of the Society of Jesus. The book is, according to the disposition of the reader, either a brilliant satire or a bitter attack on Madrid society. It is held together by the mere shadow of a plot or psychological study. *Pequeñeces* together with a collection of short stories of the nature of tracts, published at various times in religious periodicals, form the literary stock of this writer, who during the last two years has occupied a large share of public attention in Spain. The Padre Coloma's view of life, so far as it may be inferred from these works, is of the one-sided and narrow character to be expected from one who has studied his fellow-men chiefly in the confessional. His want of faith in human nature almost amounts to a cynicism which must be far from natural to him who created *el tío Pellejo*. The fact that his lash produced a smart is proved by the amount of controversy his somewhat crude religious novel has created. Valera himself came forward to reply to his strictures. Coloma's ideas, or perhaps we should say the ideas that Coloma attempts to propagate,—for we cannot quite believe that a man of his undoubted talents has allowed a narrowing early education so completely to restrict his private views,—are those of the extreme ultramontane party, and must, in some respects, be characterised as bigoted to a degree that is now happily rare in his country and among his class. Years and experience will probably produce a more hopeful and tolerant spirit, and then the writings of the witty Jesuit will appeal to a more intelligent class, and, instead of repelling, may attract those whom he wishes to influence. For the present his teaching may be summed up in the words of the Spanish proverb "*la ocasión hace al ladron*" (opportunity makes the thief), and he would have us believe that there is no salvation outside his own narrow fold.

The present century has produced no great Spanish historian. The work of Don Modesto Lafuente is painstaking and accurate, but possesses none of the elements that go to make a great book of lasting value.   While the general historian is still wanting, an immense amount of valuable work is being done among the archives and the history of particular periods.   When at last something like a final history of Spain is written, its author will owe a great debt of gratitude to writers like the jurist Don Francisco de Cardenas, the historian and critic Marcelino Menendez y Pelayo, and the statesman Cánovas del Castillo, who brought up the history of the House of Austria to the degree of perfection allowed by the documents known at the period when he wrote.   In the great archives of Simancas and in local records a great field lies open for historical enterprise, and the Spaniards, headed by such men as the learned Jesuit Fidel Fita and the members of the Academy of History, are not slow to take advantage of it.

As scholar, critic, historian, philologist, and biographer, the name of Pascual de Gayangos is held in affectionate respect by all those who during the last fifty years have interested themselves in the history and literature of his mother-country.   A long chapter would be occupied by the mere enumeration of the signal services rendered by this most learned, unselfish, and modest of workers in each of these departments.   From Prescott and Ticknor to Watts, all English students of Spanish have acknowledged their obligation to his immense fund of knowledge and ever-ready kindness.   In spite of his advanced age Don Pascual is still one of the most distinguished living orientalists, as is proved by his *History of the Arabs in Spain*, *Vocabulary of the Arabic Words in Spanish*, and his great

Catalogue of Spanish MSS. in the British Museum. He contributed largely to the great edition of the Spanish classics
published by Rivadeneyra under the name of the *Biblioteca de
Autores Españoles;* he published in Spanish an amended edition
of Ticknor's great work on Spanish literature, and has edited
several valuable works in the Spanish Old Text Society (*Biblió-
filos Españoles*).   Side by side with Gayangos for thoroughness
of method and disinterested love of knowledge may be classed
Marcelino Menendez y Pelayo, the author of a *History of
Heterodoxy in Spain* and of a *History of Aesthetic Ideas in Spain,*
the latter work still unfinished, possibly on account of its
author's early promotion to a high position among the leaders
of the conservative and traditional party which includes much
of what is best in modern Spain.

Of contemporary Spanish poets Nuñez de Arce is probably
the one who gives proof of the most genuine inspiration.
Less prodigal of his talents than his brethren, his works main-
tain a more even standard of excellence.   They consist of a
collection of lyrics, several dramas, and some short poems.
Nuñez de Arce is a man of action as well as a poet.   His
verses as well as his public conduct have played no small part
in piloting his native land through the troubles of the last fifty
years.   The watchword of his life has been ever Liberty, and
for liberty he has fought, holding revolutionary license no less
in abhorrence than tyranny.   With regard to the present age
he is a pessimist, regarding it merely as a painful state of
transition, but looking forward to a time when the problems
which now vex humanity shall be solved, and the destructive
tendency of modern philosophy shall be replaced by a faitn
founded on a higher knowledge.   He hates the sneering spirit
that has deprived the world of so much that was beautiful in
itself and good in its results ; he is inclined to think that the
price we have paid for our present enlightenment is too high a
one.   The restless and revolutionary spirit of the times he

attributes to the diffusion of dangerous knowledge calculated to destroy the existing sanctions of morality.　To his lyrics he has given the expressive title of *Gritos del Combate* (The Shouts of Battle), and such indeed they are, wrung from their author by the agony of his country's dangers and addressed to his fellow-workers in the cause which he had made his own.　Nuñez de Arce is no poetic dreamer : he saw that his country offered no soil on which an exotic republic could flourish, and he declared himself a monarchist, preferring even Amadeo's necessarily weak government to the incessant struggle of interested ambition for the first place.　With the accession of Don Alfonso the struggle ceased, and with it the *Gritos del Combate*.　Since that time the poetic muse has taken a gentler form and appeals to a different set of feelings, occupied rather in social and philosophical than in poetical matters.　Remarkable among the short poems are the *Visión de Fray Martín* and *Raymondo Lull*.　In the former the story of Lully's conversion (see p. 57) is treated as an allegory of the reckless pursuit after knowledge and of its bitter fruits.　Fray Martín is Luther who, seduced by the doubting spirit to which Nuñez de Arce attributes so much evil, drags down in his own ruin the whole fabric of the Church.　These allegories are skilfully and vigorously handled, and even those who are not in sympathy with their teaching cannot fail to be influenced by their powerful imagery and striking thoughts. Speaking of the hereafter the poet says—

> [1] ¿Quién interroga á los sepulcros? Nadie
> Sabrá jamás lo que en su abismo encierran
> ¿Es la vida? ¿Es la muerte? ¿Es el principio?
> ¿Es el fin? ¿Es la nada? . . . ¡Eterno enigma !—
> ¡Este es el mundo ! El vértigo en su altura ;
> Abajo la bullente podedumbre,
> Y en el altar la sombra . . .

---

[1] " Who gets an answer from the grave ?—No man will ever know what its depths enclose—Is it life ? Is it death ? Is it the beginning ?—Is it the end ? Is it nonentity ? Eternal riddle !—Such is the universe ! Above is the giddy height ;—below is seething rottenness,—and a shadow on the altar. . . ."

The simple love-story that bears the name of *An Idyll* has been compared to *Evangeline* and *Mireio ;* a more apt comparison would be that with *Paul and Virginia*, but the Spanish poet's conception of love is purer than that of the French priest, while his local colouring is none the less vivid. One of the most beautiful passages in the *Idilio* is a description of the scenery of Castile, which brings out all the poetry of its brown plains as seen by an artist who loved them as his home. The *Short Poems* are written in harmonious and finished verse, and appeal strongly to the higher and nobler feelings, but it is probably in his *Gritos del Combate* that Nuñez de Arce will live. Even in the present time of peace, when their echo seems to come from afar off, they cannot fail to stir deeply every Spanish heart. Should their fame, however, not prove enduring, their influence on contemporary thought is enough to justify the existence of poets in the nineteenth century. The dramas, of which the most interesting is the *Haz de Leña* (Bundle of Fire-wood) founded on the same story as Schiller's *Don Carlos*, are well written without being remarkable ; they may be fairly said to fulfil their author's intention as expressed in the words, " I have attempted to be classical without becoming a prey to mannerism, romantic yet free from monstrosity, realistic without provoking disgust ; but above all I have attempted clearness and sincerity in matter and in form."

Don José Zorrilla became, after the death of Espronceda, the chief representative of the Romantic school of poetry in Spain. Endowed with some poetic gifts, he abused more than any of his contemporaries an extraordinary facility for the production of second-rate verse. The following anecdote serves to show the mechanical and commercial uses to which he applied his real talents, as well as to illustrate the position of literary men in his country. When Zorrilla's reputation as a poet was at its height, it happened that a speculative firm of booksellers at Barcelona bought up some of the worn plates of

Doré's illustrations to Tennyson's *Idylls of the King*. Zorrilla accepted from this firm a commission to write poems on national subjects to suit the illustrations, and thus give the purchasers an opportunity of making use of their bargain. The contract was faithfully carried out.

But it is unfair to judge of Zorrilla's merits by the expedients to which he has been at various times reduced by pecuniary difficulties. In 1845 Zorrilla had already published ten successful volumes of verse and thirty dramas, but they brought their author little profit. His *Don Juan Tenorio*, though far inferior to Tirso de Molina's play on the same subject, is one of the most successful and popular dramas published in Spain during the present century. In spite of this we find him in 1854, after an unsuccessful attempt to retrieve his fortunes by means of a corrected edition of his works and an *Epic on Granada*, living in Mexico, where he enjoyed for some time the generous patronage of the unfortunate Emperor Maximilian. At the time of his protector's overthrow and death Zorrilla happened to be in Spain, and, finding himself cut off from all hope of help from abroad, he set to work to revive his somewhat faded laurels in his own country. Public sympathy was roused in favour of the old poet whose struggles against fortune had been crowned with so little success. He was warmly supported in the tours he made round Spain for the purpose of reading his own verses in public ; the Duchess of Medinaceli raised a small subscription which relieved him from his most pressing needs, and the Government finally granted him a small pension. Zorrilla's longer pieces are spoiled by haste, want of method, and a general slipshod air and lack of finish. This is the case with his epics on *Granada* and the *Cid*, in which even the sweetness of his verse cloys at length by its insipid monotony. For subjects for his poems he ransacked the legendary store of his country, but he rarely improved upon the simple and powerful traditional stories ; his ideal was something like Sir Walter Scott's poems, but he seldom approaches and still more rarely attains their standard of merit. At other times the legend under treatment actually loses dignity and point in the process of manufacture into a poem. Of Zorrilla's work very little is worth a second reading; the stories themselves remain engraven on the mind, but we are glad to forget the commonplace verse, which is all that their author contributed to them. He exercised, however, a wide influence on the minor poets of his time, and his work produced a host of imitators who accurately reproduced their master's faults—shallowness, commonplace, and lack of finish —without possessing his chivalrous heart and occasionally picturesque imagination.

Don José Selgas enjoyed during his lifetime a considerable reputation as a journalist; his sweet and amiable character had gained him many friends, and, after his death, his verses, which had appeared separately from time to time, were published by his admirers. They form a considerable collection of lyrics of great delicacy and beauty, full of deep appreciation of nature and a tender and romantic melancholy. Without containing anything of striking originality, they appeal to a large class of readers by their simplicity and harmonious versification. Their author's poetic imagination endowed each flower and rock with separate individuality; for him the voices of nature spoke in articulate tones, and he wrote down simply and faithfully the message that they gave. His manner is well illustrated in his graceful lyric :—

LA NOCHE.

[1] " ¿ Porqué la noche callada
De negras sombras se viste ?
¿ Acaso está enamorada ? "
" Está triste."

---

[1] "'Why is the silent night—clothed in black shadows ?—Is she perchance in love ?'—'She is sad.'—'Sad ! Does she soothe her woes—by

" ¡ Triste ! . . . ¿ Y su pesar alegra
   Rindiendo al amor tributo,
   Vestida de sombra negra ? "
    " Va de luto."
" ¡ Luto !   Por eso á deshora
   Camina con paso incierto :
   Ó celos ó ausencia llora."
    " Llora á un muerto."
" ¡ Muerto !   ¡ Muerto !   Triste punto
   De su amorosa porfía.
   Pero ¿ quién es el difunto ?
     ¿ Quién ? " . . . " El día.
   ¡ El día su faz esconde,
   Rotos los mortales lazos ! " . . .
   " Murió " . . . " pero ¿ cómo ? ¿ dónde ? " . . .
    " En sus brazos."
" ¡ En sus brazos !   ¡ Trance fuerte
   Que en negro luto la abisma ! . . .
   Pero ¿ quién le dió la muerte ? "
    " Ella misma.
   ¡ Por eso triste y callada
   De negras sombras se viste !
   Por eso viene enlutada
    Muda y triste."

Ramón de Campoamor, born in 1817, is a poet of a very different stamp.   An ardent admirer of Shakespeare, and, above all, of Byron, whose spirit pervaded Europe during the period of Campoamor's youth, he lit his modest torch at these great fires, and went forth into the world as their disciple.   As such he has no great pretensions to original inspiration, but his *Doloras* and *Cantares* sing in correct verse of the genuine feelings of a warm and open heart.   Campoamor's very goodness

paying her homage to love,—clothed in black shadows ? '—' She mourns.'—' Mourning !   And thus through the hours of sleep—she roams with wandering steps :—she mourns for the absent or faithless.—She weeps for her dead ' —' Dead ! dead ! Sad end—to her quest of love.—But who is the departed ? —Who ? '—' The day. — The day hath hidden his face—and broken the bonds of life.'—' He died.'   ' But how and where ? '—' In her arms.'—' In her arms !   Harsh fate—that has plunged her in weeds of woe !—But who was it that slew him ? '—' She, herself.—And thus, in sadness and silence, —she is clothed in black shadows—for this she comes in mourning garb— mute and woebegone.' "

of nature and simplicity contrast strongly with the Byronian sentiments in which he would conceal them; often do we find him like a child, playing at being very wicked, and knowing all the time that it is but play. A considerable part of his best verse consists of isolated thoughts, sometimes trivial, seldom profound, but often delicate and strikingly original in form, placed in the setting of a short couplet of simple structure that saves them from the artificiality of the sonnet. Such are the *Doloras* (Complaints), which their author defines as "poetic compositions combining lightness, sentiment, and brevity with philosophic importance."

Of his success in attaining his not unambitious object the reader may judge by the two following characteristic specimens :—

[1] Mal de Muchas.

" ¿ Qué mal, doctor, la arrebató la vida ? "
Rosaura preguntó con desconsuelo.
"Murió," dijo el doctor, "de una caída."
Pues "¿ de donde cayó ? "   "Cayó del cielo."

La Opinión.

¡ Pobre Carolina mía !
¡ Nunca la podré olvidar !
Ved lo que el mundo decía
Viendo el feretro pasar.

Un clérigo "Empiece el canto."
El doctor "Cesó de sufrir."
El padre "Me ahoga el llanto."
La madre "¡ Quiero morir !"

---

[1] "A Common Case.

"'Doctor, what was the ill that caused her death,'—asked Rosaura sorrowfully.—'She died,' said the doctor, 'from a fall.'—'Whence did she fall?'   'She fell from heaven.'"

"Impressions.

"My poor Carolina!—I shall never forget her.—Listen what the world said —when it saw the bier pass by—*A priest* 'Let the chaunt begin '—*The doctor* 'Her sufferings are over '—*The father* 'I am choked with weeping '—*The mother* 'Would I might die ! '—*A boy* 'How prettily decked !'—*A youth*

Un muchacho "¡ Que adornada ! "
Un joven "¡ Era muy bella ! "
Una moza "¡ Desgraciada ! "
Una vieja "¡ Feliz ella ! "

"¡ Duerme en paz ! " dicen los buenos.
"¡ Adios ! " dicen los demás
Un filósofo " Uno menos."
Un poeta " Un ángel más."

VERDAD DE LAS TRADICIONES.

I.

Vi una cruz en despoblado
Un día que al campo fuí,
Y un hombre me dijo " Allí
Mató á un ladrón un soldado.

II.

Y ¡ oh pérfida tradición !
Cuando del campo volví,
Otro hombre me dijo " Allí
Mató á un soldado un ladrón."

Campoamor's most ambitious work is the *Universal Drama* in which he attempts to imitate Dante and Milton. This long poem contains fine passages of verse and thoughts of a deeper character than the rest of his work would have justified us in ascribing to its author. But its whole tone clashes with the character of the somewhat sceptical, pantheistic, and epicurean Campoamor whom we know and admire, and with the *Doloras*, the clue to which is to be found in the verse—

' She was beautiful '—*A girl* ' Poor luckless one '—*An old woman* ' Happy she '—' She sleeps in peace,' say the good—' Farewell,' say the rest—*A philosopher* ' One less '—*A poet* ' One angel more.' "

"THE TRUTH OF TRADITIONS.

" I saw a cross on a desert spot—one day that I went abroad,—and a man said to me ' There—a robber was killed by a soldier.'—And, alas for the faith of legends !—when I came back again,—another man said to me ' There—a soldier was killed by a robber.' "

¹ Never will I write in my *doloras*,
Vainly and foolishly,
This untruth,
That good is infinite,
Or that love lasts for ever.

Personally, Campoamor is the most charming of men, frank and cheerful in spite of his great age, and bearing the honours his countrymen have showered upon him with manly modesty. He is a senator and a member of the Academy.

The reputation of the modern drama in Spain rests on the shoulders of a number of authors of considerable talent but little originality, none of whom has succeeded in acquiring fame outside his own country. At the beginning of the present century Tomás Rodriguez Rubí and Bretón de los Herreros imitated French pieces with some success, sometimes transforming them so completely as to give a flavour of the soil to which they were transplanted. Rubí produced several original comedies of manners of considerable dramatic and literary interest. Of these the most celebrated are *Detrás de la Cruz el Diablo* (Behind the Cross lurks the Devil) and *Castillos en el Aire* (Castles in the Air), the latter a brilliant sketch of court intrigue in the author's day. Herreros is more celebrated for witty dialogue and brilliant scenes than for well-studied method in his plots.

Gertrudis Ganez de Avellaneda, a Cuban lady, made a bold attempt to revive the old Spanish tragedy. Her *Alonso Munio* is founded on national history, and is distinguished by chivalrous and patriotic sentiment, but public taste had changed to such a degree that this really fine play which attracted the attention of literary men, and was by them favourably received, failed utterly to win popularity. Her later works were still less successful.

Tamayo y Baus, after writing a somewhat frigid tragedy on

¹ " Jamás en ellas escrito—Dejaré, imbécil ó loco,—El error—De que el bien es infinito,—Ni que es eterno tampoco—El amor."

the subject of Virginia, collaborated with Fernandez Guerra y Orbe, the historian and critic, in the production of *La Rica Hembra* (the Heiress), a historical drama modelled on the theatre of Lope, but with considerably more careful drawing of character. The heiress herself is a type of character peculiar to Spain, proud, passionate, and imperious, with strong prejudices of race and education, yet tender-hearted, brave, and reckless of consequences. Guerra y Orbe is the author of two other plays, the *Daughter of Cervantes* and *Alonso Cano*, which prove rather his historical knowledge, critical taste, and profound appreciation of the old Spanish drama, than his fitness to shine on the feebler modern stage.

Alejandro Lopez de Ayala is a well-known political character, and one of the principal movers of the revolution of 1868. Before that time he had established his reputation as a dramatic author. His talents fit him, however, for satire rather than for the stage. He is the direct antithesis to Fernandez Guerra, being essentially modern in tone. The subjects of his plays are the vices and failings of his time, and his representation of them in an odious light was intended to be salutary. A good instance of his manner is his *Tanto por Ciento* (Percentage), in which he holds up to public reprehension the struggle for money and the mania for rash speculation, with its lowering effect on the morality of the individual and on the nation. This, as well as other works by the same author, excited much attention at Madrid, which was pleased to recognise itself on the stage, but the structure of the piece is not sufficiently good to conceal the sermon which lies beneath.

The best of modern Spanish dramatists is Echegaray. His long apprenticeship has given him a thorough insight into dramatic method, and his manifold successes have taught him to a nicety what will please the taste of his countrymen. Echegaray is no great genius, but he is a conscientious playwright. Producing by dint of hard work rather than by inspiration, he seldom rises to lofty and stirring effects, but always avoids the poor and commonplace. His plays have, generally speaking, very little flavour of their native soil; if the proper names were changed, many of them would pass unchallenged on the French or English stage.[1]

After the seventeenth century literature ceased to appeal to the great body of the people. The time has long gone by when editions of the best Spanish authors such as Juán de Mena, Alemán, and Garcilaso, were printed for the use of the Spanish soldiers in the Low Countries, and when Cervantes and his fellow-captives amused themselves with acting dramas during their weary captivity in Algiers. The ballads are forgotten, and now sound strange in the ears of the descendants of those who made them. The wandering reciter of verses at the fairs or *romerías* (local pilgrimages) has lowered his tone, and tells of the exploits of the campaign in Morocco or of the execution of the latest notorious criminal, instead of the Cid and his companions, and the Seven Princes of Lara. Times have changed, and with them national ideals and literary forms, but the spirit of poetry has not departed from the Peninsula. The verses that appeal to the popular heart are the innumerable short stanzas by unknown authors composed to be sung to the guitar. Of these the most popular forms are the *petenera*, or *copla* as it is loosely called; the *jota* and the *seguidilla*, combinations of music, song, and dance; and the *malagueña*. Each one of these forms is linked to a traditional air, with slight local variations: the two latter especially bear strong traces of an Oriental origin in their weird, wild, and plaintive cadence.

The *Malagueña* belongs peculiarly to Andalucía and the *Jota* to Aragón, but all are popular in Castile, and in Castilian are written most of the verses thus sung. Their structure is

---

[1] For further information see Novo y Colson, *Autores Dramáticos Contemporáneos*. Madrid, 2 vols. fol.

extremely simple, and well adapted to the rustic poets by whom they are frequently improvised to suit the occasion. The ground-work of the *petenera*, *jota*, and *malagueña* is the same, four eight-syllable lines, the second and fourth rhymed, generally in assonants (see p. 44) ; *e.g.*—

> [1] ¡ Era tan dichoso antes
> De encontrarte en mi camino !
> Y sin embargo no siento
> El haberte conocido.

A couplet of the above form becomes a *petenera* by the repetition of certain lines of the couplet and the addition of other conventional and meaningless lines :—

> [2] Por tí me olvidé de Dios
> Por tí la gloria perdí,
> Y ahora me voy á quedar
> *Solea triste de mí*
> *Y ahora me voy á quedar*
> *Sin Dios sin gloria y sin tí*
> *Por tí me olvidé de Dios*
> *Por tí la gloria perdí.*

The above couplet may be made into a *jota* or *malagueña* by additions and repetitions of a similar kind.

The structure of the *seguidilla* is more complicated, and its movement more sprightly. The following is an example :—

> [3] Cuando voy á la casa
> De mi querida,
> Se me hace cuesta abajo
> La cuesta arriba ;
> Y cuando salgo,
> Se me hace cuesta arriba
> La cuesta abajo.

---

[1] "I was so happy before—I met you on my way,—but yet I do not regret—that I have known you."

[2] "For thee I forgot my God—for thee I lost salvation—and now I am left alone—godless and lost without thee."

[3] "When I go to the house—of my true love,—the uphill road—slopes down ;—and when I come away—the downhill road—slopes up."

Such verses as these are sung outside the barber's shop, in the courtyard of barracks, or in *patios* of inns throughout the length and breadth of Spain. Many are of great delicacy and beauty, others are coarse and indecent; their theme is principally love, but they reflect all the varying moods of the Spanish people, all its pathos and quaint humour. When read away from the country, they bring with them as it were an echo from the sunlit plains and mountain villages of Spain.

INDEX

INDEX

THE END